Underground

Underground

A Memoir of Hope, Faith, and the American Dream

By

'DEJI AYOADE

UNDERGROUND
A Memoir of Hope, Faith, and the American Dream

By

'Deji Ayoade

www.dejiayoade.com
ISBN: 979-8-9865876-1-5

For any information, please address
'Deji Ayoade at info@dejiayoade.com
or write to:

'Deji Ayoade
P.O. Box 4485
Broadlands
VA, 20148

For my wife, Tolu Ayoade

Contents

All referenced poems in this book are written by the author and also available as a separate book titled: Poems from Underground: A memoir of Hope, Faith, and the American Dream.

Introduction

In January 2021, when I received a notification from my General that I'd been selected for the Secretary of the Air Force recognition, I thought I was in a dream. In January 2022, I became the same Space Force General's civilian of the year and was also nominated for the Department of the Air Force civilian of the year. By October 2022, I found out that a new General had selected me as a Space Force Guardian of the Year at the Pentagon level. These three instances felt like a chapter in an unwritten book. Words can't capture how grateful I felt in my heart, not just for the recognitions but for every journey until these moments.

Logically, I should never have arrived here. From being raised in a small town in Nigeria to someday commanding a flight of nuclear-armed missiles in the United States Air Force, and now leading in the newly established United States Space Force. Statistically, seventy percent of men in my family never lived past forty years before my generation. Ninety percent never attended college, and ninety-five percent never left Nigeria. I barely made it past my tenth birthday, and I have cheated death more than I can count. Yet here I am. Each time I ask myself how and why? I owe it to my faith, but you will have to turn the pages until the last page to understand the answer to that question thoroughly.

As I chatted with the Secretary of the Air Force, I thought of my father's words to me as an 11-year-old kid in rural Lagos. It was six in the morning, and I had missed a spot while sweeping the hallway with our traditional African broom, my assigned daily chore. He said, "wherever you find yourself in life, whatever position, no matter how big or small, they are equally critical. You are there because you were meant to be, so you must embrace it, own it, and never compromise your integrity, no matter what, until the very last second while you're at it. You never know what it's preparing you for."

It didn't take long after that for me to figure out how every moment of our lives is connected to our future one way or the other. We never know where our NOW is taking us, even when we think we do.

Underground is my unusual journey from childhood poverty to where I am today. How the impossible became a reality. Some people try to forget their past, especially the bitter parts. I prefer to cling to every moment. They are powerful reminders of who we once were, who we are, and if we allow them, who we are becoming. Each trial strengthened me, increased my confidence, and ingrained the discipline to seek accountability for my life.

I hope my book gives voice to that population, the life-affirming hope that America offers. Through this intimate, firsthand account, I want to illuminate what so many people take for granted when we close the door on the one group of people who believe more ardently in this nation's promise than anyone else. The ones that hold on to the core values of this country with unwavering tenacity decade after decade, through setback after setback.

More hopefully, I wish for my story to exemplify how faith can prevail in the face of adversity, including poverty, betrayal, grief, and near-death. I hope it reveals how this country's promise and basic stability help immigrants heal and move forward from great loss and tragedy. To readily integrate into this new world and feel motivated to give back to the country that offers them so much.

Above all else, I want this book to inspire my fellow dreamers, immigrants, and those born in America alike. Those who might be feeling afraid or worn down at this particular moment, who are wondering if the grief and uncertainty are worth it and questioning whether America still holds the same promise. To them, I say it does.

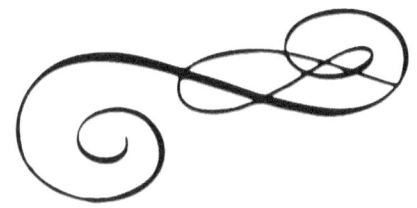

Prologue

SAN DIEGO, CA: May 2014

The Recruiter, the Investigator, and the Candidate.

*W*hen the top-secret investigator showed up at the Clinical Investigation Department at the Naval Medical Center, San Diego, I was already in my scrubs and headed into the lab. My team and I were in the midst of researching hearing restoration treatments to help our troops after some had been deafened from bomb explosions in combat zones.

I hadn't been anticipating anything about the investigator's arrival. She had long, dark hair and a sharp red jacket as she shook my hand and introduced herself as a special agent from the Federal Government Office of Personnel Management. Her last name was Italian. She was very confident and very clear.

"I'm here for your interview for top-secret clearance," she said. "We opened your investigation two months ago."

She asked me to meet her inside a facility that didn't look to me like a place where my future should be decided. Enough chairs to *host an entire fleet were stacked in one corner as she and I sat across from each other at an oval table that was far too large for two people. Everything about the moment felt too big.*

Six months before the investigator came to interview me, I had just made it past the local recruiter who had scheduled my transition interview from the Navy, to join the Air Force. At that time the questions that would scour the course of my thirty-four years and my responses, all spoken with great truth and reverence, were nothing new to me. I'd never held anything back for most of my life.

I'd always been honest throughout my education, my immigration to the United States, and my enlistment in the military. But this time, more was at stake than ever. Since I was a child, I'd promised my mother that somehow one day, I would take her and my siblings away from the country where our family had endured poverty, abuse, and misfortune for years.

I'd had to start at the bottom— in this country, and in its military— but when my mother and sister had finally arrived in the United States, I knew my sacrifices had been worthwhile.

Now, in front of that military review board, I had the chance to create an even better life for us here. That leap was in the hands of the Officer Candidate Interview Board.

I glanced subtly around me as the candidates I was up against sat straight-backed in their Air Force uniforms with their ribbons mounted high. My Navy Service Uniform sported only three meager ribbons. *Why should the Air Force take me?* I wondered as each candidate walked out of the interview room with an air of confidence, some even indulging smiles.

Finally, my name was called. I entered the room, which was much smaller and simpler than I had expected. The only décor was a dull green paint on the walls, and the lone piece of furniture, a desk, was only big enough to accommodate four people. From one side, the colonel and captain rose to shake my hand. As they resumed their seats, I took a chair across from them.

"First thing," said the colonel. "How do you pronounce your last name?"

He was a broad man, formal and direct, and intimidating.

"Ah-yo-AH-day, Colonel," I responded, hoping my intention to cooperate with his every query was clear. "Four syllables."

"Welcome, HM2 Ayoade. We've been reviewing your profile, and I have to say: it's extremely unusual." *Unusual* was a label I'd grown accustomed to since I'd moved to this country six years earlier; it was not what I'd hoped they would focus on today. I braced myself for what came next, posture deliberate and poised.

"You were born and raised in Nigeria," the colonel said. "You're a veterinary surgeon. You have all these other degrees. I might be a colonel, but you're more educated than I am. So, why did you bother to enlist in the Navy when you could have been commissioned? How did you become an American? And how did you meet a two-star admiral?"

"Admiral?" I asked, puzzled.

"Yes, your rear admiral. He wrote us a recommendation letter about you." From the stack of papers in the binder that lay before him, the colonel pulled out a document with the bold letterhead of a Navy flag officer running across the top of it. "You didn't know?" he said. "You haven't read this?"

"No, Colonel. I haven't." I replied, shocked.

The Colonel noticed how astounded I was and in an instant, he slid it across the table to me. "It's the most impressive letter I've ever received from a flag officer about anyone."

I accepted the paper, my eyes racing across the content— phrases like *"exceedingly bright and resourceful," "dedication and drive essential to excel," "an outstanding applicant with an underutilized skill set..."* I gazed up at him, at a loss. I had no idea the highest-ranking officer of Navy Medicine West had ever been watching me—a low-level enlisted non-commissioned officer, just trying to be the best sailor I could be. The United States Navy had taken a chance on me, and my goal had only ever been to prove their risk had been worth it—for them and for this nation.

"Tell us your story," the colonel demanded, now propping himself up for a listen.

Mindful of his time, I tried to sum up my journey to become an American citizen and a United States Navy sailor. I explained why I had to start at the bottom by enlisting, instead of commissioning, considering that my education and background should have deemed me more than qualified. For the sake of brevity, I skipped over some details but noticed that neither the colonel nor the captain failed to interrupt me and ask about the specifics. "What were you doing in Finland?" they asked. "How about Estonia? Tell us about your medical research. Are any of your studies published?"

I answered every question—about my education, upbringing, and favorite soccer team (Arsenal). At the end of the interview, the colonel crossed his arms. Then he stared straight into my eyes and asked, "What is most important to you?"

I paused for a moment, knowing I'd lived my entire life preparing for the moment I would be called to answer this question. My eyes locked onto his. "There is no doubt, Colonel, that my whole life, I have carried with me a thirst for something new, an inexplicable force to accomplish more than the ordinary, and an endless quest never to stop achieving."

He and the captain exchanged a glance. "Colonel," I continued, an urgency inside me needing to hold his attention. "I guess what I'm trying to say is, I can't help how I'm drawn to a life of accountability. I'm only able to give my life meaning by reminding myself that every single moment counts, and I must do something meaningful with it— so that just maybe someday, in my dying moment, I can look back on my life and smile."

For a few seconds, both men sat motionless before me. At last, they looked at each other again. Then, poker-faced, the colonel said, "Thank you for coming. Your recruiter will get in touch with you about our decision." I shook their hands firmly, accepting that I had no more clarity as I exited the room than I'd had when I'd entered.

A month later, my phone rang.

"Are you sitting down?" my recruiter said.

I sank heavily onto my bed.

"Yes." So the process hadn't gone well. I had to remind myself to breathe as I waited for the worst.

"Good. I want to congratulate you. You ranked number one in the interviews."

I was at a loss for words. My mouth wide open. My phone still glued to my ears.

He continued, "This is a good sign, doc. But the fight has only just begun. There are eighty-six of you guys from California alone and over eight hundred across the nation. The selection rate for this batch can't be over eight percent."

Quickly, I did the math: only about sixty of those eight hundred would be chosen to join the Air Force.

"The Air Force is downsizing because of funding issues and furlough. Right now, they're extremely selective, only taking people for the jobs that are in dire need of skilled officers. After we get your board results in February, we'll have to suspend commissioning boards until further notice. Let's keep our fingers crossed the results are what we want."

I understood: the Air Force wouldn't be taking any more officer applications for the rest of the year. This was the first, last, and only chance for my application to be considered to join the Air Force before I became ineligible due to the age requirement. The maximum age to commission into the Air Force was thirty-five. Next year, I would be too old.

"What can I do?" I asked him.

"Pray and pray. That's all we can do."

The results were due forty days after the commissioning board had met. Not that I was counting.

The day the results were in, I didn't go to work. I lay in bed, clutching my phone on my stomach. By 2:00 p.m., the day felt excruciatingly long. I wanted this. I wanted it for me, of course, but I wanted it for so many others, too: my mother, my siblings, my wife, my children, and one day, their children. And I wanted it for all the people who had invested so much in helping me get to this point.

The truth was, I also wanted to prove the doubters wrong. If a starving little boy who walked thirteen miles in the West African bush for his school exams could grow up and commission as an officer into the U.S. Air Force, it would prove there was no distance in life that I couldn't travel.

The phone rang. I jumped off the bed and braced it in my palm for a moment as if the phone itself could transmit news of my fate. Then I answered.

"Doc, hello!" my recruiter said. I didn't want to pay undue hope to his tone—staying upbeat was part of his job.

"The results are finally out," he said. "Now, remember, I said only eight percent were selected for commissioning."

I massaged my brow to soothe myself. "...Yes?"

"Only three candidates from California and one from Arizona were chosen from our zone. It was extremely competitive." My faith sank within me.

"But I want to congratulate you," he said. "You're one of the only three candidates from California."

The air caught in my throat. My eyes stung. I wanted to let out a joyous *Yawp!*, but he continued, "There's a direct request to upgrade your clearance level to top-secret as soon as we can, so that's the next step for now."

What? Someone must have read my profile wrong.

"I don't think you will be doing what you applied to do initially," he continued. "In fact, you've been selected for a very unusual position." Again, that word. I paced slowly as he continued, "You'll be accountable to the President of the United States himself, the Secretary of Defense, and the Commander of the United States Strategic Command in the operation of your duties. Your job is not just a job." *So what on earth was it?* "You'll be heading straight to a special duty: nuclear missile operations."

I gripped the bed and sat up. A tear slid down my cheek. I had navigated a lot of challenges in my past, but the training for this would be one of the greatest triumphs of my life. If I could complete it successfully, I could think of no greater honor as an American than to be selected for this role.

Now, two months later, inside that massive conference room, the top-secret investigator told me she had interviewed the head of my department and a few others who knew me, including my boss, who was an Army major and veterinarian, the research building senior veterinary technician, and a Navy sailor whom I supervised. She'd already spoken to my old friends, neighbors, colleagues, professors, and supervisors. And when we were done, she had more interviews scheduled in Maryland, Washington D.C, Georgia, and at my church here in San Diego.

"You know what you'll be doing for the Air Force isn't related to medicine, right?" she asked me. "At least not for the first three years."

I wasn't sure whether to acknowledge that my recruiter had told me I was being considered for an even more specialized job. She continued, "You're being considered for work in nuclear weapons and nuclear codes, dealing with the most dangerous weapon ever designed. When I finish this portion of the investigation, I have to send the report to D.C., where they'll make the final determination on your top-secret status." It was apparent she could see I had dozens of questions.

As a Nigerian kid, dreaming big was one of the few things that kept me going. Still, not in my wildest dreams did I ever imagine that someday I might be in charge of the most classified weapon in the United States Air Force.

For hours, the investigator and I sat across from each other in that cold, gray room as I unspooled my life for her. I told her about the way my uncles had been killed, how my father had beaten us and squandered his money, how he'd died of lung cancer three years after I'd graduated from veterinary school. I told her about the robbery at gunpoint—that I'd been one of the few to survive during a bus ride to Lagos. I told her about the chance encounter between my wife and me in Baltimore and about working as a veterinarian. I would sometimes stop to recall some details or to take a sip of water, and that's when she'd ask me more questions.

She flipped page after page as her notes took up sheets of paper. I watched her jot down thoughts next to some of the questions on the clearance questionnaires that I had completed two months before.

It was five hours later that she tucked her notes into a brown briefcase and shook my hand once more.

"Can I ask you one last question?" she said.

I stood prepared for anything, as I'd been trained to do.

"Of course."

"What gave you the drive to overcome all the adversities you encountered?"

I only had to think for a second before I started to explain: "When I was seven, I woke up one morning and walked into my mom's room. There she sat on her bed, crying. When she looked up at me, I noticed her left eye was bruised, and her eyebrow was slit across. I thought of my father the night before, yelling. But that morning, I'd made my mom a promise."

The investigator gazed at me intently, eager to hear my next words.

"One day, I will take you far away from here. I will become a doctor. I will move to the United States and become an American citizen, and then I will take you and my siblings away from this terrible place." I did not know exactly how I would do it, but I knew why, and that was just as important.

PART 1:

Nigeria

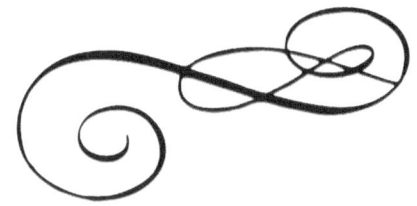

Chapter 1

NIGERIA: November 17, 1977

Oh, brothers. My heritage is one of blood, sacrifice, and tragedy.

"**I**n 1977, three years before you were born, your grandfather died," my father's mother told me. We called my grandmother *Alhaja*, the revered name for Muslim women who had made the pilgrimage to Mecca. I had always hung on Alhaja's every word, but this story about how my grandfather had died and the aftermath of his death was one of the most intimate things she had ever shared with me.

"It was traditional for him to be buried where he came from. And he was laid to rest next to his father, who was buried next to *his* father." She said.

I understood the honor in this tradition since my family came from a royal heritage. Alhaja was the figure in my life whom I felt safe to trust the most, and she felt that helping me understand the events in our family's history would shape my identity and help me discover who I was.

Often, whenever Alhaja told us stories, it was usually at night in the balcony, on her muslim praying mat. Otherwise, she prayed in the mosque or in the corner of our living room. I rarely saw Alhaja's hair as a child. Her hair was often covered in hijab and only uncovered when she was weaving it. She often wore an Abaya and usually had a 100-count Subhah in her right hand while sitting on her praying mat.

"Your grandfather was a successful businessman with a loving reverence for his heritage." She explained. "As was customary in his Muslim faith, he had four wives, and I was the fourth and youngest wife."

Although Alhaja had three children with him, he had nineteen children from four wives: eight boys and eleven girls, but one of the boys was a twin from his second wife who died young. My father was the sixth of the seven sons left.

"Your grandfather made his career in Lagos's retail and wholesale industries, but his heart never left Ijaye (pronounced *EE-jah-yay*), the tiny rural village where he was born." Alhaja continued.

"You see, early memories of our childhood are like river tributaries. The rest of our lives not only flows through them but is rather built around them. It doesn't matter how well we do at running away from our childhood. Our guiltless years cling to our hearts like a mother coddles a nursing baby," Alhaja usually spoke in proverbs or parables to add emphasis to what she had said, or to provide a lead-in to alert us that what she was about to say was very important.

"Before your grandfather passed away, he implored all his sons to return his body to his birthplace—all of his sons, that is, except for your father." I noticed the disappointment on Alhaja's face. "Your father was the absentee son, but your grandfather asked his brothers to find him. No one knew where your father was. It had been over seven years since he vanished, and it wasn't the first time." Though it had been many years, I could sense Alhaja reliving the pain of her disappearing son as she took a pause to listen to our endless questions about dad.

Stories about my dad as a lad often sounded more fictitious than not, mostly too captivating to be real. However, they were accurate accounts of his past. As fascinating as they were, there was no doubt that those were Alhaja's toughest years as a mother. She thought it was incomprehensible how my father was so different in so many perturbing ways. "Raising him as a child was one of the most difficult periods of my life," she often said.

From Alhaja's stories, what I remembered most was that there wasn't much of a right or wrong depiction of him. He was just a different child. A very different child lost in the world of an emerging civilization where things once considered the "norm" were no longer acceptable.

My father was born prematurely, two months before his expected birth date. Alhaja carried him around in a basket because he was too fragile to hold. It scared her as she beheld almost every vein beneath her son's epidermis. She was anxious about his survival, but he sure made it - the reason I can tell this story today.

My father grew into a very eloquent, charismatic, and noticeable character. He caused a lot of trouble in his early life. As a result, his father enrolled him in boarding school at a young age. In 1960s Nigeria, enrolling primary school pupils in boarding schools in western Nigeria was often a desperate action parents resorted to after exhausting all other options. It was a pseudo-military education system designed to enforce discipline and moral character in children. You could call it a place to break and rebuild a child's character to fit into more socially acknowledgeable cultural values. Our country was still struggling to balance cultural over-diversification and the introduction of British Westernization that was to stay in Nigeria.

"Academically, your father was a genius," Alhaja once told me. "Regardless of your father's behavioral issues, the school wouldn't expel him because he was their best student. By the time he graduated from primary education, he knew the nitty-gritty of the boarding school system. He figured out how to get away with doing things his way while evading the consequences of his actions. He wanted to live his life the way he saw the world, and no one was going to stop him. He refused to accept rules from anyone, especially the school administrators."

My father's high school was in the city of *Ife*, located in present-day *Osun* State, a significant historical landmark of the *Yoruba* tribe of Nigeria. Often lauded for coming home with several prizes and awards for his achievements in sports and academic competitions, it didn't change the painful truth that he was unpredictable—a ticking untimed bomb waiting to explode. It didn't matter how bad his conduct was; he always told the truth in a manner that made people wonder if he ever gave any thought to the punishment for his actions.

"Overwrought with what the next report about my son would be," said Alhaja, "I tried to have many eyes keep watch over him. It didn't do much for me, though."

Alhaja often called me by my first name, *Ramon*. However, most of my friends called me by the short colloquial for my middle name, "'Deji" as to "Adedeji" or simply "Dejavu" several years later.

"You frequently ask why I pray several times a day," she smiled gently, but looked disheartened, like she did prefer to hide the sad truth from me. "It's because I needed consolation for the great loss to this family. I can only find solace in many grandsons. He gave you and your brothers to me; a much better version of your father, which makes all my prayers answered. So, if you see me always on my knees, it's because I can't stop thanking him." Alhaja looked up and pointed at the ceiling as if she was referring to someone living up there.

I looked up at the ceiling but saw nothing.

"I've seen all your father's good qualities in each one of you boys, but you are all nothing like the troublemaker he was growing up. I am telling you his stories, so you know how far he'd come and how much I went through with him as his mother."

The most shocking tale Alhaja ever told about my father as a teenager was about his time in high school. The first time he disappeared. He surprised everyone who knew him. It was so shocking that the local news broadcast his story.

"When your father was in high school, for a few weeks, he moved a few scraps of broken furniture from the school into a remote forest, which was a few miles away. No one could explain how he pulled it off. He built a shack for himself in the jungle, a home far from the worst of the civilized world. There was no doubt it was a domain for many wild animals. After he successfully moved his possessions, as well as the utensils he needed to cook, he soon stopped going to school."

"He stopped going to school?" I asked, unable to hide the shock in my voice. I knew my father as a strong proponent of education. In fact, my father would employ a private home tutor to give extra classes to all the children that lived in his house. My father emphasized the need for further development in English and mathematics if a child was to be sound academically. "A real application of both is the foundation for a successful education," my father would always say. He understood how quickly the world had evolved since his childhood. He frequently talked about how his children should be part of the change the world anticipated many years before, especially during his time as a father.

"Do you mean Dad dropped out of high school?" I asked again. Alhaja knew I anticipated "no" for an answer.

"No, he did not, Ramon. You should listen to the rest of the story. There is a lot for you to learn about your father."

According to Alhaja, it didn't take long for my dad's school to report his disappearance to his parents and the local police. They searched for months without success. It had been three months, and Alhaja was beginning to accept the likelihood that my father was either dead or killed.

Games and the delirious lines,
And yet, you play some pranks.
Loved ones turn a record of warning.
Conceit narrows your edges.
Learning by experience,
Not by obedience.

Then the neck breaks.
The game is now a bane.
The head falls off,
Marking the end of the race.
And the world turns to hear a bitter tale...

One day, a hunter showed up at my father's school. He wanted to speak with the principal.

"I believe one of your students is living in the forest," said the hunter.

"What? In the woods?" the director exclaimed.

"No," said the hunter. "I said 'forest'. In fact, more like 'jungle,'" the hunter attempted to correct the principal. "He told me he'd been there for over three months."

"Oh my God, that must be *Lani Ayoade*!" Dismayed, the principal continued, "Bloody 'ell! We've been searching for him for months now! Can you describe him, just to be sure it's really who I'm thinking?"

His description matched my dad well. Lani Ayoade was quite infamous in school, even more so since his disappearance. "Frankly speaking, I'm amazed that he survived the forest up till now," the hunter said.

My grandparents immediately left Lagos upon receiving the news. Upon arrival at Ile–Ife, they set out to find him in the forest, along with the principal and the hunter, who came back for them the following day. After driving a few miles, they came to a bush path where they could no longer continue by car. They had to trek through the jungle.

"The hunter brought an old rifle and a machete with him," said Alhaja as she described the scene. "However, it didn't rid us entirely of our fears as we continued to disappear into the sinking forest. The bushes were so tall none of us could see to both sides of the forest path. Sometimes, the bush path discontinued into freshly grown tall grasses showing that no one had been around for months. Not even the hunters. Thanks to the hunter, who continued to clear out the path for us with his machete."

"Finally," Alhaja said, "we arrived at a secluded area where we found a shack. We could hear a waterfall. We knew it had to be nearby, but we couldn't catch any glimpse of it from where we stood. We stared at one another, petrified that this could be the spot Lani called home." Alhaja paused and gently turned her head sideways like she was trying to hide her face from me, but I continued to listen intently.

When she turned to face me and opened her eyes, they were filled with tears but she quickly dabbed them with the tip of her hijab before they could roll down her cheeks. She gathered herself and then continued.

"There was a small area that resembled a kitchenette. I called out his name, hoping when the response came, that it would be my son's voice. No one answered, but I tried a few more times. We stepped into the shack trying to search for any proof our son was truly alive. Behold, there was a snake on his bed. We weren't sure what kind of snake it was because we didn't stay long enough to find out. Nevertheless, it must have been about 20 feet long and half the width of an electric pole."

"Wow! So what did you do?" I interrupted Alhaja. "Did the hunter kill it?"

"No, we took to our heels but returned about half an hour later. This time, we found Lani drying up. He must have gone swimming in a nearby river, probably where the sound of the waterfall was coming from. Initially, he staggered at the sight of us, then let out a disappointed sigh when he saw the hunter standing in our midst. I broke into uncontrollable tears."

"And what did Grandpa do?" I asked Alhaja.

"Grandpa was dumbfounded. We simply came to terms that our son was genuinely troubled. We told him we found a snake in his bed, but he laughed it off like it was nothing. He strolled into the shack to grab a shirt and said as he puts it on, "they come around to play sometimes.""

"What? He played with animals in the jungle?" In my childish mind, I thought that was exciting and movielike.

"Yes, he did. All sorts of wild animals. It was hard to accept what we witnessed about your father firsthand. He was no liar, so we knew all he told us about the jungle was nothing but the truth. It was hard to believe our ears, and it wasn't easy to accept what we saw. It seemed like a fairy tale—Tarzan in the jungle, but without Jane. My son was the boy who found comfort in a world of danger." Alhaja said.

"So how did he survive?" I asked Alhaja.

"Good question, Ramon. The principal asked him the same question. He told us that he had a lot of food supplies and kerosene for his stove when he came down." He then added: "I cooked until I ran out of food items a month ago. I now live on fruits and whatever food I can harvest from the forest or fish from the river. Look around. I could never starve around here." He pointed to the improvised stove containing firewood he had built with three big stones in the kitchenette.

"Your grandfather and I goggled at each another when he said that. Your father exuded a type of confidence we hadn't anticipated. He almost convinced us he understood exactly what he was doing." Alhaja said.

"If you are worried about schoolwork," my father said, "I can guarantee you I'm ahead of my classmates, probably by two academic years. I brought all the texts I needed with me from school and have the school syllabus with me. The education system moves at too slow a rate for me," he concluded.

This part of the story made more sense to me as a teenager - why my father bought the academic syllabus for senior high school for us to study with while we were still in junior high. He made us study well ahead of every academic school year while in high school.

"Your father took pride in being ahead of his classmates in school," Alhaja told me. "Nevertheless, what we saw was very unorthodox, considering he was just a kid. He did articulate his case intelligently, a witty attempt at displaying a non-written right of freedom to live wherever he pleased. To leave the civilization that the world desperately craved for? The western liberty and education so many died for? He preferred primeval convictions to achieve his innermost desires rather than give the norm a try. He resorted to bringing his fantasy world to reality."

As Alhaja continued, I quietly thought I might have something in common with my father after all. If only Alhaja knew of my nightly drifting off into another world of my own, unknown to them.

I slept on a mat in Alhaja's room every night while we lived in the family house. It was the type of mat weaved from dried palm fronds. Alhaja's mattress could only accommodate her and my two female cousins, *Tola* and *Toro*. I liked to sleep on the right side of the mat. It was the closest to Alhaja's cupboard. Her closet was laminated in plastic Formica. My fantasy world existed in this Formica.

Every night, I lay on my left side, staring at Alhaja's closet, completely immersed in my fantasy world. It was my solace. Although I never shared my interpretation of the blueprint on the Formica covering Alhaja's cupboard with anyone, I silently craved that moment every night. The cupboard had indefinite interlocking connections of varying depths of brown shades. Every design from the base of the cupboard to the top was meaningfully connected in my imagination. It was more than a printed meaningless silhouette on a plastic material to me. It was a masterpiece of an imaginary world.

Gently touching the smooth Formica, I often thought to myself that I could live in the shade that looked like a tree with a smiley face. I imagined the rooms, well carved out and hidden in its branches. I would have smaller rooms for all the birds chirping outside on the tree. The path that led from the tree through the meadow would be my solitude. The animals could continue to graze or perhaps chew cuds while sitting quietly on the lawn. I wondered if they had any thoughts on their minds.

In my solitude, I would also contemplate the still river. The flowers by the shore were of many colors. They never withered. I could sit there all day making ripples with the pebbles sitting around me.

Oh! I thought to myself, *I should keep away from the upper part of the cupboard because there are several little huts inhabited by the*

Lilliputians. I could live there in peace forever. I could disappear into that world and come back to my family whenever I wanted to. If Alhaja or my parents were to know my fantasies, what would they have thought? If they knew how much I craved the magical ability to transport myself back and forth between worlds, they might have thought I was disturbed, just like my dad. As much as they wished to respond to my father's passionate idea of what education should be in the mid-twentieth century, they were lost for words.

Alhaja continued her story about my dad and the forest: The hunter, with much discomfort, rippling from his inability to comprehend my father's points said, "You must get this boy out of here! Take him back to where he belongs! I am a hunter! This is what I do for a living! I only hunt this way with my friends when we really need to do serious hunting. In fact, it's not uncommon to get lost around here sometimes. You all witnessed how difficult it was to get here. As far as I am concerned, I still cannot fathom why and how this boy is still alive! Our fathers often say, *A word to the wise is sufficient*."

Alhaja said she made my father leave the jungle after they allowed him to pack his books and clothes. They brought him back to Lagos, and boarding school was over. He was schooled closer to home from that moment on, while my grandparents made him take more classes at home to keep his mind engaged. He graduated high school a year earlier than he was supposed to.

My father did almost everything right for his family for the first time. He was expected to soon leave the country for college in England, along with some of his brothers. For the first time, my father's family didn't have to worry much about him until one morning when he was nowhere to be found. He had disappeared again. The search for him continued into a three-day brouhaha without success. My father's younger sister, *Aunty Modina,* was the baby of the family, six or seven years old at the time. She was Grandpa's last child. It was not surprising that it took the little girl quite a while to understand what the hullabaloo in her house was about.

"I saw my brother wash his clothes, iron, and pack them in his bags," she said to Grandpa. "He woke me up when everyone was still sleeping and told me to help him with one of his bags."

Alhaja thought it might have been about 4:00 a.m. because most of them were usually awake by five in the morning due to the call to prayer from the mosque.

"He carried the other two bags by himself," the little girl continued. "When we got to the bus station, he gave me some money, kissed me, and told me to go back home."

"Did you see which bus he got on?" Grandpa asked.

"No, I didn't, but he said, 'Tell them I'll be okay if they ask for me.'"

No one had heard from my father ever since.

Grandpa owned two large buildings in one compound, right in the center of Lagos. It was a common trend for men who had multiple wives.

"Your father," Alhaja said, "of the seven sons, was always the different one. His early life was such a riddle, so difficult to understand, that he was never able to explain the reasons for most of his disturbing actions. Although your father was a lot of things, no one could argue that he'd possessed a special gift—*a sixth sense*."

Young Alhaja

Grandpa before he died in 1977.

My dad Lani Ayoade after he
returned home

My mom Rafat Ayoade and I at my
naming ceremony in 1980

"Your grandfather's first wife had two girls, and the second wife had eight—four boys and four girls. She was the one who lost a boy from her set of twins. The third wife had six, two boys and four girls, and of course, three from me, two boys and one girl. The six sons fulfilled your grandfather's wish. If only we knew the price for doing so, we could have forestalled the havoc that followed his burial. It's such a shame you never met any of them. Is it the resemblance amongst them or the way they loved one another? You could not tell they were from four different women."

Alhaja paused for a few seconds as her eyes filled with tears. She tried to smile as her face broadened, but it was well masked by the teardrops from the corner of her eyes. I knew for sure that there was nothing pleasant about the story.

"On their way back from Ijaye," Alhaja said, "some of them needed to use the toilet, so all the cars pulled over to the left shoulder of the highway, the *Abeokuta* expressway. There were two cars and one pickup truck. Your father's brother, *Bayo,* drove the first car. He was the only full-blood brother your father had. There were two women with Bayo in his car. One of them was one of his two wives."

"*Toro's* mom?" I interrupted. "We've never met her!"

My father raised all three of my late uncle's children, and Toro was the only child of the three with a biological mother that we had never met. A woman often visited the other two, *Tola* and *Tope*, from time to time, sometimes bearing gifts for them. She was their mother.

Alhaja nodded and continued the story.

"The second woman was my sister. My only sister. Your grandfather's first son was not with them on this trip, but the other four brothers, one of their sisters, and two other in-laws were in the next two vehicles, three in the second car and four in the pickup truck. The truck was fully loaded with empty bottles and plates from the funeral. Some of them exited their vehicles, trying to decide where to piddle, while others were still trying to make their way out of the car. An eighteen-wheeler from the other side of the road lost control and crashed into the three vehicles. The first car was completely crushed so that you couldn't tell if there were human bodies left in it. Your uncle, his wife, and my sister were still in this car when the truck crashed into them."

I gasped, "What? you mean they got crushed in the car?" My mouth fell wide open in disbelief. Alhaja paused, nodded to my affirmation rather than a question, then continued. But tears was beginning to fill her eyes again and her voice began to shake.

"The impact on the first car continued into the second car and the pickup truck. Two of your uncles and their sister standing in front of the second car also died instantly, squashed between vehicles." The pain in Alhaja'a heart was undeniable as tears rolled down her cheeks as she struggles to continue the story in a clear tone.

"Unfortunately, one of the last two of your uncles died in transit to the hospital. Only one of your uncles, *Abey*, and the two in-laws made it to the hospital alive. Although Abey was your father's half-brother, he was a splitting image of your father and also his best friend.

"He would die three days later from undiagnosed internal bleeding. We also found out later that he was the only one who knew where your father was but never disclosed it to anyone because he had promised your father. So, before you interrupt me, yes, your father named your brother after him. He vowed to name his first son after him." Although Alhaja thought she answered a question I might have asked, I was imagining how my family had lived with such a tragic experience - the pain and suffering they had endured before I was born and still silently living and dealing with it in different ways.

As the clock ticked,

I wept in the solitary idleness of my mind,

Wishing I could take one more glance,

But I couldn't.

I wished I could wipe my tears,

But they fell on my heart.

With every step closer to my sanctuary,

Distance crawled in between.

I thought I found a new home,

But how could I survive a new Love?

Don't blame my fragile heart for growing in sorrow.

My hope was taken from me long ago.

"A tanker lost control and killed all those people?" I asked Alhaja in a frustrated and angry tone. Although I was a little boy, I understood those were my family members that I would never meet and I couldn't stop imagining what each one of them looked like, what their personalities were, or what memories I could have made with each one of them.

"What happened to the driver? You know, Alhaja, he didn't have to kill all those people. He could have done something to avoid such calamity if he was experienced enough to drive a tanker!" I imagined what the driver could and couldn't have done, faintly hoping that I had some control over the tapping steps of fate and time. I imagined him driving drunk, dozing off behind the wheel, or perhaps driving a truck not fit for the interstate. I was sure in my mind that he killed almost half of my family members due to irresponsible driving.

"There was no way he wasn't rotting in jail." I thought aloud. Nonetheless, Alhaja often had real answers to my questions.

"You know, *Ramon*." Alhaja seemed like she was about to explain the most agonizing part of the story, but then, she took a deep breath, a long pause, wiped her tears, and then quietly began to say prayers with her 100-count subhah that had been in her right hand the entire time, as she sat in her usual sitting yoga position on her praying mat. She managed to control her breath and her tears, but I could feel every pain in the tone of her voice as she continued.

"Before we talked to the survivors at the hospital, many people prematurely accused your late uncle of the accident, especially the other three wives. They imagined he must have pulled over too close to the highway, readily conceivable because he was the one leading the group. However, your father's half-brother would prove them wrong before he died at the hospital.

"Abey and the two in-laws explained that Bayo wasn't responsible for the accident. He pulled over because some of them needed to use the toilet. The tank driver must have lost control; maybe he was drunk. He came out of nowhere, probably from the other side of the road. It all happened so fast, no one had time to think. Bayo, his wife, and other passengers died instantly. Only three people survived because they were in the rear vehicle, the pickup truck. The doctors said Abey was in shock from the accident but could go home in a week. The boy had shown no visible injuries. It almost seemed like he wasn't in the accident. However, the other two in-laws: your grandfather's first daughter's husband and one of my relatives would spend months in the hospital."

Noting the pain in Alhaja's voice though she still managed to compose herself, I asked her again in an angrier tone, "So what happened to him? The driver? Did he go to jail?"

"Nothing, Ramon," Alhaja said with a sad smile on her face and an acceptance of her misfortune.

"Justice is pretty hard to find around here. It's all about socio-political status and who you know. Besides, what difference would it make? Whatever we do to the driver won't bring back the dead. We let him go. It was for the best. He will find a much bigger war to fight with his conscience."

"Conscience? What if he doesn't care?"

"Trust me, son, what happened wasn't an easily forgettable thing for any man. A few people may try to prove stone-hearted sometimes, but I know a man with a conscience when I see one. The accident will haunt that driver for the rest of his life for almost wiping out an entire generation of a family. You know, your uncle's first wife was four months pregnant with his only son, your cousin."

"Tope!" I quickly interrupted.

"Of course, he's the youngest and the only boy of the three," Alhaja mockingly replied at my unimpressive display of wit, very much acceptable for my age. "Imagine if she had gone with them. Bayo wanted one of his wives to stay with the kids in Lagos, so he insisted she stayed because she was pregnant. She could have been in the first car."

Looking back and seeing Alhaja's composure, I still cannot comprehend how much faith it took to accept such a catastrophe. How do you move on from the loss of a husband, a son, four stepsons and one stepdaughter, a sister, and a daughter- in-law, as well the accusation of a slain son by those he loved the most—all in one day? In fact, besides Alhaja, who mustered enough courage to unfurl the tragic story to her grandchildren, I can't recall any Ayoade that ever talked about the incident. It was my family's best-kept secret.

"So, Ramon, this is how all your uncles except one died on the way back from Grandpa's funeral, a tragedy that will linger forever in our hearts. It also explains why your father never allows any of his children to visit his hometown."

"How did my father get the news since no one knew of his whereabouts?" I asked.

"Unbeknownst to us, he started a new life in *Kaduna*, the north-western part of the country. His then-girlfriend read about the accident in a newspaper. She didn't know much about your father, but she thought his last name was the same as the family reported to have suffered such a great tragedy. The resemblance between your dad and grandfather was indisputable, so she knew as soon as she noticed the picture on the newspaper page."

"So, he came back."

"That's right. Your father came back home. News of losing his father and brothers brought him out of seclusion and back to Lagos, but the damage of this loss would haunt him for the rest of his life. He was devastated. It'd been seven years, and no one had seen him until after the death of his father, six siblings, aunt, and sister-in-law.

"He asked for Abey as soon as he returned. He hoped it was only a bad dream. My sister was his favorite aunt, a childless woman of whom your father often claimed that his best years were those spent under her nurture." Alhaja said. "It was the first time I saw him shed tears in the many years that I have known him as my son. A very bold and brave boy, but the loss of his brothers broke him."

Although my father was quite young, he quickly learned to assume responsibility for his stepmothers, female siblings, nieces, and nephews.

"He promised never to leave his family again," Alhaja said. As tempting as it can be to conclude that my dad's impulsive behavior appeared to have continually yielded to his incredible instincts, it might sound premature because there was no proven record of the havoc that he might have evaded. His perturbing decisions preserved his life from the accident that would have wiped his entire generation from existence. There is no doubt that he would have traveled in the same car with his brothers.

So, I often wander through the maze of my father's life to discover how thrilling it was. Did he have instincts as an unreligious prophet that he was too young to understand at the time? It was probably safer for him to be alone than to be with his loved ones. Who knows? Maybe he knew, or maybe he steadily yielded to the unwavering convictions he had no control of. All I know is that my father always knew something was coming way before it actually did.

Cold winds, runny noses.
On a restless pavement, I
stand.
Miles, I traveled,
But here I am.

Staring eyes, teary eyes.
Where have I placed my will?

This day isn't mine,
But I promised not to remember yesterday.
However bad,
However sad,
This scar in my heart must fade.

"Your father remained in Grandpa's house. He chose to stay in a separate building from where his late dad and I lived. He wasn't close to his only surviving brother. He was much older than him and lived far from us. However, ever since your uncles died, the family history of violent accidents continued," Alhaja said. "By 1979, less than two years later, your dad tried to devote himself to providing for our family as he saw there was big business in automobiles at the time."

The oil boom had given Nigeria the opportunity to partner with a few European countries and America to establish an automotive industry. My dad began to consult in auto sales, and over the next few years, his business thrived. However, in our country, there was a cultural superstition that dictated many people's lives: *every time something good happens, you can expect something terrible to follow.*

"That's what came in 1979." Alhaja said. "Your father had been involved in two fatal car accidents in Lagos and almost died. While he recovered, the family house caught fire with me, your dad, his stepmothers, and sisters all there. We barely made it out before it burned to the ground."

After he surveyed the damage, my dad built another home on the same property. After my father rebuilt the family house from the ground up, the only son left to move into my grandfather's home in the city, he married two women. My mother was the first—a gorgeous 18-year-old girl with dreams of a career in fashion. Born on October 1, 1960, the day that Nigeria gained independence from Great Britain, she embodied a spirit of freedom and excitement that would ultimately be whittled away by her marriage to my father.

Three years later, he separated from his second wife. I was only three and too young to understand why they separated. My father swore never to allow any of his children to visit his hometown. My mom, Alhaja, my four siblings (one boy and one girl from my mom and two half-brothers), and I lived in my grandfather's house until I was seven.

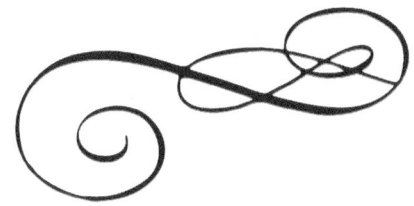

Chapter 2

NIGERIA: March 1987

The Housewarming.

My earliest childhood memory begins with tripping into a roadside gutter in front of my late grandfather's house. The gutters in my neighborhood were never covered from the public, so they were constantly littered with all forms of rubbish. It was the same with many parts of Nigeria, especially those on residential streets and local roads. Sometimes, only the driveways were covered for vehicles and pedestrians to cross.

I should have been three or four years old to have a faint memory of the incident, but my mother insists I was only two. I don't remember much about the accident, but the picture in my mind starts to form with my mother snatching me from two burly men that probably rescued me from the detritus-laden gutter.

"What happened to him?" she screamed.

"He fell in the gutter!" the men replied, almost in unison. I was completely submerged in sewage from head to toe, which was very much expected for a city deprived of an efficient sewer system.

"There were lots of broken bottles in the gutter," Mom explained much later. "One of the glasses had cut deep into your right forehead." I remember my mom wiping the sticky dirt from the sewage off my face. She was taken in horror at the sight of blood spurting out uncontrollably from my forehead to my face, and down to the floor. I don't remember feeling any pain but everyone trying to help my mom were in utter shock.

"Our effort to control the bleeding was unavailing, so we hurried to the hospital," Mom said. "Given the severity of the skin torn away from your head, the doctors had to graft before stitching the laceration."

My scar turned out more evident on my forehead than I was aware of. After all, what does a child make of a thing like that? For years, the other children made fun of my scarred face. I always let their taunts roll off my back; maybe they thought I was weak. As I grew older, I endured the early mockery of my scarred face, especially by classmates. Although the stitches were gone, I needed to be reminded of it until after the incident that occurred on my first day in primary school.

My first day in primary school wasn't exactly what you would expect from a typical five-year-old. I showed up at school with my brother, Abey. At the time I had no idea Abey was, in fact, my half-brother. For some reason, I thought we were twin brothers, and he thought the same. My brother and I are only a month and a half apart, and my mom had raised both of us as twin brothers.

A few years later, we found out that Abey and our brother, Lateef, were from the same mother. She and my dad had separated when Abey was three years old, and Lateef was only eleven months old.

40

Sometimes, I am surprised by how I had a vivid picture of my "gutter-accident" when I was about the same age as when this woman left but had no memory of her.

Biola, the only girl, is two years younger than me, and *Tunji* is five years younger. Both are from my mom. As for my half-brothers, *Abey* is a month and half older than me, and Lateef is a year younger than Biola.

St. Thomas Aquinas Catholic Primary School had a great reputation for excellence and discipline, considering it was an all-male school. Most mothers also seemed well attracted to the white shirt and khaki short uniform along with a ball cap. The school badge was tailored on to the left breast pocket, while the ball cap also had the same badge sewn to the front piece. I can't remember what our sandals were called at the time, but the item was in vogue for primary-school pupils in mid-eighties Nigeria. Our socks rolled all the way up to just below our knees, just as they did for soccer players.

Abey and I couldn't wait to get in those uniforms every morning, at least for the first few years in primary school, until we figured it was because we didn't have to do our own laundry back then. There weren't washers and dryers in Nigeria in the mid- eighties. Considering how neat and sharp we appeared every day of the week for kids in white uniforms, my mom and cousin must have done an unbelievable job handwashing and ironing our uniforms, even if they had to use a coal iron or fold and place them underneath the mattress overnight.

My dad often came down from his building every morning just before he left for work to scan through our uniforms in an almost military manner. I remember Alhaja requesting that he drop us off at school on the first day, but he declined.

"They will have to get used to walking to and from school by themselves, come rain or sunshine," my father said. "They need to learn to be independent; otherwise, they will expect me to drop them off every morning. Besides, they are boys."

Alhaja seemed disappointed, but she knew her son well; not even in the rain would he drop his kids off at school in his car.

As my brother and I walked to school, my father drove past us on the street. I remember neighbors paused to wave at us. *"You boys look so clean and sharp!"* they yelled. Although I didn't know much about what it means to start school, I loved being in my uniform and, more importantly, the proud look on the faces of my family members.

We got to school at about 7:30 a.m. All the kids were dressed up the same. I admit it was very military in my primary and secondary school years in Nigeria compared to the education system in the United States. In Nigeria, students mustered at a designated assembly spot every morning at 7:45a.m. and left the premises at 1:00 p.m. for primary school and 2:00 p.m. for secondary school. Formations on the assembly ground were by class—designated in alphabets, grades, from the most junior to the most senior, and respective student heights, from the shortest to the tallest. It was amazing how every student knew exactly where to go, in front of whom and behind whom. You could easily tell if someone was missing at the assembly.

After the prayers and announcements, students sang to the drums as they marched off to their respective classes, one class after the other. New students were directed to their respective classes, and fortunately, I ended up in the same class as my brother. Two students were assigned to each desk and bench. My brother and I were excited, but we weren't allowed to sit on the same bench. The class desks were designed to meet the same requirements as lockers in developed countries.

Abey was a lot different from me; in fact, he was quite the opposite. Though we very much had the same daily routine, dressed the same way, and made the same friends, he was more introverted, calm, quiet, and gentle. On the contrary, I was very curious, energetic, and fearless. Earlier in the morning on the first day in school, I noticed some students in slightly different uniforms from ours mustered separately, so during lunch break, I tried to walk around the school, attempting to figure how many schools were within the same compound. I noticed my brother walking away, about a few meters from me, crying.

Someone must have hit him, I thought. I ran up to him and asked what happened. He told me a bigger and older pupil had bullied him. I asked him to show me who it was, so we walked around for a few minutes while he searched for him. It didn't take long for him to point at one of the students. He was truly bigger and looked much older. Later, I found out he was a class ahead of us. Apparently, John had a reputation. My brother wanted us to turn around and walk away.

I walked up to John, tapped him on the back, and asked why he attacked my brother. He pushed me away and took a swing at my face before asking, "So what? What will you do about it?"

I don't have a vivid picture of how the fight started, but I do remember that it took two male teachers to get me off John. When the teachers pulled me off John, I watched him bleed profusely from his nostrils. His white shirt was stained with blood. Later, I found a few blood spots on my new uniform as well, but it wasn't my blood. I was taken back to the class while the young bully was attended to at the sick bay. My brother tried to explain why I defended him, but the principal handed me a letter to take home to my parents a few minutes later.

All the members of my family feared my father. He was a tough disciplinarian, and we never wanted to cross his path. "You must be punished when you misbehave," was a slogan of his. No magnitude of pleading by anyone else, not even his mother, could change his decision once it was made up. My father could be unpredictable, so that when you expected the worst from him sometimes, you barely got a warning.

My mother and Alhaja read the letter after we got home. After a short silence, with the letter still in her hands, Alhaja looked up at both of us, still in our uniform, and said, "Tell me what happened?"

She listened intently while my mom watched us tell our side of the story. Alhaja sent us away to change out of our uniforms and stepped aside to speak quietly with my mom.

As much as Alhaja tried to keep quiet about the incident, especially because she believed in her grandchildren standing up to defend one another should the occasion arise, my mother made it clear there had to be consequences for being involved in a fight.

It wasn't my mom that I was worried about; it was what my dad would do to me when he returned from work. I was only five years old but old enough for punishment. After all, I was old enough to fight a bigger kid. My mom was right; if they had kept the incident from him, he would have found out one way or the other since everyone knew him in our area.

When my father came back, I heard everyone greeting him as he climbed the stairs to his room. I hid in Alhaja's room though he had not received the news yet. When Alhaja called me to dinner, I shook my head and told her I wasn't hungry. I was more worried about the *Koboko* whip in my dad's room, so I didn't bother to touch my food.

It felt like an eternity of worriment between when my father arrived and when my mom called me and Abey to his room upstairs. She had waited for my father to finish his dinner before she showed the letter to him. Alhaja went upstairs with me and Abey. When we entered his room, he was still reading the letter from my principal. My mom sat in a sofa across from him while Alhaja stood behind me and Abey. I stood still, quiet, scared but not shaky, expecting my father to pull his Koboko from underneath his chair as soon as he finished with the letter. Abey also stood behind me, terrified and jittery.

After my father finished reading the letter, he looked at me, poker-faced and asked, "What happened in school today?"

I turned my head to catch the reaction on Alhaja's face and then back to my dad. *Is this a trick or an opening to whichever punishment he's about to serve us?* I thought to myself. After stuttering my way through explaining to him why I got involved in a fight, he turned to Abey, looked at him but didn't say anything, and then dismissed us. Shocked, my mom, Alhaja, Abey, and I looked at one another. *So that is it?* We could almost hear ourselves in the dead silence that followed.

A few days later, we found out that Dad was glad I stood up for my brother though he would have expected Abey to defend himself being the older one. As I got older, I would understand why in my culture, fathers would more than anything love their first sons to turn out tough and strong, so they could take their place someday. Not that Abey was weak - he was just a very patient kid who tried to avoid violence at all costs. Many years later, many kids in school would come to fear Abey after we witnessed his anger first-hand with another bully in school.

For the rest of my time at St. Thomas Aquinas Catholic Primary School, I became famous for breaking John's nose. No one poked fun at my scarred face, nor did anyone try to bully my brother and me. We sensed mutual respect as John and the rest of the bullies tried to make friends with us.

On weekends, the entire Ayoade family would huddle together in my dad's living room to watch movies from dawn to dusk. However, when night called, we left for the warmth of Alhaja's chamber. I spent more time with Alhaja than I ever did with my parents while living at the family house—a status quo fueled by the constant intrusion of my father's apartment by other family members residing in the same compound. There were extended family members in the house, mainly my dad's sisters. Some of them were married with children, while others were high-school or college students.

I'm not sure if my parents had much privacy, given how difficult it was to break away from the constant knocking on my dad's apartment door. When neighbors needed money or a place to hang out, they came to our home.

My dad was known to be very generous to the people in our community. He handed out money to families that needed a little extra help, and he always brought home VHS movies. Our entire family and groups of neighbors would crowd into our living room, watching films like *Rocky, Karate Kid,* and *Top Gun.*

Through these films, I saw America as a place where people knew exactly what they wanted out of life—Rocky went from being a no-name underdog to training, humbly and hard, and then eventually becoming a world boxing champion. I remember when we saw Rocky I through III, all on the same day.

It was a Sunday, and as on most Sundays, after breakfast around 9:00 am, all the kids went upstairs to my dad's living room. Not long after, my aunties, cousins, and some neighbors began to knock at his door and my mom let them all in to join us. When my dad inserted Rocky I VHS cassette, the excitement was at its peak and the crowd in the room was almost twice what it could accommodate. Most of us had heard or read about the Rocky movies and couldn't wait as we whispered amongst ourselves.

After watching Rocky I halfway, I felt connected to the story so that when Rocky became the heavyweight champion in Rocky II, the entire room went into a frenzy. Even my dad seemed genuinely happy as he inserted the third installment VHS cassette. When the Mayor of Philadelphia celebrated Rocky in Rocky III, and said, "Every once in a while, a person comes along who defies the odds, who defies logic, and fulfills an incredible dream," I thought to myself, *That will be me someday!* It wasn't the boxing that I connected with, it was the sheer determination in Rocky's story.

In *Top Gun*, I loved watching Tom Cruise fly the fighter jets the way he did, his confidence and his quest to be the best, to fight and defend his country.

When you're a child living in circumstances wildly beyond your control, books and movies make America seem like the perfect place. The theme in Hollywood is so often about dreams; how a family can go from nothing to something when one of them decides to give everything and commit their life to that goal. How even in situations of corruption and abuse, good can overcome bad. And for a child living in a world like mine, the impact of that message is immeasurable.

These men endured, persevered, and worked relentlessly toward that dream until they came out on top. I related to them because there was so much that I wanted to experience, too. I was a Nigerian kid, but in my heart, I felt like an American, dreaming about a better future and determined to make it come true.

When I turned seven, my father built his first house. It was my third year in primary school. The memory of the longest short drive was a lifetime of vision for me, though I didn't very well understand the uncanny feeling behind the trip.

The new house was about thirty miles away from the family house, and it was a mansion compared to grandpa's house where we moved from. Besides my dad, mom, Alhaja, aunt, and now five siblings with the birth of Tunji, my three cousins from my late uncle also moved in with us.

After driving halfway, I perceived a changing aura, from the initial excitement of moving to a new place to how bleak our future might be where we were headed to. Maybe I discerned this earlier than the rest of my family. Soon, we would be rocking in the mysterious boat for many years that followed.

For inexplicable reasons, I became more downhearted with each passing mile we drove. Although I was little, I knew things wouldn't be the same. *Surulere* was where the life of the Ayoades was rooted, and it flourished as the years passed by. It was the central part of Lagos, the heart of urban life on the mainland, and influenced by decades of Western development.

For every mile we drove, we noticed only about five houses for the best part, most of them poorly constructed. Then, the little huts. You wonder how they survived the rainy season. The brick and mud houses were mostly defective, patchy, and sometimes shockingly fragmented. I would have rather kept to the mat in Alhaja's room in Surulere than take a much bigger room with a king-sized bed in a place that felt so barren, almost lifeless.

Is my father running away from something, or perhaps someone?

The question remained in my thoughts as we drove further into the rustic little town called *Ejigbo*.

The convoluted roads weren't tarred. The earth was covered with clay that was mostly dusty, staining the atmosphere red as cars drove in and out of the uneven roads. Many kids ran on the streets in underpants with no shoes or slippers on.

Sometimes I noticed women sitting on footstools or benches outside unpolished buildings fanning wood-fired three-stone stoves. They sometimes looked like mini bonfires after the fire was fully grown. It felt like a different planet - and one I didn't like.

I had only seen them on local television shows. As dangerous as a kitchen with a mini bonfire might sound, it was the wonted way of life for these people. I needed to remind myself that we were still in Lagos. There were so many trees, forests, and farms. Only randomly did we notice completed buildings.

There were many kiosks made with dry local woods on the streets. Next to the kiosks, you found two or three men in dust-covered clothes, smoking cigarettes while they prattled away their lives. We had left the world we'd always known in exchange for an entirely different and unnerving one.

Finally, we arrived at the new house. My father's house was one of only four on my street, a crescent that spread over a mile and a half. Our house was also one of the only two houses with fences or any form of security. Most houses had no electricity, so my father had secured a generator.

The village also had no government water supply. There were very few borehole systems, and those who had one sold drinking water to the rest of the community. Most families survived on well water, drawn with a local rubber bag with bare hands.

When the wells ran dry from extended drought, the river - which was several miles from where we lived - was the only option.

It was the Year of the Rabbit. The house was prodigiously ahead of its time, very modern for the eighties, and an exquisite sight to behold. The precision of the construction plan was apparent, while the design was undeniably unique. Why my father picked this location to plant such an edifice was a mystery to us then, but it wouldn't stay that way.

My dad had a stepbrother from Alhaja's first marriage, who was many years older than him. As he stared in wonder at his first sight of my father's house, shaking his head, he muttered a question that I believed was for no one.

"What could be the possible motivation for a man as interesting as my brother to build a mansion meant for the city in a jungle?" he asked. "What sort of a place is called Ejigbo?"

After a moment, he added, "Apparently, Lani's obsession with the wilderness has returned."

I asked Alhaja what he meant by Dad's obsession with the wilderness. Alhaja, knowing how inquisitive I was, answered, "It's the same story that I told you once, remember? Remember when he was in high school?"

When we later searched the map of Lagos, Ejigbo was omitted. My siblings and I didn't find it too shocking when we found out Ejigbo didn't exist on the map. We figured it made sense that a place that rural, embedded in the middle of nowhere, couldn't be known to most *Lagosians*.

I rock in my boat
As the waves glide beneath us.
The shimmering image of the sun
Sparkles upon my face in the gentle dusk.

Peace and joy are my friends.
We paddle with ease and care.
The sea smiles at me, and the blue sky's
Reflection is her beautification.
I smile back,
And we salute each other.

I'm tossed in my boat!
I cannot see him,
But how he deals with me...
Dark cumulus o'er my head gather.
Bright swords are blinding my way.
Driven by reckless tornadoes,
Black waters slap against my boat.

Marked and dampened,
A rugged flare—my face.
I am alone—who watches me?
I am torn—who mocks me?
But she stands firm, my feet held—Love.

When my beloved boat broke,
After high seas and low,
Currents, canals, and caverns
Around the small globe,
I rested with her.
Then I landed on the mighty's land,
Before the king whose eyes are keen,
For scales appeared in it.
How did you keep her?
Forlorn. Here I am now.

My father carefully planned every aspect of the new house. All designs were executed to the very last detail, with no mistakes except one: the housewarming party. My father believed inviting every member of his family and all his friends to the housewarming was the single most critical mistake of his life.

When I found out he had already begun to use both flats on the first floor for soap and nylon production for months before we moved, I wondered if my father ever wanted to live in that house. He found the unprecedented struggles that later befell his family traceable only to one event—*the housewarming party.*

Friends and family members traveled from various parts of the country a week before the housewarming celebration. Dad's three stepmothers and many half-sisters that I'm not sure if I knew at all were also invited. There was enough room in the house to host all the guests that arrived to spend a few days. Looking back, we must have had about fifty guests on any given night that week, but a little over three hundred would attend the actual housewarming party.

When they began to arrive. Most of them would stop outside, admiring the house for a moment before walking through the massive gates, or drive past the house not believing my father could afford such a property. A party that was meant to be a celebration of my father's achievement did witness a few that genuinely hugged and congratulated him, and so many more that conspicuously begrudged his success - friends and family alike.

Now my father, the one who caused so much worry when he ran away as a teen, had begun to do well and went on to build something that, to his family, was a resentful reminder of all they had lost. Even though he had taken financial responsibility for a lot of them after my grandfather died, tragedy had made many bitter, and from this point, there was nothing he could do to please them. It was incomprehensible for me as a child, how much love, care, and generosity my father lavished on his friends and family, yet they did not want him to attain even that level of success?

Many of those he considered close friends, instead of congratulating my father, stared at the house and broke down in tears or became dejected, verbally accusing him of not advising them to invest in a property when he was doing so.

"We hang out together almost every night and partied most weekends," they chastised him. "How could we have known you were investing in something this big despite how much money you spent partying with us? How could you not tell us?"

One of his closest friends would not eat or drink the entire party which lasted a little over twenty-four hours. He rested his head on a table in our living room for the most part of the day, increasingly looking despondent until he left the following morning.

In my culture, the size of your house is an instant measure of how successful you are. Throwing a housewarming party is like welcoming both your friends and enemies into your private life all at once, and the result is often a silent mayhem waiting to explode into your future.

These women had lost their sons almost ten years before. Most of them did not only envy my father's feat, but they also envied Alhaja as well. Watching them berate Alhaja, and his friends castigate him, I began to see that no event in our lives could ever be completely happy. If something good happens to you, others will wish you harm.

If they knew my father bought another house from government housing, how would they have reacted? He would later handover the keys and papers of that house to his half-brother who was married to seven wives and needed a place for two of them when he could no longer afford housing for all of them.

I remember my dad arguing with Alhaja days later about not wanting to live in that house. All he wanted to do was use the building for business, and continue to live in his father's house, but with the help of the head of the family, his mom would convince him to move to his house. As I got older, while Alhaja never denied encouraging my father to leave his father's house, she argued that the elaborate housewarming party wasn't her idea. she had only supported my father's desire to have one.

As I got older, it became even more unclear who persuaded who to have a housewarming party. Neither my father nor Alhaja would ever give a direct answer but they both invited all those people to our home.

When my dad lost his father, five brothers, one sister, an aunt, and a sister-in-law, he desperately wanted to stay clear of the rest of his family altogether. But due to the absence of a man in the family house, he knew he had to pick up the responsibilities.

His sister and a good number of his ten half- sisters, nephews, and nieces all depended on him as the man of the family. Although this made it impossible for him to abscond like he always wanted to, he decided to stay out of his inheritance altogether. He believed money begot enmity even between siblings, and he wanted to prove to them that he could care for them without taking a dime from his father's stakes. So, he relinquished his right to his mother, sister, and other wives.

Despite such a gesture from my father and the undeniable fact that he remained generous to his friends and family, they didn't stand behind his success. It was shocking for me because these were the people that I considered family. How justifiable it was then that he always wanted to make a getaway from his family, constantly trying to flee before the unfortunate incident that claimed the lives of his brothers? He was probably aware of how much duplicity he was surrounded by, so it was reasonable for him to reckon he was better off on his own.

Nonetheless, he trusted and loved his friends much more than they did and when the housewarming revealed the few on his side, it was a hard pill for him to swallow given how much he celebrated his friends publicly.

It didn't make any difference if it was either his or Alhaja's idea. My father was the type of man who made his own decisions, at least to the best of my experience with him.

It is impossible to appease people's practical demands, and so it was between my father and the rest of his friends and extended family members. Post-housewarming, my father was excommunicated from the family. He and Alhaja had not only unintentionally reminded the women of the tragedy that took their sons away; they had awakened the darkness and anger that often comes with bitterness in people.

There was nothing he could do to please them, a lesson he had learned too late. However, they tried to pin their actions against my dad on other reasons. Initially, for not showing interest in the monthly meetings, and later, for his consistent absence from the annual remembrance of his father and brothers at Ijaye.

On several occasions, Alhaja tried to persuade Dad to heed the call of the family. It was his responsibility to do so as a surviving son. What never occurred to them was that my father secretly visited the graves of his father and brothers in Abeokuta every year. I never blamed him for always turning them down. He was only trying to make sure he didn't suffer the same fate as his brothers. Still, there was nothing he could do to please them.

Hurt you, hurt me,
We both must feel.
Hate pain, love pain,
She will always have a place.
How long, how well,
You must be stronger at the
end.

Don't get me wrong
'Cause my pain won't last long.
Sorrow won't last forever,
But I can choose which memories
will linger.

Finally, the lessons
Will open your eyes to your blessings.

It's all for a purpose,

That which fate proposed.

You may never realize

Until the right time—

Your time.

From left: Abey and I at a birthday party in 1983.

From left: My mom, dad, Alhaja, and the Imam praying at the housewarming ceremony in 1987.

A prayer session at the housewarming ceremony. On the right: I was the kid in front, and my cousin Tope was behind me.

Grandpa's four wives. From left: Grandma, third wife, first wife, 10-year-old Toro, and second wife at the housewarming ceremony.

Side view of my dad's house on the day of the housewarming.

Dad and his half-brother from Alhaja's first marriage.

Dad and some of his family members.

Dad and his half-brother (from the same father). The only two surviving brothers after the accident.

My mom.

Judging from my dad's troubled childhood and all that he went through to survive, no one expected him to make it to the top on his own. There was so much envy and bitterness in the air that Alhaja, Mom, and my aunt had become worried for my dad. Knowing what some of his friends and family were capable of, they puzzled over what they intended to plot against my father after the party.

My dad didn't seem too worried about the drama. He continued to quip around with a drink in one hand in disdain of the obvious.

He later said to his mother, "The damage is already done."

It was prescient, like he knew what was coming. My father came to believe that his father's wives, or someone in his family, or someone he calls a friend, had put a curse on him. A year later, we lost all three of my father's cars. One to an accident and the second to a knocked engine. I can't remember what happened to the third, but I do remember my father started riding to work on the back of an okada - a motorcycle used as a taxi, for a long time before he finally got an old used Peugeot 504 to get to his office. He still worked in Surulere, which was very far from home.

My mom gave birth to a baby boy, *Salam*, following severe complications as my father's business started to take a downward turn. Though he'd become known in the community for his generosity, a man who'd helped so many, no one would come to his rescue.

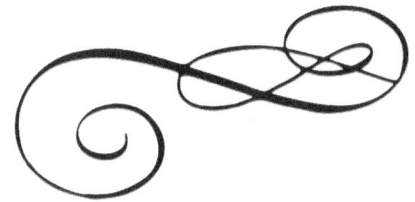

Chapter 3

NIGERIA: July 1990

A Needle to the Heart.

"It will be three years next week since the accident!"

Tears filled my mother's eyes as she spoke, and her voice trembled terribly. Anxious about what was to come, she gaped at me and then back at the doctors. She turned her gaze from one doctor to another, her eyes blurred with tears.

There were six physicians in the room. Two of them were Americans. One was undoubtedly Indian, while the other three were Nigerians. It was easy to figure out, just by listening to each one of them talk. They sounded quite different, yet they clearly understood each other. I assumed most, if not all of them, were pediatricians.

The oldest was Dr. Lander, an African American, who was the chief pediatrician at Ikeja General Hospital. She was my pediatrician. She had summoned five other doctors to her office while I sat in the lobby with my mother. They had talked for approximately twenty minutes before we were invited in to join them.

It seemed like the end of the world to Mom as she anticipated more information from the doctors. She had not completely gotten over the loss of my two-year-old baby brother. Memories of the severely jaundiced baby crying in severe pain for days remain vivid even now.

Both Mom and Dad were in and out of the hospital for weeks until one morning, while my mother gave him a bath, he began to gasp for breath. They rushed him to the hospital, and when they came back, my brother wasn't with them. Salam died on the way to the nearest hospital. I couldn't entirely comprehend the pain my parents were dealing with as I was taken away from the living room by Alhaja while several friends tried to console my parents.

As our entire household went into mourning, I came down with a deadly case of pneumonia that would lead to a startling discovery. It was around this time that I began to have terrible nightmares.

Although I was too young to make anything of the nightmares, they became more consistent, often before something terrible happened to me or someone I loved. I equally had dreams that were good and those that weren't bad but hard to understand. Irrespective of how long I forgot about these dreams, I remember them almost in detail once they happen in reality. Sometimes, they were déjà vu-like, though I couldn't explain where or how.

My mother continued to sink into depression. What happened to me and the news she was about to receive on my health following such an agonizing loss of a child could only make life more unbearable for her.

The physicians continued to stare at me, astounded by the radiologist's report. I had been admitted into the same hospital. During the course of that illness, I stayed in the hospital for two weeks. Recovering in the hospital bed gave me a lot of time to read any book I could get my hands on, especially books from America.

I loved to read and to think there was so much around me that I wanted to learn—so much happening in my life that I hated. But at ten years old, I knew I couldn't change any of it: the way my mother was treated, the notion that it was normal to treat others the wrong way, the place we lived, the fact that we often had very little to eat.

While our community knew my father as a successful and generous man, we knew a very different side of him. It was also around when I was seven that I woke up one morning and walked into my mom's room after hearing my dad shouting the night before.

When she raised her gaze, her left eye was bruised, and a slit in her eyebrow was gaping open. I knew without a doubt that this was my father's doing. He got drunk, and he did this often.

In a year or two, he would start using my four siblings and me as his punching bags. There would be several memories of being whipped until my skin was torn off my back. That morning, I made my mom a promise.

"Mummy," I said, "One day, I will take you far away from here."

Both her shame and her swelling made it impossible for her to fully look at me. "Where will we go?" she asked.

"We'll go to America. One day, I will become a doctor. I will move to the United States and become an American citizen, and then I will take you and my siblings away from this terrible place."

Until I was seven, we lived in the city and were close to everything we needed. Now, we didn't even have electricity. Even the most basic things in life felt harder, and there was nothing I could do to change it.

While these thoughts orbited my mind, I gazed at my mother as I lay in the hospital bed. Despite the lingering pain of the untimely death of my little brother, she never left my bedside. Even on nights when the hospital staff ordered her to let me rest, she slept in the cold of the night outside the ward.

I imagined how much fear she was dealing with. The loss of another child would, without a doubt, kill her. As we regarded each other in the silence of my hospital room, I maintained that promise between us: *I'll take you to America.* The way I'd come to see it, life in Nigeria meant making ourselves vulnerable to the worst.

My admission had commenced with fifty-three antibiotic injections, none of which I thought my father had witnessed. The first and only time he visited me was on the first day of admission to the children's ward. To date, I still don't know if it was due to work or if he'd showed up a few times when I was asleep.

My in-patient experience left my gluteus maximus severely swollen, painful, and tender to touch since the doctors and nurses could not decide on an alternate injection site. As a result, I lay in a prone position as I endured my two-week confinement to the hospital mattress.

Here I was on my fourth appointment in two months following my discharge from the hospital. It took the radiologists a few weeks to finally come up with something definitive, considering how I'd been exposed to X-rays more than six times in ten weeks. Whatever their discovery was, they were staring at it.

Across from where I was seated were eight X-ray images hanging in the X-ray fluorescent light box. They looked identical to me, but I thought there might be something different about the X-rays as two of them were from three years before. The doctors continued to whisper to one another as they slowly moved from one X-ray to the next.

Finally, they uncovered a mystery about the ten-year-old 'Deji! I thought. I remained quietly seated, watching my mother shed tears in the chair next to me. It was the third time I would see my mom like this. The doctors seemed too stupefied to speak.

I have been with you,
And you said, "Certainly, I do know."
The sea tide is rising,
So let's go home.
Home is in the end—
The end of a long road.
It haunts me to tell,
That this, you must tread.

It's so uncertain—
I'm sorry,' urn request.
The thorns must be there,
Including the starless midnights,
And as in the beginning,
You don't have to find me.
No! You'll never walk alone.
Everything is alright.

These bloody drains—
Is it that of domestics?
She looked at me and sighed.
"It may be cruel as you see it.
Perhaps as you take it or live it
It has little purpose—
To bother or worry.
There will always be tomorrow,
So please don't hurry."

My son… my help!
Well, it's just me now.
The road, this road we're on.
No cars, no flight; so dull.
I won't be afraid of surprises.
I'm full of it.

"Looking back is bad.
There's no need to look around,"
She whispered from afar.
"Well, then, help me to not look down.
And if I look inside,
Tell me it will be alright."
"Hey, son!" she whispered aloud,
"But these rights include so many ways of life:
The thins, crooks, and smooth.
Teach me to look up."
Then she said, "That's all right."

As I tried to recall the times I had seen my mom that shattered, I wondered if the gutter event was the first time. *Perhaps this is like the needle incident from just three years before when I was just seven years of age,* I thought. It seemed almost like *déjà vu* sitting in a room filled with pediatricians.

"I can't believe my son is still living with a needle in his chest," said Mom. She finally broke the silence, dolefully glared at her hands and away from the doctors. I felt responsible as well as guilty for my mom's predicament as I recollected the night of the needle incident when Mom rushed to the scene.

My mother was a seamstress, and I'd been a little obsessed with her sewing machine since I was five. However, her tools were inaccessible because she was working as a fashion designer in town. She never kept her tailoring tools anywhere near the kids.

It was her biggest dream at the time to own a business. So, my father built her a small investment boutique to start a tailoring and fabric business at the new house. I would watch, mesmerized, as she flawlessly cut the clothes into different shapes and sizes and sewed them together into *buba* and *iro*, the traditional attire for Yoruba women in Nigeria.

Buba is a loose blouse worn on top of iro. Iro is a wrap skirt referred to as a *wrapper*. My mother specialized in this type of attire for women. Oftentimes, she would get very crafty with the fabrics, creating intricate designs depending on her clients' requests. I never saw her outline male attire except when she made me a male Buba from leftover materials.

It was no surprise that, in Mom's absence, I played around with her sewing machine and some of her tools. Eventually, my curiosity would get the best of me. A few weeks later, my older cousin caught me with a sewing needle.

We had been horseplaying, and she'd tried to take the needle from me, so I tucked it into my front shirt pocket to hide it from her. The house was always hot in the evenings, so after dinner, we children often congregated in the living room, where I loved to lie on the center table just because the surface was smooth and cool. But as I'd positioned myself to lie on my belly, the needle angled upright, and because my shirt was too tight for me, it penetrated my chest.

The pain was initially sharp and became more intense and stabbing as it penetrated my chest. It felt like when the nurses administered my doses of injection but forgot to take out the needle when done.

I screamed out in pain. "Pin! Pin!"

Alhaja and the rest of the kids, alarmed and confused, screamed back, "Where? Where?"

The commotion was unexpected for the family as Alhaja yelled out for Mom.

"My chest! My chest!" I continued to scream.

There was no electricity, but we had a few lanterns in the house. My brothers grabbed the lamp from the table where I was lying before my screaming episode began. Alhaja held me by the shoulder while she searched but couldn't find the needle. The lantern wasn't bright enough for anyone to find the needle. We could barely see each other's faces, so they had no other choice than to helplessly continue to search as carefully as they could.

"Where is it? Where is it? Show me, Ramon!" Alhaja continued to ask.

"My chest! My chest!" I continued to cry. "It was in my pocket!"

Alhaja carefully tried to remove my shirt, knowing whatever I was crying about must be hanging somewhere. That was when Mom came into the scene.

She heard my cries, and as my cries got louder, she became more agitated and, in panicked haste, accidentally broke off the protruding end, leaving the rest of the sharp needle embedded in my chest.

Not long after, my father arrived. I remember lying in his arms in stabbing pain as he rushed me to the back seat of his Peugeot 504 and zoomed off to the hospital. The closest hospital to my father's house was the *Isolo Health Center*, about twelve miles from the house. The doctors took two X-rays after the incident, and I was admitted for a week.

For weeks after, I felt a sharp tenderness beneath my ribs, but the X-rays immediately following the incident had dismissed the possibility that anything was wrong.

Now, three years later, six new X-rays for my pneumonia revealed a piece of the needle situated dangerously close to my heart. My mother, who was still grieving the loss of her youngest child as I—often her protector, her confidante—fought for my life, blamed herself for all of it.

"Mrs. Ayoade, we looked into the two X-rays you brought to your son's last appointment. I told you to bring them over because I wanted to compare them with what we have. You said they were from three years ago?" Dr. Lander reconfirmed.

"Yes, they are," Mom replied.

"You are right. We did not find this needle in those X-rays," Dr. Lander continued. "However, if you look through these radiographs, at the lower left side of the chest, there's a needle of about two inches in length, pointing towards the apex of the heart." She pointed to the radiographs with the tip of her pen. It took the radiologists a while to finally come to a conclusion.

"As you can see, these six radiographs were taken at different times between his admission to this hospital and his last appointment at my office. The most shocking part is that the radiologist's conclusion is accurate based on the short story you just told us. Ramon did have a needle accident in the past.

"It was hard for us to believe as much as it is for you, Mrs. Ayoade," the doctor continued. "The truth is, Ramon has a needle in his chest. I'm afraid we must act quickly. How he made it this far without problems or complications is still a mystery. I wanted these doctors to witness your son's case. That's why they are here. I'm sure they have questions for you. We will be deciding today on the best step to act on to achieve success with the new development."

Tears rolled down my mom's face as the doctor continued to talk to us. If I didn't understand the conversation and had just observed my mom's reaction, I would have thought they just told her I wasn't going to make it. The doctors paused for a moment for my mom to comport herself before one of the residents continued.

"Mrs. Ayoade, can you give us a little history about why your son was admitted here?" My mom, still overwhelmed with guilt and obviously trying to gather her thoughts, turned to the young doctor, but I could tell she wasn't entirely there. It seemed to me the doctor had asked a question that had become less important at the worst possible time.

"He could barely take a full breath," my mom said, speaking slowly but with an obvious disconnection between her words and her thoughts. Her right hand cupped in her left hand, resting on her handbag. I sat next to her, quietly observing.

"He couldn't lie on his back either, so we took him to a local health center," she continued. "The same hospital he was admitted into three years ago. The doctors referred us to your hospital because they could not treat his condition. He had severe pneumonia, as your doctors later diagnosed. His pneumonia was too advanced for delayed treatment, so he was admitted to this hospital. They had him on antibiotic injections every six hours for two weeks. He was discharged after his pain and breathing got better. We have since been on bi-weekly appointments with Dr. Lander to monitor his progress."

My mother still had concerns that were more pressing to her. She abruptly switched from her short story, which the resident was paying much attention to.

"Forgive my diversion," she said. "I'm still trying to place how a needle resurfaced on six new radiographs." She turned to Dr. Lander, trying to get an answer from her.

Dr. Lander attempted to explain a possibility to her, but clearly, her medical explanation didn't do much for us.

"You mean there's been a needle close to his heart for three years?" Mom asked, still in tears. "Will my son die from this needle?"

She turned her teary eyes to me. She seemed amazed by my presence. Meanwhile, I tried to hide how special I felt about such gargantuan attention I was being showered with by keeping a blank face. I would be boasting about carrying a needle in my chest for three years in school the following Monday while my friends thought I was a superman.

"It's my fault. I should have been more careful."

"Mrs. Ayoade, there is a way out. Your son will not die," Dr. Lander assured.

"We have to refer you to another teaching hospital where they have more experienced cardiothoracic surgeons than we do. They could operate on your son successfully. I know someone in *Lagos University Teaching Hospital*, LUTH. We used to have the good ones here, but most of them left for greener pastures if you understand me."

"You mean they could remove the needle successfully?" Mom asked, desperate for some assurance on her son's life. It seemed that Dr. Lander understood this. However, her face remained the same. It wasn't going to change until the possibility of my survival was a certainty.

"I will write you a referral. I'm sure the surgeons will do their very best to help Ramon."

I gazed at Mom's swollen face and puffy eyes as we rode quietly in a taxi.

"I'm sorry, Mom. I'm sorry."

She didn't seem to understand what I was so sorry about. I'm not sure what was going on in her mind as I poured out how much I regretted my behavior. I finally had an outburst of sincere apologies. My actions did not influence the remainder of a quiet, emotionally charged day. Not better or worse than it had been by any means.

"It's fine, Ramon," Mom said, offering a watery smile. "You were just an innocent seven-year-old. We all make mistakes sometimes. I made a big mistake. This wouldn't have happened had I been more careful. I mistakenly broke the needle because I was confused. I should have been more careful." She continued to blame herself as her eyes filled with tears once again.

"I heard the doctors say the pin is near my heart, but it won't kill me. Right?"

"No, you won't die."

"Say that again, okay?

"You will not die," she repeated the second time in a lower tone without looking at me like she needed to believe what she had just said.

Never underestimate
The beauty of the morning sun,
The gentle breeze found in the wilderness,
Love between father and son,
And an orison from mother to a child.
Never underestimate
The ability to understand spirituality
And to be better aware of an ultimate presence,
Within and around you.
A mother's sacrifice.

Between our departure from Ikeja General Hospital and arrival at LUTH, I thought Mom might have replayed the needle incident in her head several times. I knew she wished she could erase the scene where she accidentally broke off the needle that fell into her son's thoracic cavity. Perhaps she would pause at the scene just before she touched me, so she could get another chance to handle things differently.

Fortunately, we found the surgeon we were referred to. He carefully read the letter after inviting us to have a seat in his office.

"Okay, Mrs. Ayoade, here's what we'll do. I need you to bring your son exactly a week from now. Make it 10:00 a.m. We will be ready for him."

"Just like that?" Mom asked, evidently still disturbed about the urgency of my predicament. She moved on to the next question without waiting for an answer to the last. "Are you serious? He's got a needle in his chest!"

"I understand, Mrs. Ayoade. He's also borne this needle for how many years? Three years? That's an indication that the needle will not kill your son overnight. He will be okay. We will review his record and make plans for the surgery. We will also have to keep him here for a few weeks after the surgery, so prepare for a short stay as well."

Soon we were out of the surgeon's office, my hand in Mom's. She continued to stare at me, silently crying. "I should have been more careful."

"Don't worry, Mom. I will be alright. The doctor said I would be alright," I tried to assure my mom, all of ten years old.

I was only four

When she told me they were stars.

Up in the night sky,

They never stopped shining.

That's where I wanted to be,
But there was no one to take me there.
For years, I watched so intently,
But I could only see my reflection
Down at my feet.

I'm twenty-eight,
And I still haven't stopped.
I have the picture of a blue rose in my star,
And it makes me think of who you are.
I see a shadow of a woman watching me,
And it reminds me of what your Love is.

So many times, I've thought about my life,
And how much pain it's caused yours.
I could live without everything else,
But not without your Love, mama.

On surgery day, both of us were anxiously sitting in the operating room waiting area. A nurse came over, called out my last name, followed by my first and middle names. A little boy about five years old jumped off the chair and ran off to the nurse. Astonished, I turned to my mom, who smiled back at me.

"Sorry dear, how old are you?" the nurse asked. "I am five years old!" the boy replied.

"Well, this patient is ten years old, so I guess it's not your turn yet, sweetie."

A forced smile radiated briefly from the nurse towards us as Mom and I got up to approach her. Apparently, we shared the same names, except that the little boy's first name was my middle name while my first name was his middle name.

A momentary ease in the air at the young boy's display of enthusiasm, the tension on most patients waiting to be seen seemed to be lifted for a few minutes.

"How are you?" she asked. Without waiting for a response, she said to Mom, "I'm not sure your son's surgery will hold today anymore."

"What? What do you mean? His surgery's been canceled?" Without giving the nurse a chance to explain, Mom continued, "His surgery is very urgent! The surgeon promised today!"

"The doctor would like to talk to you in his office, ma'am."

A simple line that rescued the nurse from a desperate mother. She knew there was no turning back for the mother of the patient at hand. She walked away as she escorted us into the same office we had visited a week before.

"Mrs. Ayoade, there's good news and bad news." The doctor said as soon as we entered. "The good news is, your son can live with this needle without possible danger to his life. However, you must prevent him from strenuous activities that could potentially cause the needle to move further up toward his heart. The sad news is that LUTH is currently having the same problem Dr. Lander's hospital has. Our most experienced cardiothoracic surgeons left the country, leaving us with, I believe, those not skilled enough to operate on your son, including myself. After carefully reviewing Ramon's case, I must be honest with you, Mrs. Ayoade." He paused for a few seconds and continued, "I prefer not to take any risk on this surgery, especially knowing your son can live with the needle without the surgery."

"So, you mean my son will be perfectly fine with the needle inside his chest?" She seemed somewhat relieved as she sat up in her chair.

However, her expression was still very troubled by the fact that I could live with it.

"How is he supposed to live without doing all the things kids his age do? Like playing football?" Mom countered out of frustration.

"Mrs. Ayoade, if you and your husband can afford surgical treatment for your son in the United Kingdom or the United States of America, I can guarantee he would get care from highly experienced cardiothoracic surgeons," the doctor said. "The chances that your child will live a healthy life with the needle in his chest are much higher than the likelihood of a successful surgery if we went ahead with it."

Now my mom seemed more confused, frustrated, and helpless at the same time. Of course, she knew we couldn't afford surgery in a developed country, and how could she live with the fact that I had a needle inside me with unpredictable outcomes? She was left with the option to trust the doctor and believe I could live with it, provided I didn't engage in strenuous activity. My life would be different, but she was happy that I would live.

Chapter 4

NIGERIA: 1990

No One but Alhaja.

W hen I was released from the hospital, the doctors advised me to stay away from rigorous activities, including soccer. I was indifferent to hear the news, all I wanted was for my mom to be happy and stop worrying about me. Soccer had been a favorite pastime among my siblings and cousins, but now I sat on the sidelines of our yard's makeshift field and watched them all play together.

It was there that I noticed we'd all begun to regard each other a little differently. Maybe it was because I was still recovering, or maybe it was because we were all still grieving Salam, but it was noticeable to me, and I think to all of us - we children had begun to take very intentional care of each other.

Back in school, the classrooms which were already dilapidated finally collapsed. The school made us go to the bamboo swamp to cut down bamboo and palm fronds to build classrooms on the school field.

We moved our desks and benches into the sheds with raised bamboo sticks tied together, and the roof was covered in palm fronds. Most times, the sun found its way into the sheds, but we were indifferent. All that mattered was that we had a school to attend.

When the rain came, and we had no classes for the teachers to teach, the biggest church and mosque in Ejigbo town then offered their buildings for us to go to until the school buildings were fixed. It was further from home, and my brother and I went from trekking six miles to eight miles every day.

By the time the government finally came to the school's aid two years later, I was about to leave for junior secondary school, where the buildings were also deteriorating.

Slowly, my brothers brought me back into our soccer games, passing the ball to me gently and encouraging me as I grew stronger. In our home, we all grew more supportive of each other in this way. It was as though Salam's death and my illness had proven how quick and easy it would be for any of us to lose a sibling. We looked out for each other as the aftermath of events like these played out painfully between our parents.

While my parents were suffering, Alhaja made it her job to uplift us children. She was our consolation, the only adult in our lives who always had time for all of us children in the house. She was calm. She sat down to our level and told us stories.

Alhaja made a point to remain playful and maintain a veil of innocence for us children. Sometimes in quiet moments when it was just her and me, she told me about her husband, my grandfather, who'd died just a few years before I was born. She talked to me about faith and death and the struggles she'd been through and survived.

One of the lessons Alhaja once gave that stayed with me to this day was about knowledge.

"Knowledge can be so complicated," she said. "We understand circumstances best through life experiences. Otherwise, they are mere words. We can speak words, write them when prompted, and pretend we thoroughly understand them because we learned to use them in context. No matter how we use these words when we ought to or not, or how long these words are taken for granted, we will never comprehend them entirely without a happening: a personal life experience."

Alhaja tried not to over-expound on subjects such as love, life, and death. Despite having life throw more than her share of rocks at her, she believed that the most complicated topics could be explained to any child.

"Even when a child assumes an adequate knowledge of these three gifts, it is an entirely different story when they finally become the subject," Alhaja explained. "It remains ambiguous what differing life experiences do to our understanding. A better understanding might be earned just like it will for most men, but not every child will come out of what they know the same way."

"It could be sweet, such as in the case of a boy and a girl in love for the first time. It could taste bitter for a child lost in an iniquitous, wicked, and vile world without a loved one. It is a different ball game when a child loses a loved one for the first time. Then the child will understand how sad life can be. How love can make life so gratifying, and when death can ceaselessly, or sometimes abruptly deprive it of any meaning."

At a more personal level, I was aware I had just come very close to death. But my grandmother's teachings, along with the pain of losing my little brother, led me to start thinking very deeply.

My first understanding of life was *curiosity*, and it sure got me into a lot of trouble.

One day, my dad came back home with a plumber and a policeman, along with two of his friends. He was furious. The cop and his two friends tried to mollify him. He had paid the plumber more than a few times to fix some broken water pipes in the house. However, the plumber had absconded, and it had been months without hearing from him. My dad was able to track him down with the help of his friends and a cop.

He wanted the plumber arrested for fraud, but his accomplices had a better suggestion for him. Since the plumber had been crying and begging my dad not to have him locked up, they suggested they make him sign a contract stating what he'd been paid for and when the job must be completed. It seemed like a good plan until after the contract was drawn and it was time for the plumber to sign.

They discovered he couldn't - he was illiterate. He could neither read nor write. So, they all sat in a circle at the center of the living room, trying to figure what to do with the man. I was working on my homework while observing the incertitude that was beginning to infuriate my dad once again.

I walked towards the middle of the grown-ups with my *Bic* pen pulled out of the plastic holder. My father turned towards me from where he sat. He knew I was up to something, but he didn't have the time for it. He yelled at me to leave the parlor. As I started to walk away disappointed, one of his friends stopped me and called me back.

"Go on, Ramon. I think you've got something on your mind," he said, curious what I was up to.

I nodded, walked to the plumber and ordered him to extend his right thumb. There was extreme silence in the room as I pulled the head of my biro and blew two drops of blue ink on his thumb. I turned and walked back to the dining table, where I was finishing up my homework. I couldn't help but notice how the men eventually broke the silence, started to laugh and made fun of one another.

"Imagine a six-year-old not only understands we could use a thumbprint in place of a signature, he knew exactly how to get one," my dad's friend said jokingly. I knew beneath my father's stern demeanor that he was proud of what I did despite my intrusion, but he said nothing.

My first experience of deep affection wasn't until my third year in primary school. It was bitter-sweet because I admired a girl in my class from a distance.

As hard as it was to describe the kind of love between my family members and me when I was a child, I discovered that I couldn't afford to lose them. Regardless of what I liked or disliked the most about each one of them, they were still part of me. I realized that once humans die, we never see them again.

This understanding brought my family into sharp perspective for me. I couldn't afford to lose them—Alhaja out of all the people. In the dark moments of my childhood, it was only Alhaja who could grant me comfort.

If I lose this woman, I thought, *what's going to happen to me? She can't go anywhere. If she does, my life will be over.*

So, as life continued to bring death in our paths, I watched people cry from time to time, and then I wondered only about Alhaja, no one but Alhaja.

This love, as I realized, was different and much stronger than the type of love I'd felt for friends, or for the girl in my class. When I could no longer contain the troubling thoughts of losing Alhaja, I knew it was time to talk to her.

"Alhaja, are you going to die? Will you ever leave us? How long do you have left to be with us? Can people tell when they will die?"

Finally, it was a perfect moment to unleash such questions to Alhaja. I thought she was the only one who truly loved me. She understood me more than anyone else. There was no doubt that I would run into a raging fire to rescue Alhaja if I had to. I loved her that much.

Alhaja was my interpretation of love. Without her, I believed life wouldn't be the same. I had no idea how old she was, but she seemed ancient to me. My confusion was further complicated by the tremendous respect that comes with old age in my culture. Alhaja got a full truckload of those. Looking back, she must have been in her late sixties, much younger than I thought back then as Alhaja turned ninety-nine thirty years later.

"Alhaja, I want to know how much time you have left before you leave us," I persisted, sitting next to her on her favorite brown cotton couch where she often rested when she was not praying on the mat.

She was quiet for a few seconds, probably wondering what prompted a seven-year-old to worry that much about death. With a steady, intent stare, she asked, "Why do you ask, Ramon? What did you see? What's your worry?"

"If you die, we can't see you anymore! We will be miserable without you!"

Alhaja struggled with tears rolling down her face. With a scarf, she concealed them as she brought herself to her feet. She did not respond. After a little quietude, she began to walk toward her son's room, my father. I went back to watching television, my question unanswered.

You are my haven.

I could burrow up and down

In the letters of your words

And find clarity in your wisdom.

Your Love is my refuge.

I could reminisce

About all that was more than words

And burn in memories of you.

Between joy and sorrow is time and knowledge,

And I could still pour my heart out

Just to find

How to live right by you—my solace.

A few minutes later, I heard my dad walk down the hallway. I could feel the vibrations from the terrazzo-laden floor as he took each footstep down the hall. A sturdy man, my father was. About five-foot- eleven, but he appeared taller than he really was. He was light- complexioned and well-built but not overweight. At thirty-two, he seemed much bigger than he was, probably because of the way he walked and talked. He walked like a giant and spoke like a king, born with a rare, enchanting charisma.

My dad knew who he was and never settled for less. I thought he was the strongest man that I'd ever seen. He was fierce, brave, and never showed any sign of pain or weakness no matter what.

"My father can move mountains," I'd boast about him among friends. "The ground trembles at the steps of my dad, and the world quivers at the sound of his roaring voice when angered."

Alhaja must have invited him over to the living room.

He walked in and sat on a couch across from where I was sitting. Alhaja returned to her seat that was next to mine. There was a center table between my father and us.

"Your son wants to know how much time I have left before I leave them. He wants to know when I'm going to die!" she announced to my dad like they hadn't debated the issue in private.

My father paused for a moment. He allowed some silence to settle in after tuning the television volume down. He leaned forward as much as he could from the couch like my understanding of what he was about to say depended on it. He smiled gently and stared into my eyes so that he had my full attention. This was one of the few intimate moments I ever got to share with my father.

"Alhaja is going nowhere, Ramon. She will always be around and will stay with us for a very long time. I can assure you there is nothing to worry about. She will be around long enough to see your children. That's a very long time."

He must have noticed my dissatisfaction, so he added, "You see, when we are young, it's okay to think older people are more aged than they are. But they are much younger than they seem, and you will grow up to see them age less as you become a father someday."

A little confused about Dad's explanation, Alhaja intervened, "I love you, Ramon. I love you all. I will always be around. If I must leave for any reason, nothing will happen to you. Nothing will change."

I knew she understood the implication of my question better than my father ever would. She was the pillar that held my family together in an enormous house—not my dad, mom, or my aunt. She made the house a home. Even when everyone else forgot to show love while they were busy with the different challenges life was hurling at them, Alhaja never faltered. So I knew, should Alhaja depart for any reason, be it death or illness, nothing would ever be the same.

Alhaja would often encourage us to dream.

"A dream is like a roadmap," she said. "Without it, you will be lost in mottles of life's purposes. You know, like when you watch a mouse on the television, adrift in a maze? The mouse either keeps treading the same path repeatedly or makes a wrong turn when it's closest to its destination."

She also encouraged us to have goals. "Even when you think you have goals, it might be harder to realize your true purpose in life without dreams. But remember, dreams are impossible to achieve without goals," she added.

"Your father might be a hard man, but he sees things. He knows you have dreams, and he wants to make sure you don't lose that gift because you will achieve them. You need to know also, every great thing comes at a cost. However, beware of chasing after dreams that already came true. It's like placing a roadblock on your destiny with your own hands."

Alhaja loved differently. She showed it. She lived it. Her love felt tangible. She kissed us on both cheeks every morning and when we returned from school. She told us stories by the moonlight, taught us how to pray, cook, and improvise with what we have whenever we needed anything we couldn't afford. Alhaja spoke in a clear, gentle, smooth, and calming voice even on her worst days.

I remember her doing so much more for us and everyone else that we knew or not, than she did for herself. She gave us reasons to believe in love. She defended us, often even from my father.

Alhaja, 1990.

While Alhaja was unconditionally caring and affectionate, our father's love was much tougher. He showed love by providing for his family. He believed fatherly love rested on fulfilling his responsibilities. He would go to any length to protect his family. His interpretation of love was different. Fortunately, he was blessed to have children who understood him quite a bit. We totally believed in his advice despite his contradicting way of life.

My father was very unpredictable. He was strict and short-tempered. Nothing about him was passive. His anger quickly soared into aggression that frequently ended in violence. His temper was uncontrollable each time it rose to a boiling point, so those that knew him well did their best to avoid prolonged arguments with him. Looking back, it was as though he thought he was preparing us for the harshness of life without realizing that we as kids were already feeling it too.

The older children had the luxury of avoiding my father, but the younger ones weren't that lucky. After an episode of bellowing in anger, he would reach for his Koboko. My dad's Koboko was only a few inches shorter than the Australian stockwhip. A single stroke was capable of ripping off your skin and inflicting more pain and wounds than you could ever imagine.

Once when I was fourteen, he had my shirt removed and beat me to the point where I stopped crying in pain. He was enraged, completely out of control. No one dared mention a word or tried to stop him. He continued to flog me as mercilessly as he could, like he desperately needed to beat the life out of me. My siblings would later explain how they had lost count of how many strokes landed on my back. They thought I was dead when they stopped hearing my screams, and they started to cry when he kept thrashing.

Afterwards, everything was hazy. I tried lying on my back after teetering back to my room, but the sheets stuck to the bleeding bruises on my back. The bleeding from my back continued for days while it took weeks of lying procumbent for my wounds to heal. Most scars from my father's whip healed over time; most disappeared completely into my skin, but not from memory. I still bear the scars that won't go away on my back no matter what I do.

I have no idea how we made it through such a degree of physical and psychological abuse, though corporal punishment was the norm in school and in my tribe.

Today, especially in the United States, my father would by no means be considered fit to be a father, or worse still, to raise children. There were times when we doubted if he was truly our father. He never treated any child differently from the other. There were five of us from two wives and three other kids from my late uncle.

My cousins desperately sought to escape to their mom. They would rather go through a financial struggle with her than continue to suffer from recurring abuse from my father. At least, they had a second option. It was not the same for the rest of us.

My dad would not entertain the idea of his kids sleeping over at someone else's house, not to speak of traveling for the holidays.

When I turned eleven, my father hired a tutor. I was in my first year of junior secondary school, which was the equivalent of seventh grade in the United States. The tutor focused only on Maths and English: Mondays through Fridays, from 4:00 p.m. to 6:00 p.m. after we arrived from school, usually at about 3:30 p.m.

He was quite a disciplinarian, very confident in his strict teaching methods, but not anywhere close to what my father was. He would realize that after his first major encounter with my father in action.

It was one of such evenings we wished the tutor wouldn't show up for the evening classes. It was the second term of my first year in secondary school. The clock ticked on the wall of the children's parlor as we waited patiently for him to arrive. The time was a quarter before 4:00 p.m., so he would be coming in 15 minutes.

As usual, we all settled around the dining table and went over the homework he had given to us the evening before. The dining table had eight dining chairs, and there were seven of us being tutored—my brother and I, with whom I shared the same age and class in school, my three cousins and two young uncles that were three and six years older, respectively. The younger of the two uncles had just moved to my dad's house following his father's death. His dad was Alhaja's younger brother.

The tutor usually sat in the middle dining chair where he could clearly observe each one of us as he gave us work to do. We knew better to be settled and ready before he arrived, a requirement we never needed to be reminded of. We were the youngest at the table. My cousins and young uncles were about two to four classes ahead of us.

As he perused our assignments, there was disappointment written all over his face, but he waited until he checked the very last person's work. Then, his disappointment was quickly followed by confusion, anger, and frustration. Apparently, every single one of us didn't do well in the same work he thought we'd already mastered a while back. He got louder, and my mother and Alhaja could hear him, but they didn't know exactly what to say. They stood in the center of the parlor waiting for him to handle the situation; after all, that was what he got paid to do.

The earliest my father ever returned from work was 6:00 p.m., and most times, just when the tutor headed out the gate. Unfortunately, that day, he returned an hour early. He walked into the hallway just when the tutor was still chastising us for forgetting things we'd already learned.

Instead of heading straight to his room like he usually did, he paused for a moment, turned to where the noise was coming from, and listened for a few seconds while the teacher, who took no notice of him, continued. The more he continued to express his disappointment, the longer my father listened, and the more we knew the trouble was getting worse.

My dad resumed walking towards his room instead of walking over to the dining table, where we all sat quivering at what was about to happen next. The tutor had no idea what was about to flounce us, but we knew, and we were getting ready for it while he talked.

Of course, at this point, it wasn't as obvious, but we weren't paying much attention to him except my younger uncle, who was still new to my father's house. He had never been whipped before with my dad's koboko. When my father came out of his room, it was as expected; he had his usual white knicker on, no shirt. He stormed the hallway and walked straight into his living room.

All of us except the newbie uncle and the tutor jumped off our seats, waiting for the beating. The two seemed confused about why, but it was too late. When he came out of his living room, he had his koboko in his left hand—the stronger hand. He started off with one of my cousins, who was already waiting right next to her chair. The tutor and my uncle jumped off their seats and stood behind the chairs, perplexed at my father whipping the living evening out of every one of us, one kid to the next.

Now, we all had tricks to escape my father whenever his group-whipping session ensued. When you get whipped about five to six times, you want to run away from him into an open space where he could not reach you while you allow him to be distracted by someone else. We all knew exactly what to do, but my poor young uncle had no clue. He crawled underneath the dining table only after two strokes—the biggest mistake you could ever make whenever my father had his koboko in his left hand.

My dad leaned lower and underneath the table towards him and continued to lash him until he probably landed his usual number, twelve strokes. Meanwhile, he had forgotten about my brother and my other uncle because they sat closer to the sliding door, which was closer to the balcony. They had taken off to the balustrades along with the rest of us that already took a few lashes of the leather.

The tutor was now standing a few feet away from us, the dining table, and my dad altogether. With his arms dangling by his sides and mouth wide open, he stood next to my mom and Alhaja who couldn't do much about what was going on but to watch.

When my father finished with us, he stormed out of our parlor and back into his living room while slamming the door behind him. As some of us continued to cry while others that escaped my dad's whip pretended to cry in pain, Alhaja turned to the tutor and asked him, "Did you expect what just happened?"

He turned to her with his mouth still wide open, unable to utter a single word. Alhaja continued, "I guess next time you know what to do. That's why we don't report the kids to him half the time. That's his way."

Later at night, while recapping the thrashing episode from my dad in the boys' bedroom where we all shared beds, we made fun of the new guy: what his mistake was, and what he needed to do next time such an occasion presented itself.

As far as he was concerned, it was still difficult for him to understand why my father had to go that far. His father had never laid hands on him while he was alive, so he was pretty much in shock while the rest of us laughed off the incident as one of many. My brother and other uncle mockingly thanked him for taking up just enough strokes for my dad to forget about them.

The following evening, we all scored a hundred percent on our homework, of course. However, the tutor apologized to us. He didn't think our dad would go that far on an issue that he'd expected him to simply warn or advise us about. At the end of the academic year, I had the highest score in math in the entire school.

My father demanded we be the best intellectually and toughest emotionally. We felt the constant need to impress him academically. However, the growing feeling of dejection and increasing need for affection were undeniable. Initially, for me, it was clearly out of fear of what would happen if I came home with the second-place result at the end of the term. But over time, it became a matter of pride.

One morning, it was 6:00 a.m., and I had just missed a spot while sweeping the hallway with our traditional African broom, my assigned daily chore. He said, "Wherever you find yourself in life, whatever position, no matter how big or small, they are equally very important. You are there because you were meant to, so you have to embrace it, own it, and never compromise your integrity no matter what. Till the very last second while you're at it—you never know what it's preparing you for."

In everything that I did, mediocrity was not an option. My father perceived my confidence level had skyrocketed, so he ceased to worry about me academically. I took the bull by the horns, not out of love or compensation for all he provided as a father or to earn his respect, but as a matter of personal goal when it came to being the best in my class. It was the only place I could channel all my frustrations from the imprisonment of my father's world.

We didn't get many opportunities to see the city like we used to. My initial sadness that came with our relocation to Ejigbo did not fade. It sprouted uncontrollably into depression, though I was too little to understand what depression was back then. We had been subjected to reclusion. We weren't allowed to meet other kids after school. We couldn't leave the gate or play with other children in the neighborhood.

My father timed us each time he sent us on errands, sometimes in the middle of the night, miles along a bush path, and mostly pitch-black, you could barely see what was ahead of you. He did everything he could to ensure we did not have any playtime outside his compound. Since we could do nothing about our circumstances, we accepted our fate—destined to live and adapt to our pristine environment and its conditions without choice.

He warned from time to time, "Do as I say, not as I do." How my father behaved and treated us was in no way close to being right. How could a father claim to love his children and treat them the way he treated us? You want your kids to be happy, but you can't emotionally express your love to them? You don't want your kids to smoke cigarettes and drink alcohol, but you are a chimney who takes to the bottle all weekend? You want your boys to grow and become gentlemen, but you controlled their mother like a puppet and continually turned her into your punching bag before their eyes? You don't want them to become bullies, but you hit them at the slightest irritation? You want them to be smart and have self-confidence, but you shout at and whip their confidence out of their brains? It's a child's nature to observe what their parents do. We couldn't help it, despite his warnings.

During this period, I would isolate myself more deeply, always shrouded in worry about my life, my family.

"You're only eleven years old!" my father would say. "You have no kids. You have no wife. What do you have to worry about? You don't need to save the world!"

Yes, I did. Every one of us has a soul and feels pain. Our family's life and the things I witnessed had planted a seed within me to protect not only the ones I loved, but anyone vulnerable. He didn't understand that about me—I knew he would think it was weak.

"Do you need a book?" he said. "That's it. I'll buy you a storybook tomorrow."

On days he returned home with something new for me to read, I would lock myself in my room for hours, submerging myself in any tale that would take my thoughts away from life at home.

Every morning, I noticed my father staring into a big mirror in his room while dressing up for work. It was usually about the same time I completed my morning chores before getting ready for a three-mile walk to school. He often left his bedroom door ajar while I swept past the hallway to the stairway with a broom.

I wondered what he saw every morning staring at that mirror. Was he doing everything he could to change himself, or did he prefer the easier way? To keep warning us not to be like him? If my father succeeded at anything, he had exceptional children with a natural ability to discern what was right from wrong.

None of us wanted to be like him. His prayers and ours were answered, for sure. At least, none of us inherited his anger. My father only wanted us to follow his words, and we did. We managed to bury all our grotesque experiences and try to heal completely from the wounds of our childhood memories. How ironic that we looked up to our father, but we never wanted to emulate him.

It was a remarkable thing that we comprehended that wasn't a normal way of life—that expected from any kind, peaceful and loving family. Thanks to Alhaja, who often told him, "You are fortunate to have wonderful children. It's not every day men like you end up with kids like yours."

My father was quite happy with his achievements as a youngster. However, he knew he was too weak to get rid of his demons. As we grew older and understood our father better, we longed for an escape route. The only way out was not until college. This meant we still had many years to go.

My brothers and I would often fantasize about how we wanted to live our lives far from our father's house. I never stopped dreaming about a life for me, my mom, and my siblings in the United States. My father, in spite of being such a terrible role model, he did manage to achieve what he wanted: to raise truly good, self-reliant, and intelligent children. Though he set a lot of bad examples, he indirectly provided a perfect example of who not to be, but who to aspire to be, as most fathers do.

Staying alone is a task to deal with.
Staying alone—O, for a man to be
Like red coal sinking into the still sea…
Staying alone amid turmoil.
Staying alone, yet amidst many.

Not all days were bad days with my father. He told me he loved me as a son on three occasions. The first was at about 6:00 a.m. after he'd returned from all night partying in a drunken stupor. It was the same on the second and third occasions. My father needed some sort of booze to muster enough courage to tell his children how much he loved them. However, his words came out very differently whenever he was drunk. They were idiomatic, discerning, and much deeper. Simply put, my father was still the secular prophet I thought he was.

On rare occasions, my father would enter my room and remain there, standing over me in quiet contemplation.

"I want you to decide your path," he said. "Choose your path. Choose your destiny. Don't ever try to be anything like me because your future is undeniably great."

Memories like this, recalling his time and affection, are profound. I loved my father, but we agreed on one important thing: that I should be a better man than he was. I was too young to understand most things he talked about, but he assured me that I would understand his words someday.

"You are smarter and wiser than you think, son," he said to me once. "I know you like the back of my hand. You will find yourself remembering my words even in old age. You are a good son. You have a good heart. You need to know the world is not as you see it. You are too sad for your age, and I know why. You want to change everything. You desire to change the world. You believe everyone could have a good heart, but you will understand better when you get older."

He continued, "You must pray and be very patient. You know what your grandma used to remind me about every time I misbehaved?"

"No, Daddy," I answered.

"Alhaja told me, never leave a shoe by itself with the face down; it brings bad luck! Superstition it was, but here I find myself today with lingering uneasiness at the sight of any shoe upside down." He looked down, shook his head, like he was ruminating about what he had just said. I sensed he'd wished it made sense to me the way it did to him.

"It tells me, son, we don't have to necessarily believe in some adventures that make us, be it from our past, present, or future circumstances. However inherent a superstition has come to be by virtue of either trust by innocence, force by order, an upbringing that we couldn't change—in the end, you still have the choice to change anything" Many years later, these words from my father are still empowering for me.

I often observed other families, in particular on television. I saw how much love they shared with one another and wondered why that was missing in my family. I envied the passion and emotion between parents and their children, and more importantly, amongst the children. I craved and longed to have that much love within my family.

Although there was the family type of love amongst us, it was the unspoken kind of love. I wished that we could tell ourselves how much we loved one another, but we could not. For starters, I couldn't initiate such things because it would sound out of place and unusual to everyone in my family. Besides, even if I did, I knew the boys would give me the *what the heck?* look.

I continued to read books and watch movies, often about life in America. When my siblings and I were alone, I would tell them, "You see that place on TV? One day, I'm going to take us all to live there."

I promised them that one day I would become an American citizen and bring them with me to the United States, taking us out from poverty and the physical and mental abuse in our father's home.

Why is everything about life
Full of little bites?
The larger ones
Usually are the painful ones.
And just like a flash,
The euphoric ones crash.

As soon as you have a taste
Of what brings so much joy,
Regret stealthily crawls up this bait
Like the Trojan horse of Troy.

Why does our pain last for so long?
Sorrow almost never departs.
Happiness lasts just for a moment
Like joy hardly even existed.

Eventually, I stopped worrying about how long Alhaja was going to live with us. I believed her when she promised never to leave us, a promise she was eventually forced to break. I feared when she died, my father's house might turn into a graveyard. It didn't take Alhaja's death for my dad's house to be referred to as the fortress that kept the Ayoades from the rest of the world. Alhaja's consolation got us through many years.

I made many promises to Alhaja on the condition that she stayed long enough.

"I will never be anything like my dad when I become a man," I promised her.

"I will love everyone, hug them, and kiss them."

"I will change the world and put smiles on people's faces."

She told me she knew. She was convinced none of her grandchildren would turn out like my father, with his demons.

"You children must also know that your dad loves you all to death. Unfortunately, he can't change who he's become. His biggest fear is to see his worst reflection in any one of you. You must learn to take the best from him," Alhaja said as she reflected on the right side of the coin.

For a child in Nigeria, life was not easy. For a child in our home, life was sometimes worse. Even at that young age, I knew my father's good qualities and his bad qualities would one day call me to make my own choices as a man.

Chapter 5

NIGERIA: 1995

Idolatry with Cozeners.

By the time I became a teenager, my father was fired over a dispute with the managing director at the car dealership where he worked.

This put a lot of pressure on us kids. For a couple of years, Dad had been running three other businesses on the side: an office business center, a nylon bags factory (that sealed dry goods for the markets in Lagos), and the third, a soap factory.

Before losing his job, his businesses had been failing for a couple of years, so he diverted all remnants from the office business center and soap factory to the nylon business.

The tedious production process of the nylon business was assigned to us. My siblings and I worked long hours for my father. On weekdays, we worked in the nylon factory from 6:00 p.m., immediately after the home tutor left, until 9:00 p.m. when it was time for bed. During weekends, we were only allowed to step out of the factory for brunch. Otherwise, we often worked from dawn until Alhaja called for dinner.

We often sustained burns on our hands from sitting next to the spools of nylon and using a red-hot metal razor that ran along the top of the machine to slice off and seal the nylon into pouches of different sizes. My father would deliver the small pouches to town, where market sellers would pack them with sugar or salt, rice and nuts. He couldn't afford to pay us.

My three cousins had gone to spend the holidays with their mother and refused to return to my father's house. In the midst of our hardship, my mom gave birth to another boy. My father named him *Salam*, after my late brother. We drifted from poor to impoverished as we scavenged on profit from the nylon business, which had begun to dwindle completely.

I was too young to understand how troubling my dad's financial situation really was, but not too young to see that he was desperate. My grandmother was a devout Muslim, but my father had never been the religious type. As he grasped for a solution to his troubles though, he started to rely more heavily on God.

At this same time, the bricklayer who'd helped my dad build his house a few years prior resurfaced in our lives. He'd been aware of my dad's former financial position and now, recognizing him as a man in distress, took advantage of my father's misery to turn him to paganism. In the Yoruba tribe, there are a few pagan idols, and my father was introduced to several of them.

Unfortunately, Dad's newly discovered faith was financially demanding. His idolater friends deluded him into believing that through spirituality, they could help him regain all that he had lost—if only he would offer up some cash, then some more, then his car. The list of items they demanded didn't stop until they bled him dry.

There are consequences for every action we take in life, be it virtuous or peccable, just or nefarious. My father soon suffered these consequences. He wouldn't listen to the bitter truth from anyone, nor did he attempt to take any precautions. Friends quickly became foes for not supporting his outlandish decisions.

My father once said, "Always heed the warnings of the aged, for if their words don't come to pass today, they most likely will tomorrow."

It was shocking to see my father ignore Alhaja's warnings for the first time. She didn't give up easily on him; I stood witness to the many cautious and relentless prayers for her son. My father seemed wide awake, yet we knew he was in deep slumber.

"You are walking into a trap!" Alhaja said. "How can you not see it? They will continue to extort you till you have nothing left."

The problem was not primarily with my father's dance with the pagan faith but with the men who introduced him to it. There was more to them, and Alhaja saw it before anyone else did.

Undeterred by Alhaja's warnings, my dad remained obstinate as he continued his quest to quench his thirst for answers. He detached himself completely from the wise counsel of his mother and all those that truly cared about him, the same guidance that had brought him this far.

Understandably, Alhaja suffered a massive blow she couldn't change, the costly one-time credulity of her son. She knew he was too desperate for answers to many eluding questions, but he followed a very unwise course, a path from which many never found their way back.

It wasn't long after Alhaja's incessant warnings proved futile that my father began to take from his investment. I didn't quite understand how he expected to hear from the God he believed in by glorifying paganism. As far as I was concerned, his actions negated his belief. He was taking directions from the unknown.

His decisions were strange, irrational, and unstoppable. Everyone except my dad knew he was making an irreparable mistake. At this point Alhaja must have had it with him and so had my aunt. My aunt, who was the company manager at the time, was a devoted Christian.

No faithful Muslims or Christians could share the same roof with "idolaters" or allow paganism in their homes even if it was their family, especially knowing the beliefs in question were fake. They waited long enough for my father to listen to reason. Instead, he reached deeper into the rabbit hole, despite the warnings from his loved ones.

I thought Alhaja must have threatened to leave if he didn't reconsider, since she knew he was fond of her. But to her bewilderment, her threats were weightless. They changed nothing. My father was neither listening to her nor making his own decisions, so she left, hoping her departure would stir him awake from his stupor. He lost what was most important to him—and as a result, so did I.

I wondered if a little more maturity explained why I didn't break down in tears as Alhaja left in a bus. Sometimes, I thought maybe it was her assurance to always be around. Alhaja left our home and returned to Lagos's mainland, to my late grandpa's house. There she stayed for good.

My aunt always complained about signing too many checks while my father refused to disclose what they were for. No one could be fooled any longer. Following each withdrawal from the bank, he would disappear for days only to return with bizarre traditional markings on various parts of his body. It seemed to us that my father believed his bankrupt businesses were due to spiritual influences.

Crashing financially was the least of his problems, however. He feared there had been multiple incorporeal attempts at his life, and he sought spiritual solutions to those as well. He could not prove why to anyone, so he kept such frightening experiences to himself.

The brave Lani Ayoade felt the need for protection. He was going to give a good fight for his life. A group of people promised to offer a desperate man spiritual protection, and he would give all that he possessed financially for it. He became the only blind one in his house as many words of wisdom went through one ear and flowed out the other.

It was the only time I wished my father could for once adhere to his own teachings when he once said to me: "Life is made of ups and downs. There comes a time when all that was good and given might be lost, but he who gives and trusts in the provider will be replenished of all that was lost to this changing world."

These were the values and belief systems my father was raised by. Then he would ask, "Do you know the motto of the United States? It's printed on every currency and engraved on every coin!"

I had never seen a penny before, less so a dollar, so I had no clue what to say when he asked this question for the first time.

"In God We Trust! Even the greatest country in the world today put their trust in God. Do you think the country would be where it is today if she only relied on men? In God We Trust, son! Trust only in God!"

One love, one heart, one life,
Everyone.
Humanity and its reproach.
The dint in that eye.
That look that besmirches.
She can never be yours.
Not for the times,
Not for the procedures,
But for a faith that stands firm.

What we made makes us—
What we believe separates us.
The blood and the water,
The numerous sacrifices
In the name of Christ,
Or perhaps a God that can't fight.
The enmity of humanity sits
With ethnicity and self-belief.

The freedom we cry about
Is not in the loosened
Shackles of independence.
Independence lies in
The freedom of our minds.
It's better to be a free-thinker
Than a heavenly murderer.

It's better to be originless
Than to be a kinsman killer.
I would live in all the darkness
Rather than hate in lightness.

I won't serve a God who has
No better way to the truth,
Nor will I be a brother to
Those ethnocentric fools.
I would be an island
And live free, serve free, love free!

My father persistently warned us not to place all our trust in man but to have faith only in ourselves and in one God. He tirelessly urged us to wait patiently as we persevered during tough times and to never quit praying to God. The one source of stability in our home was now gone, and my faith in my father started to waver.

Around 10:00 p.m. one night after Alhaja left us, my father called me into his room. "I want you to go to *Idimu* (pronounced Ee-dee-moo*)* and pick up a medicine for me."

"The chemist at Idimu junction?" I asked him, trying to confirm it wasn't the herbalist who lived in the far end of Idimu, to which the shortest route was a four-mile walk along a thick bush path.

"No, the herbalist at Idimu. Not Idimu junction."

Although shocked, I nodded and listened to his instructions. First it was late, and the bush path was dangerous to travel at night. Sometimes, human sacrifice sorcerers lurked in the forest, as well as hungry wild animals.

I tried to hide my fears so I did not complain to my dad as he described to me what to ask for when I get to the herbalist's. I believed my dad had already dismissed my fears along with the risk of sending his young son into the bush at night. My slippers were torn, so I would have to walk barefoot.

Although there were no street lights throughout the trip, I walked past a few houses on my street for the first mile. Some of them had lanterns hanging in their passageways. The houses were built in bricks or mud, unfinished for the most part, defective, and rather unlivable, but people lived in them. It was so quiet that I could hear almost every footstep beneath me as I walked past the last hut and disappeared into the long walk along the bush path.

The path was pitch-black. I could barely see what was in front of me. The further I walked, the taller the grass seemed to have grown so that I couldn't see anything to my sides, ahead of me, or behind me, except that I could feel the earth beneath the sole of my feet and sometimes the tall grass rubbing over my face and shoulders.

The moon seemed to have withdrawn into the night sky, so I wasn't getting much help, and the stars were much smaller than usual, as if it might rain. I'd been warned never to hold fireflies at night because the snakes feed on them, but I needed their delicate glow to light my way.

When I could no longer risk what the next sound would mean for me, alone in the dark, in the middle of the forest, I ran and ran like a wild animal was chasing me the entire way to the herbalist's house. When I arrived at the herbalist's house, he was in a white robe, getting ready for bed.

"Good evening!" I greeted the herbalist, panting. "My father sent me."

"Why are you breathing hard? Did you not come on okada? Did a car bring you?" He asked, surprised.

He recognized me because I had been there in the daytime before and he knew it would be dangerous for me to have trekked all the way to his house at night.

"No, I ran all the way." I replied, and continued panting.

"What?" He asked, still looking shocked. "What is so urgent that couldn't wait till daybreak?"

I described what my dad wanted. He rushed in, came out and handed a small bag to me. Still dumbfounded, he shook his head, "so you have to walk all the way back?"

"No, I think I will have to run. It's too dark and scary to walk." He went back in again, and when he came back out this time, he handed a flashlight to me and said, "go now."

When I returned home panting, my father slowly examined the bottle I'd delivered.

"No," he said. "This isn't what I wanted. Go back, tell the herbalist he gave you the wrong thing."

By now, it was past midnight. This time, I didn't think I would make it back home alive.

For the first time in my life, as I resumed my running, I doubted that this man was indeed my father. No loving parent would ever put their child through something like this.

After Alhaja left, we drowned in increasing fear of what would happen to us if our aunt left too. Her wedding was getting closer and closer. Those that were bold enough to look my father in the eye and tell him the unwanted truth were already gone. She planned on resigning from the managerial position in the family business. She was weary of the constant fights with him.

Soon the wedding came, and like that she was gone only to hear from her once in a blue moon. After that, it was just my dad, mom, me, and my five siblings left in the house.

About a year after my aunt left my father's house, the financial situation had gotten out of control. We scavenged on what was left of the nylon business until it was ruined completely.

After that, my father gave away all the equipment to his half-brother. He was too ashamed to sell it. Only the house was left, the smartest investment of his life. We could have been homeless. We fed on the reserves from Mom's business until she went bankrupt as well.

Eventually, we could barely afford one meal a day. For years, we'd been brushing our teeth using chewing sticks or salt. Alhaja showed us how to, so we all thought it was cooler, not because we could no longer afford toothpaste or toothbrushes.

She had shown us how to cut out the stored rice sacks in the house into sponges to take our showers with and make a local black soap using unbelievably cheap ingredients. We never even considered it might have been because we couldn't afford even the traditional Yoruba sponge, *kankan*, made out of straw, and the regular bar soaps we used before then. It would continue for years.

The truth was, Alhaja always found a way to extinguish any fire that could potentially burn her family, as we later understood. She borrowed if she had to and sold her jewelry as long as there was dignity in our home and food on the table for her grandchildren.

A year later, as our financial situation finally hit rock bottom, the national college examinations season came. The General Certificate Examination (GCE) was a national testing required for all qualifying high-school students to be eligible for college education.

My father had registered my brother and me to test a year early from the actual high school finals—the Senior Secondary Certificate Examinations (SSCE)—so we could have a good shot and twice the chance at getting into college immediately after high-school graduation. At this time, it was not uncommon for my mom, dad, siblings, and I to go without food for days. Hence, the most grueling weeks were the 1996 GCE weeks.

With both of our exam centers thirteen miles away, and no transportation fare, we walked those thirteen miles on hot sunny days, sometimes in the rain and without shoes because we couldn't afford new school sandals, and the old ones could no longer be mended.

Sometimes, we got on the back of pick-up trucks if the drivers let us or we hid and hung on the back of the petrol tanker trucks just to shorten the trek to the exams center; trying not to think that a good number of my family members had been killed by the same tanker many years before. The following day, we would do it all over again, all with empty bellies.

This was the period my brother and I had to make a lifelong decision: to keep pursuing our dreams for the future by performing exceptionally well in exams or give up because we were too weak even to lift a book?

This period culminated into an unprecedented level of respect for me and my brother from my father. Despite the circumstances, we were relentless in our studies. We would set off for exams hours before dawn because of the distance we had to walk.

When things were at their worst, we had to do what we knew was wrong. We snuck into nearby brush and farms to find some cassava, yam, or coco-yam tubers. Sometimes, we plucked vegetables by roadsides, usually after dark, so no one we knew might see us. Whatever we found that was edible or nearly edible, we brought back home to our family.

Among our siblings, whoever found any food, we all shared—no matter how small the portion was. We had nowhere else to go and no one else to turn to, and we'd all witnessed so much in our home that by now, it had granted each of us a maturity beyond our years.

With Alhaja no longer around to show us an adult's care, this was the period when every single one of us stopped being kids. Though we had each other I was still so lonely in my sadness, sure that it sat more deeply for me than for any of my family. During this period, I became numb to hunger. I never complained, and I never liked being around people who did—it didn't change how hungry we were.

At the end of the GCE exams, we went back to our routine. Despite the hunger, we woke up early every morning, completed our daily chores and proceeded to a three-mile walk to the dilapidated buildings we called school.

No one suspected the magnitude of poverty in my house, not even our closest classmate with whom we walked to school every morning. Sometimes he was shocked to see us walk miles to the river or the open well near his house a few times to fetch some water. It was more shocking to him to see us tote the water back with buckets on our heads while walking miles back home. If only he had known we did so on empty stomachs most days.

Not only was the water machine broken, but the television in the living room had also stopped working, and the last time we watched television as a family was closing on to three years. Almost everything that was broken in the house stayed broken because we couldn't afford to fix them. The only thing that mattered was putting food on the table.

This was the time in a boy's life when he needed to look to his father for guidance more than ever, but I was losing all faith in mine. He continued to make decisions that tore my mother apart, and he was blind to how his actions affected us all. But as I entered young manhood, I resisted pointing my finger at him. Beneath his tough exterior, I began to see that he was scared.

He had been responsible for taking care of so many people, and his worst fear was to lose his ability to provide for us all—and that was exactly what happened. I didn't understand him, but I worked very hard not to judge him.

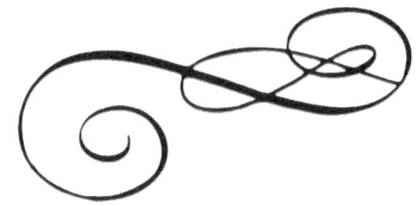

Chapter 6

NIGERIA: 1997
Moonlight over the Balcony.

"Hey, Ramon! Are you okay? You look pale. Your eyes, they are sunken!"

"I'm okay, Aunty. Nothing's wrong with me."

"No! Something's not right. You look sick."

She walked closer to me, trying to make a better assessment of my lean body.

"Tell me, what's going on? I saw your sister earlier today. She looked scrawny and pale as well. What's going on with you kids? Are you all sick? Hasn't my brother noticed?"

I now had five siblings. Salam, our youngest brother, arrived in early 1995. Fifteen years younger than me.

My aunt had recently been contacted by my high-school management to cater for lunch for all students. Without the responsibility of my father, she was finally back to doing what she loved—catering.

"Well, I don't think we are sick, but things are really tough at home."

Instantly, I realized I had said too much already.

"What do you mean things are tough?"

"I'm sorry. I can't tell you, Aunty. I have to go now."

"Come back here! I'm still talking to you!" My aunt yelled.

I scurried away from further interrogation. Sometimes, we thought our situation might become obvious to others, but my father's demeanor as a stoic disciplinarian successfully camouflaged our suffering to a great extent. Otherwise, our silence or short fake answers to prying questions always sufficed. As long as our father's honor was protected.

Very few people in the community suspected the magnitude of our poverty. We still couldn't afford electricity and had to study by lantern if we had kerosene. Otherwise, we resolved to the moonlight, which often reflected well across the balcony. Beneath our smiles and fun times with friends, we were repeatedly engulfed in fear of returning home to empty pots at the end of school hours. We found ourselves always praying to God for a sort of miracle before leaving school, frightfully hoping there might be food in the kitchen this time, or if not, at least, some bread to dip in sugar and water.

The home tutor had stopped coming for years after realizing my father would not make up for the several months already owed. None of us begged for food, nor did we complain about the penury at home. We weren't turning pale because we were sick, but from malnutrition and gastrointestinal bleeding. Now, as an adult with years of medical training, I'm aware that it's not impossible we could have died of starvation. Begging for food wasn't an option for my family.

Through all of this, my mother cowered behind her husband. He still brutalized her physically, even when he was sober. The daily stress of his finances caused him to be meaner in more mentally and emotionally damaging ways.

When they met, she was a teenager who had just gone through trade school to work as a dressmaker. She was so vibrant and beautiful that film producers in Lagos had approached her to appear in their films. Now, she'd become a shell of her former self. My father forbade her to have a career or any kind of freedom, instead making her responsible for going out and begging for food on credit at the markets.

Even for her purest efforts, he dominated her. When Dad's friend informed him that he'd run into my mother when she tried to get food in town, my father beat her for having left the house without his permission.

Ever since they got married, my father had managed to subjugate her to his dominance, which would span over twenty- four years. Sometimes it was physical abuse, but more often, mental and emotional. Quietly I approached her, asking why she couldn't stand up to him.

"Why are you still here?" I'd whisper.

"Because if I leave," she murmured, "I don't know what will happen to you kids."

But she was supposed to be his wife, not his slave. It sank my insides to think she endured all of this to protect us. As her child, I felt terrible about how my dad treated my mom, and I couldn't begin to imagine how she felt. When I was seven and knew what was going on, I still needed her around and couldn't even consider the thought of her leaving us. But as a teenager, I wished she would leave him.

When I got older, it made more sense.

My mother had met my father when she was only eighteen. She was very naïve, and my father was the only man she had ever loved.

He wasn't just her husband; she looked up to him. Undoubtedly, she endured his demons, heedlessly hoping he would heal from such a terrible family experience and change for the better as a husband and father.

More than a few times, I'd listened to members of my father's family calling her my dad's puppet, sometimes lazy. They'd witnessed how far my dad had pushed his overwhelming control of my mother's life and concluded my mom was weak.

There were several instances when she left temporarily for one or two days but at the most three days. She would always return in my father's car after, we assumed, he apologized to her.

Sometimes, it was shocking to see her return, considering the extent of physical abuse he rained on her. Once, she was rushed to the hospital, and they had to stitch the back of her ankle over her Achilles tendon, which tore from a broken glass my dad had thrown at her. And the incident I could never forget was when he slapped her, as hard as he could, while she was almost at full term with my youngest brother.

If my mother was silent, that was because she had no say in virtually any decision that was supposed to be made between her and my father. He was the monarch of his house, and the rest of us were simply his lickspittles, including Mom.

My father's supposed friends were gone. What was so convincing about the new doctrines for a man like my father, who once had a strong faith in God, was unfathomable for me. There was no guarantee that if my dad came out of his tough years, he wouldn't return to his mistakes. I wasn't convinced about how clear-headed he was.

All his friends who knew of our financial difficulty deserted us. No help came from the few close ones he swallowed his pride for to ask for help. Life became harder with each passing day. All the friends and relatives, who ran to my father for help when they needed him at one point or the other, were nowhere to help him.

This was one of the darkest periods in my life, but it strengthened my resolve to fulfill my promises to my family. I focused my frustration on excelling in high school to make it to college, become someone, and change what I could for my family.

Down my arms,
Roll the tears
From the corners of my eyes.

On the radio
Is a young rodeo
From a sad little town.

In the rhythm of the music,
I feel an empty life hanging on to a wish.
My soul's heavy
And my eyes are teary.

There have been
So many disappointments,
And I dread this could be the life meant for me.
I wish I had all the answers to my questions,
But all I can do is pray for a vision.

"If only my aunt had the slightest idea of our circumstances, we might get some help," I murmured to myself as we all lay quiet, too weak to talk to each other.

We had just returned home from school. My father was in the living room, now forty years of age. He'd lost enough weight so that he sank into the three-seater couch he once intimidatingly occupied.

He looked as pale as my brother and sister, more evident than my mother and me because we were darker in complexion. The atmosphere in my house was gray and bleak, too pensive and too sad to spark up any light. Suddenly, we heard a voice. It was a familiar voice.

"Is anyone home? Why is it so quiet in here? Where are you, boys?"

It was my aunt. My wish was granted in just a few minutes. I was filled with consolation not because I was sure she would provide food - it had just been a long time since a loved one had visited.

"She must have been curious about our discussion from earlier today," I mentioned as I tugged at my brothers. "Hey, it's Aunty *Modina.*"

We walked out of our room, which had a big notice on the front side of the door with a bogus inscription *Boys' Room.* By the time we made it to the living room door, my aunt was already there.

She stood at the edge of the three-seater couch harboring my father's shrunken body, speechless with both hands over her mouth. Tears rolled profusely down towards her nose. She had seen my dad, Tunji, who was only ten, and my sister, who was only thirteen. They were all light-complexioned, so it must have been terrifying for her to see all of them looking so pale on sight.

"What happened? You all look so pale and weak."

While she was struggling to put herself together, my sister stood up to rush to the toilet when bloody mucoid discharge dropped from her underwear.

"Oh my God, what's that, Biola?" My aunt cried louder.

I knew my sister was too young to understand what was happening to her, so I answered my aunt's question.

"We are excreting the same thing. It happens especially when we shower."

Immediately she knew it must have been either food poisoning, or gastrointestinal ulcers, or both. As kids, we thought our body was devouring itself because of starvation.

My aunt, clearly in distress, turned to my father.

"Oh, brother!" she cried. "How could you not tell me this is happening? I could have helped! How long has this been going on?"

But she knew her brother too well. He was too proud to beg. He wasn't the begging type. If only she knew this had been going on for years.

"And you, fools!" My aunt turned to us in anger. "You see me in school every day. Not one of you took the initiative to tell me!"

"It's not their fault," my father interjected. "You know my kids will die before they beg or steal. I lost my job a while back." My father hadn't lost his charismatic tone, but I sensed guilt and sincerity in his demeanor.

She turned to my mother in anger.

"What kind of mother are you? You've always known how pig-headed your husband is! How could you sit back and let this happen to your children?"

My aunt wiped her tears as scantily as she could and dashed out of the living room. We heard her footsteps down the hallway. Soon, the gate slammed after she stepped out of the compound.

If only she'd known how many avenues my mother had exhausted, from her sister to her nieces, friends, and even local food sellers. For her, for both of them, there was nowhere and no one to turn to.

My father stayed on the couch, his eyes almost teary. We slowly walked back to our room but not for long. My aunt soon returned in less than an hour. She brought food items with her. Some were cooked, ready to eat. She administered a combination of antibiotics she procured from the pharmacy to everyone after we finished our meals. She suspected we needed antibiotic treatment. To our amazement, no one would pass bloody discharge after three days of dosing.

"Every morning, I want you all to report to my tent for breakfast before assembly. You do the same during lunch breaks! Is that clear?" my aunt said, as my father watched quietly.

He didn't say a word, but his countenance spoke volumes about how grateful he was to my aunt. My aunt understood him utterly. After all, they were siblings.

She turned to my father.

"If it weren't for your generosity, I'm not sure where I would be today. The same for my three friends you took into your house without question, only because of your love for me. You should let me help you for once in your life! You are the most generous man I've ever known, but right now, you need help, brother!"

A year later, it was the last day of registration for our final year exams in high school, the SSCE, and we had just gone past the deadline to pay. My mother had been out early, walking countless miles to beg and borrow from any friend, family, and anyone she could, just enough to register us for the exams.

The GCE results from the previous year were out, my brother and I did well, but my father wanted a more outstanding result. The SSCE was our shot to secure admissions into one of the best universities in the country, so it was important that we took the exam.

My brother and I returned home but didn't take off our school uniforms. We both hoped for a miracle when Mom returned, sitting patiently and praying in the living room. Not long after, we heard Mom's voice in the hallway. We ran towards her.

By this time, my dad had left the couch he was sitting on and walked to the doorway, awaiting the news from my mom. As soon as my mom stepped through the door, she looked at my dad, too exhausted to talk, she dipped her hand in her bag and brought out the cash in her bag: she had borrowed enough to cover both of our exam fees.

Without wasting time, my father said, "You have to rush back to school! Now!"

It had been almost two hours since the school closed for the day. However, my father insisted that my mom, my brother, and I took the money and rushed down to school; hopefully, the principal would still be in the office to register us.

When we arrived at the gate, my mom was jittery as she talked to the school gateman.

"Good afternoon! Please, is the principal still around? She asked from behind the gate.

The gateman turned around and pointed to the principal who was just leaving his office, about to head home.

"Abeg wait for the principal here," The gateman instructed.

When the principal arrived at the gate, he asked the gateman what was going on My mom explained instead. Without asking any further questions, he ordered the gateman, "open the gate and let them in".

The principal walked us under a tree and had my mom sit on a bench; my brother and I sat on student chairs with movable writing tops. As he took the money from Mom, he smiled.

"Mrs. Ayoade," he said, "I am just glad your sons aren't going to miss the SSCE. They are really smart kids, you know."

My mom smiled but was visibly tired - she had walked all day just to help secure our future. The principal handed over the

SSCE identity cards to me and my brother to complete so he could laminate them.

As I completed my identity card for the exams, my eyes met my mom's when I looked up. She returned a smile. Her eyes filled with pain and exhaustion, but she smiled just enough to acknowledge me. She wore an old Buba and Iro and a pair of old slippers. Her feet were quite dusty from all the walking.

After my brother and I returned the completed identity cards to the principal, he looked at my mom. He understood how tired she was and what she might have gone through to pay for our exams.

"Today is the absolute deadline to pay for your kid's finals," he said, "and you barely caught me at the gate on my way home; that must mean more than something." Then he turned to me and my brother. "You see what it means to be a mother?"

He turned back to my mom and said seriously, "You will reap the fruit of your labor."

That was a beautiful wish for my mother, but in my heart, I'd always wished differently. I'd grown up in a country where customary subjugation of women existed to a large extent and sometimes hardly able to build a career outside the confines of raising kids.

Watching how my mother lived her life up to that point, I only wished that she would get the chance to live her life the way she'd always dreamt of as a young lady: to explore every boundary of her talents and gifts, and live her life to the fullest potential. When I looked at my mom that afternoon, I prayed to God to keep me alive long enough to see that happen.

The principal gave us our laminated cards and we began to walk home. Although my entire family had had only one meal in two days before that very moment and no dinner waiting for us after using all that money to pay for our exams, our faces beamed with smiles. I felt the only way I could truly express my gratitude was to strengthen my resolve: *No matter how tough things get, quitting is not an option for me.*

When the results came out a few weeks later, out of 285 students that took the final exams in my high school, I was one of the only two who passed every exam with outstanding results. I was the only one who secured college admissions that year.

My high school was only a community high school with few teaching resources. The teachers sometimes tried their best but often gave up out of frustration from minimal government support. Though we were all teenagers, we knew that what we learned in our high school wasn't good enough for us to do well in the national exams—the SSCE. You had to do a lot of extra work on your own.

In my case, I realized early in senior secondary school that what I was learning in school wasn't enough, so I began to study ahead of the school's curriculum by using the national science syllabus for the three years of senior secondary school. My dad had bought the syllabus to monitor our studying about two years before. I borrowed all the texts I could from my classmates, studied late on most nights after school, while using the syllabus as a guide.

Three months after my SSCE, many friends, teachers, and students saw my name in the newspaper. I had been admitted to the University of Ibadan to study veterinary medicine, the most respected university in the country.

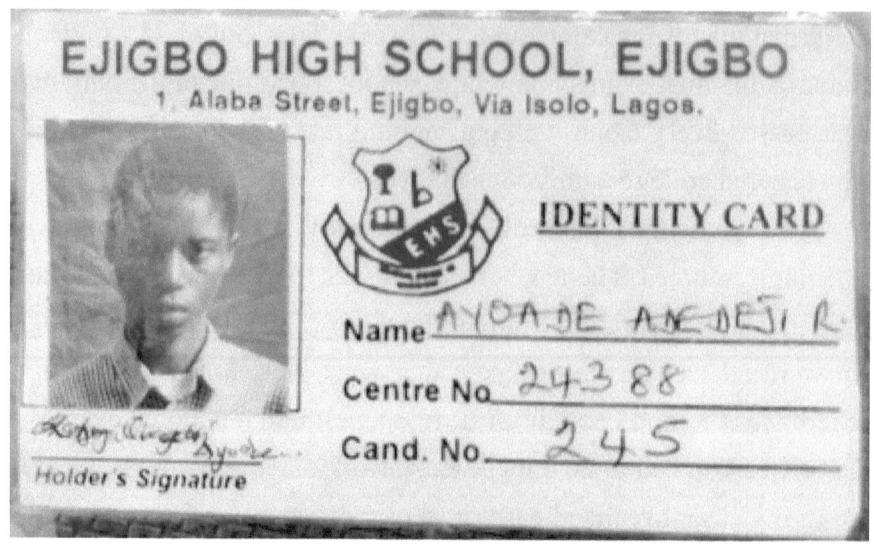

Final year high school exams ID card, 1997.

Ejigbo High School fence/entrance – Road to high school.

Road to Ejigbo High School – high school to the right.

Ejigbo High School fence – Road to high school.

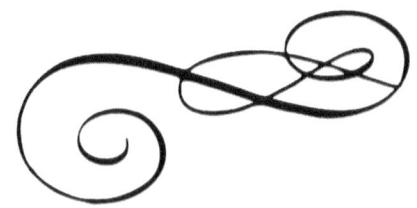

Chapter 7

NIGERIA: August 2001
A Stranger We Called Father.

> *It's father's first night away during New Year's Eve.*
>
> *He's no longer the man we used to know.*
>
> *There he goes, shedding empty tears.*
>
> *Father's gone, we know,*
>
> *But who's the man we now call father?*

At the end of my final high school exams, my godmother—my late uncle's wife and the mother of two of my three cousins—took an interest in me.

"You're a different kind of child," she'd told me from the time I was little. I was curious about life, always asking a lot of questions. She had a sister in America, and this intrigued me as I often reminded her that it was my dream to go there one day.

"I believe that you'll go to America one day," she said. "*Americana*."

It meant "American" in the native language, a nickname they called Nigerians that thought optimistically. That my godmother saw this kind of potential in me was always the most thrilling compliment.

After I graduated high school, she talked to my father and told him not to worry—she would feed me and help with my finances when I left for the university. But when I arrived at the University of Ibadan, I knew it would be a tall order.

The University of Ibadan is Nigeria's premier university, the country's oldest college. It was founded in 1948, much before Nigeria's independence in 1960. The British colonials did not only build the school, but they also designed the training programs. There was a high regard for the premier university students in Nigeria, comparable with how Harvard students are perceived in the U.S.

For many years, the school had the best medical training programs in the country, including veterinary medicine. In fact, the University of Ibadan was the sole producer of veterinarians in Nigeria for more than a decade before the establishment of more tertiary institutions following the country's independence.

I stood outside the front gate in reverence, this unexposed kid from a rural village, about to enter the Harvard of Nigeria. I was excited to be so far from home for the first time, but I could already sense there was a lot I'd be learning.

I wasn't sure if I was built for my new journey or smart enough to survive the academic demands of the school, but my initial nervousness was quickly replaced with curiosity about the school and what my life would be like as a student in such a reputable university.

I hadn't seen so many young people from different parts of the country in one place before. I found that most of my peers had graduated from the best high schools in the country, while I had graduated from the lowest ranking public high school in Lagos State, where only two of us out of 285 passed the high school finals. And among my classmates at university, their parents could afford to sponsor their full tuition. I knew this made me different. I kept my head down and chose to isolate myself in my studies.

During my early holiday breaks, I went home to check on my siblings and work in my aunt's restaurant to repay her generosity. Each time I was due to leave for school again, she always handed me cash and a load of groceries—sometimes enough to last me a month.

I knew there was no way I could navigate school without her support, and her kindness spurred me to focus on my schoolwork. In my mind, getting good grades was the most meaningful way for me to repay her.

Staying busy with my studies met another need: it helped keep my mind off my family's struggles at home. Each time I went there, the situation was worse until it reached a point when I rarely visited home. I thought I would be an extra burden they could do without.

When we were all little, we'd all sit on the mat in the balcony or stretch out in the living room as Alhaja told us long tales about what a dignified line of royalty we'd come from. Even in the ugliest moments, that had given me a sense of worth in who we were.

But now, my family had very little dignity. I couldn't imagine how depressed each of them was, and I hated to see my mother and younger siblings in such a sad, hopeless state when I knew I could do very little about it. At least for now.

I continued to study, and I set my sights on getting into the Veterinary Teaching Hospital. I would make good on my promise to my family to become a doctor, but as a veterinarian, that was more rare, prestigious, and could learn enough to care for several different species. I believed that in some way, this could make me more effective in caring for humans someday.

As I continued to focus on my future, I came to view my father in a more jaded way than ever before. The month before I registered for my first year of pre-med in 1998, he finally found a job. My family was still poor, and sometimes I found myself asking, *Who did this?*

I'd tried to understand my father, but by then, I'd witnessed too many years of my family's suffering. The pain I felt from being able to do nothing about it had hardened to anger inside me. I'd reached a point in my life where I believed it was time someone should have to accept the blame - especially when my chances to finish university became jeopardized.

Nigeria wasn't a country that had any functioning national education programs that offered financial aid to students. There were neither government nor private student loans. If you were from a poor background and determined to stay in school, then you fell into the category that no one cared about. You had to find a way to support yourself in school, which was tough to do in a country like Nigeria.

After three years in college, I completed the final preclinical examinations. I returned to my godmother's house during break and received a package that had arrived for me.

When I opened it, I had been selected as a winner of the American green card lottery.

Words could not capture how I felt that afternoon. For the first time in my life, I felt like all my prayers had been answered. As the months followed, I waited for my interview letter but it never came from the U.S. embassy, so I decided to visit the embassy as I approached the deadline for interviews for 2001 fiscal year winners. That was when I found out that for some reason, the U.S. immigration stopped processing immigrant visa cases for Nigeria that fiscal year before they got to my case number.

There was no way to fight it because the disclaimer on the diversity visa winning notification clearly stated that being selected did not *guarantee that the immigrant visa would be issued.*

I thought they might have exhausted the diversity visas allocated to Nigeria for that fiscal year before they could get to process the rest of us. I never got called for an interview.

I remembered not knowing exactly how to feel. One moment, I thought I had seen the light I'd been searching for my entire life, and just like that, I was back in the dark, frustrated and confused.

I thought I must have been cursed. Not surprising for a boy of my age and background. It had indeed been the case for many Nigerians - not just our family but others must have been cursed as well, I thought.

I returned to school, but the disappointment lingered in my heart for a long time. A few months later, I was halfway through my first year of paraclinicals at the Veterinary Teaching Hospital of the University of Ibadan. One day, in the middle of the semester, I visited my godmother briefly to help with the restaurants. On the day of my departure, she called me as I was grabbing my bag.

"I can't support you anymore," she told me quietly. She had just remarried for the first time to the same man she had been with since my uncle passed.

She had two kids with him, a boy and a girl, now grown-ups and about my age.

I could hear this hurt her even more than it hurt me. Deep down I had known this day would come but I'd prayed that I have an alternative source of financial support when it does. I had barely recovered from the major blow of losing my opportunity at the U.S. green card, now I was losing my biggest financial supporter in college.

"Your father has been working for more than three years now. He should be able to resume full responsibility for your school tuition," she said.

I'd felt guilt through those years knowing she had financial commitments of her own, but I knew it would also be hard to survive without her support since I wasn't getting much from my dad.

My godmother was clearly disappointed with my father, but I could see through her downcast eyes how hard it was for her to bring up such a topic.

"My business hasn't been thriving as it used to for a while, and you are aware of my ongoing financial responsibilities. I'm sorry, things are hard right now," she explained.

If only she had known how guilty I felt about her situation, she wouldn't have needed to apologize. I knew it was about time for her to let go of burdens that weren't hers.

No one really knew why she took a significant interest in caring for me during my preclinical years. Some people said she thought I had a special gift, and she couldn't stand by and watch it go to waste due to my family's financial struggles. Others thought she was just a generous woman who sincerely cared about others. She did her best to help me become successful. Sadly, she didn't live past the first two years following my graduation from veterinary school. I never got the chance to pay her back for her love and kindness.

Earlier in the same year, I left home after a fight with my dad out of frustration with his unwillingness to support our education. It was evident there was something different about my father. It wasn't just me. My siblings weren't getting much from him either.

He used to be the father who had no qualms about borrowing if he had to, as long as it kept his children in school. "Education is the best legacy," he'd say.

My mother often begged me not to come home. Ibadan was only two hours away from Lagos, but often took another two hours to get to my father's house. She thought it would be a waste to spend borrowed money on transportation back home when I might probably have to borrow to return to school. I knew there was more going on at home that she didn't want to disclose to me.

She tried her best to prevent the big fight between my father and me. My mother would instead scavenge whatever she could from my dad or borrow, no matter how little, so she could visit me in school.

I desperately wanted to know what was happening back home. Although leaving in the middle of the semester wasn't a good idea, I knew I could catch up with my studies. My dean was aware of my problems, so he gave every support he could if it helped keep me in school.

The two days I took away from class would turn into five long days of emotional torture in my father's house.

He came home late every night, always claiming to have no money, but I knew it was a lie. The little faith I had left to hold on to, believing that my family situation would eventually get better no matter how bad it was, was now gone

My experience at home was exactly as I tried hard not to imagine. Everything was different, far worse than it had ever been. Could you imagine my father's house worse than it had ever been? The house we once considered hell as kids. What could be worse than hell?

"The man you're living with isn't your husband anymore!" I screamed at my mother in frustration. "He's gone! This man is possessed! He has no clue what he's doing!"

It was the fifth day since I arrived home.

"The father that I knew, despite his short temper issues, would always put our education first."

Meanwhile, his close friend confided in me about my dad's recent shenanigans with random women.

"There is no good reason why your dad should be broke. Why do you think we come home so late every night? He's been sleeping around lately, and it keeps getting worse. Your dad is losing control, and I can assure you that he needs help. I heard him complain to you about how poor the family finances are.

"It's not true. You see, almost every night, he lavishes an ungodly amount of money on different women. Sometimes, it's hard for me to admit he's the same man I've known for years. He's really changed, but not for the better. He's blessed with such a great family, but it's been a while since he last had that in perspective."

It was hard to assume my father's childhood friend was lying. What sort of man would be happy about coming home to his family in the middle of the night for no good reasons?

"I have no money," my father continued to say. "You have to wait."

I stayed up till midnight every night for my dad to return from the office he'd left eight hours before. It was heartbreaking to see him drunk every night while I waited up late, in anticipation that he might provide me with some money to return to school. Instead, he reeked of alcohol as he dropped exhausted on his favorite couch.

"Sorry, son. You have to wait another day. I can't kill myself. I did the best I could, but I still don't have anything to give you."

I became sick with worry. I was supposed to write a major exam in school the following day and still needed to make the journey back to campus.

Earlier on the fifth day, my brother, Tunji, sat next to me as I weighed my options.

"Whatever your decisions are, brother," he told me, "I understand. We all understand. We need you to be strong for us."

Then he went back to his room, returning a moment later.

"Here, brother," he said, handing me five hundred naira, which was just enough for me to get back to school. "I borrowed it from a friend. Please, take it and return to the university. If you wait for your father, it might crush your dreams." Then he left.

I couldn't help but quietly wipe away my tears. My brother, once so little. Why had he been forced to grow up so quickly? He'd just turned fifteen and already learned how to fend for himself. I wondered what would happen when it was time for him to leave for college.

While I waited to confront my father, I thought about his words and how my actions would affect each member of my family. My mother still couldn't decide for herself without my father's influence.

My half-brother was also in school, preparing to look for a job with his industrial chemistry degree. My sister had just begun to study computer science and math, and in a few months, my brother would be leaving to study Physics Electronics. My second half-brother had gotten a job in the city and had gone to live with Alhaja right after he'd graduated high school. Only our youngest brother, now six, was still home with my dad.

Determined to confront my father when he returned, I packed the rest of my belongings, ready to jump on the first bus back to Ibadan. At that point, I did not worry about how I was going to survive all by myself. Even as I considered them, I knew stating the truth was long overdue.

I was ready for the worst possible scenario. I was determined to make it work for me one way or the other. However, my survival plan details of which I had no clue, I reserved until a silent moment with myself on my way back to school.

At about 2:00 a.m., the sound of the noisy honk came as usual. It was my father and his driver. After my father lost his brothers to the truck accident many years before, he began to experience auto accidents himself whenever he drove.

As a result, he never drove again since his last accident in 1979. He hired a driver from time to time whenever he could afford one. Otherwise, his friends or neighbors drove him around.

So, I went downstairs to open the gate for them. He took the keys from the driver as soon as he pulled into the compound.

"You can go home," he said to the driver.

I went back upstairs without waiting for him. I was back on the couch where I'd been watching television. As expected, he sank into the couch.

"I'm doing my best. You just have to be patient."

Without turning to him, I replied, "Patient till you are done sleeping with all the prostitutes in Lagos, or drink yourself to death? Which one is it, Dad? You come home at impious hours every night telling me the same thing like I can't read between the lines."

Enraged, he rushed into his room. I slowly got up, walked into my mother's room which was directly opposite his room and grabbed my bag. When he came out, he was in shorts.

"What insolence! Since when have we become mates?"

He raged towards me. He must have been more infuriated by how condescending the stern look on my face was. I was calm despite his fury. I knew what he would do next, so I remained as poker-faced as I could.

"I'll leave this place and I'll never come back!" I looked at my mother, shrunken behind him. "And you should do the same!"

She lowered her head.

"I will choose my next words very carefully, Dad. If you so much as touch me, I'll be gone from your house this moment. Not one minute more. This will be the last time you'll see me in your house."

Parents have been known to disown a child out of frustration. In my case, I was ready to disown the man I called Dad.

My father thought differently. I was threatening him, and he would have none of it.

His anger got more intense as he lurched towards me, throwing several punches, most of them missed. I tried to shield my face with the back of both forearms, just like professional boxers do on the television.

It was effective. My mother stood a few feet away from us, helplessly watching my father rain punches on her son.

He walked away from me while I was still leaning on the wall next to the stairway with my arms still shielding my face.

My bag was by the door to the stairwell. When I finally let loose my guard, he had disappeared into his room.

My mother hurried through the door of the living room towards me, crying uncontrollably. I leaned towards my bag, grabbing the handle with one hand while I opened the door to the stairway with the other.

In a manic phase,
Five young busters race.
Every element is possessed.
Too small was the closet,
Yet you're locked all the way in.

Shako, the brave one!
A man of heart and Love.

Mighty in frame, fearsome in stature.
To his fears, he never turned his back,
And to the weak, he sacrificed his life.

Shako, I see tears in your heart;
You're about to end your own life.
You're in there,
But your world couldn't see you.
You will walk through that door,
But you will never make it back.
And the rest of us
Can only mourn you
For the rest of our lives.

My mother's voice shook with tears.

"Don't leave, Ramon!" she said, still crying. "Don't go! See? This is why I told you not to come home. Every time you come back, there has to be a fight between you both."

"Mom! You need to pack your things and leave! If you don't, it's only a matter of two weeks before he kicks you out at the most, and that's if you're still alive by then."

Of course, my mom didn't want me to see what he'd become. She knew I was capable of looking him in the eye and telling him the truth no one else could.

"You don't want me to know how he has reduced you to his housegirl? I can't believe you let all this continue like it's normal. The worst part is that he brought another woman into your matrimonial bed. The father that I knew might be a little crazy, but this one, in this house, has no soul. I looked into his eyes, and I can tell that's not my father.

"Well," I finished, picking up my bags, "I'm on my way. I'm not coming back, Mom. This is it for me. If anyone wants to see me, I'll be in school. And tell that man I don't need his money to make it out of vet school."

I knew I was making a bold move I wasn't ready for. However, I also knew I would figure something out eventually.

"I'm doing this for all of you, son! Think about what will happen if I leave! What will happen to Salam with another woman in this house? He's only six! You know damn well he would kill me if I try to take my baby with me."

In our country, a woman doesn't have the legal right to be the guardian of her child. We all knew she couldn't leave my six-year-old brother in my father's care.

"I'm sorry, Mom, but that's not the reason you refuse to leave him. You're still in love with him despite several years of abuse," I said, looking at her. "You've been giving the same excuse since I was only six years old, remember? See, you aren't doing this for us anymore! Without you, Salam will survive, but you need to stay alive for him. I know my father was aggressive and violent sometimes, but the one you're living with has no conscience, nor does he have control. In plain words, this one can kill in cold blood, but my father couldn't."

I took one last look at her before saying, "Goodbye, Mom."

Some people walk And others run,
But I move like a rolling stone.

It never stops;
It's the reason I never give up.

Some people keep their eyes open
Or leave them closed.
Others prefer their eyes wide shut,
But mine are like that of an eagle;
I see what others don't see.

Some people cry
And others weep.
Tears can only be wiped off the face
But can never be stopped from shedding.
I still give thanks for my sorrow.

Unleashing the anger I'd penned inside me for years gave me some relief, but when I returned to school four hours away from my siblings, I wasn't proud of the way I'd behaved. I worried our father would transfer his frustration toward me onto them and deep down within me, I knew his problems were beyond his control. I was beginning to learn how that felt as my own financial struggles worsened.

My struggles in college sprouted beyond control, much more than I had bargained for financially. I was blessed to have a few good friends, but one cared for me the most: Tola.

Tola loved me like a blood brother. We had a strong connection between us, the type known to be found between identical twins. He was always there for me during my toughest moments in college.

Tola came to my rescue more than once, when I least expected it and when I couldn't put together enough funds for my tuition. He wasn't from a very wealthy home, so it meant the most generous gesture any friend could offer whenever he gave from his college funds meant for his survival in school.

Considering the academic rigor of veterinary school, it wasn't a place for anyone struggling financially as the scholastic consequences were grave. It was almost impossible to study, knowing my next meal was not guaranteed. The era that afforded two meals a day were happy days.

Once again, I was back to those tough years with my family, except that I would be starving alone while in school.

I hated it, but I was ready if it was going to cost that much. Quitting wasn't an option as far as I was concerned and I did a pretty good job hiding my financial struggles from the rest of my classmates.

I began to breed dogs. I sold carpets. I accepted any sales job that friends and acquaintances could help me work out. My mom borrowed money and brought it to me whenever she could; my sister sometimes made the two-hour trip from school to bring me meals she cooked for me there.

I would continue to focus on my education. For the remainder of my advanced education, it would be up to me to figure out a way to pay. My roommates left money on the reading table with a note for me to "*Get something to eat!*"—especially when they noticed I'd been living on bread and water for days at a time.

After seven tough years came graduation day, in March 2005.

I achieved my dream of becoming a veterinary doctor and graduating from the country's most prestigious veterinary medical school. The induction ceremony comprised the veterinary surgeon's oath as well as the induction into the veterinary profession.

It was then that I recognized a face in the crowd that changed everything.

Tearily, I gazed like a child in disbelief as I ran to hug my father. He came with his friends too, mostly his childhood friends that had avoided him years before. The years he had been someone else.

"Congratulations!" my dad said. "You made me proud."

I stood there, still teary but smiling, in my induction gown. Beneath it, I had a green shirt, tie and suit on, all that I had borrowed from a friend. I couldn't even afford a graduation suit. However, I'd never been so happy in a long time. I realized I'd missed my dad a great deal after all.

"Today is a great day, Ramon. We've waited for this moment for a very long time. Remember all my friends?" He waved to about six of them.

"They always ask when the doctor will be graduating," he said. "I'm glad they are all here to witness this moment, from holding you as a baby to when you're finally my doctor." He looked up and raised his hands to the sky.

My father slowly pulled me aside from everyone else and said, "Ramon, I am sorry for everything. I can see now with much clarity, son. Once again, I am myself. I ruined everything. I know it's much too late now, so I won't be dragging any of you into my problems."

For the first time, I was convinced of the truth of the saying *Blood is thicker than water.* I detested my father for years before that day, but in a flash, I forgave and forgot every terrible thing he'd ever done to us. I loved him.

My mother was at my induction ceremony, but my parents did not say a word to each other. They kept as much distance as they possibly could from each other. There was a wound between them only time and unexpected circumstances could heal.

Accurate to my prediction, he'd attempted to kill my mother in cold blood.

Just a little short of two weeks following my departure, he accused my mom of infidelity with his childhood best friend without proof. He choked her with a pillow in her sleep until she was more than close to passing away before he let go. Overpowering her and threatening to do it over again, he forced her to admit to his accusations. Otherwise, he would have killed her. My mom did exactly as he demanded, only for him to send her packing the following day.

That was the last time they ever spoke to each other. With a severely bruised face, bloodshot eyes, and bruised neck, my mother had visited me to confirm she was separating permanently from my dad.

"You were right, Ramon," she said. "Everything you said before you left was true. I wish I had listened to you early enough. Now I feel lost without him after twenty-four years of marriage."

I thought it was good news that my mother had finally made the right decision. She was by far better off without him, but she needed time to accept that reality.

I'm sorry.
Don't worry;
A stronger man, I have become.
Jesus walked on water,
And I wasn't even a swimmer.
You left me in the middle of the sea, helpless.
But I learned to find my way, breathless.
Though it was the hard way,
I have learned to survive — my way.

After I graduated from veterinary school, my relationship with my father became what I'd dreamed of since I was a kid. He began to take pride in me openly, and I could see how humbly he longed to make up for all the difficult years.

We communicated constantly, sometimes by text, and with each message we exchanged, I knew we could both feel the distance between us closing. For the first time, my father also became my friend.

University matriculation – my first year at the university, 1998.

My dad and my godmother, 2002.

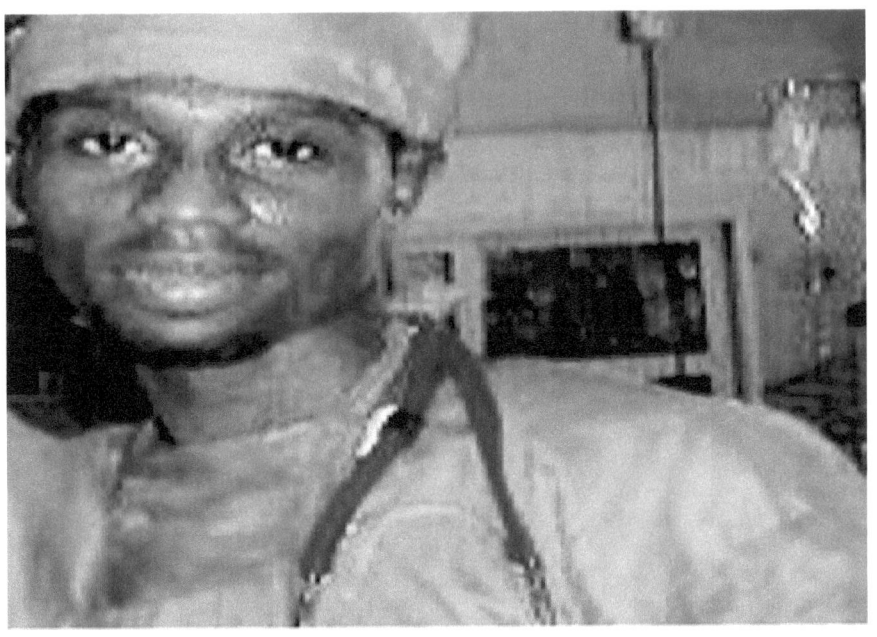

My first surgery at the veterinary teaching hospital – final year in veterinary school, 2004.

Tola and I, final year in veterinary school, 2004.

Mom and I, my swearing-in induction ceremony into veterinary practice, 2005.

Chapter 8

NIGERIA: November 2006

Dead Man's Purgatory.

I sat next to a severely dehydrated, emaciated, weak six- month-old calf in a local cattle barn.

He was too weak to stand, and his rear was smeared all over with watery feces. When I finished his treatment, I leaned back against the muddy wall. I was still dressed in my large green coveralls, mud boots, gloved hands, and holding a huge syringe. I rested both of my arms across my knees as the calf and I stared at each other.

"Poor thing," I whispered. "How much pain you must have been in for days."

As I leaned in to pet him, a little boy walked in. I looked him over; he couldn't have been more than five. His abdomen was severely distended, and his limbs were skinny.

Kwashiorkor, I concluded. He was suffering from malnutrition, common in young children due to protein deficiency. The locals in this area raised animals, but they rarely ate them. I remembered my life when I was about his age, how a Nigerian child's wellbeing was sometimes gambled in the name of customs and beliefs.

Even in his state, it wasn't his condition that caught my eye as much as something else did: his sharp blue eyes.

Earlier in the morning, a woman had shown up at my veterinary clinic with the same mutation—a local African plateau woman with a hijab around her head and those ice-blue eyes. She spoke Berom, not English, so one of the technicians had interpreted that she needed help with her calf.

With concern, she had informed us that she lived in a village on the outskirts of Jos City that she feared may have been too far for me to travel. I had assured her I was used to going out on long-distance calls. After the sixty-mile trip, I'd discovered there were about eight mud houses in the village, along with a well, a few dogs, about a dozen cattle and goats roaming a farm, a couple of chickens, and no electricity.

An older woman entered the barn behind the little boy. I shielded my gaze from the sun to meet her eyes—also blue, but hazier and less sharp, than the little boy's and his mom's. This had to be the grandmother.

These villagers intrigued me, but they also worried me. The condition of the little boy and the other kids I'd seen running around, the worm infestation in the animals, poor general hygiene and possible zoonotic infections.

After graduating from veterinary school, I'd fulfilled Nigeria's requirement to dedicate a year of service work to a community employing the background I'd gained in school. I'd organized a community health project, providing my veterinary services to the animals that belonged to families like these and bringing in a host of medical specialists to help the villagers themselves.

As I eyed the sick calf, now showing a little more activity, I knew I couldn't abandon this place. Days later, when I returned with a translator, the villagers gathered around as we pulled in on the singular road that ran through the area. It was then that a man approached me and asked if I'd be interested in an opportunity with Turner Wright, a subsidiary of a French company based in Lagos providing solutions for humans and animal health.

So meek, life's journey can be,
And what couldn't be averred
Makes it contrastive.

I once took off like an eagle,
Soared so high,
And held everything beneath
In the palm of my hand.
I touched the sky,
And no soul could comprehend how.
I stood in the sun,
But didn't get burned.
I wined and dined on the moon
And shared a crown.

Still, nothing's changed.
The pieces of every path seemingly lost
Only lead to the break of a new dawn.
How much more time will I squander
While plying the road to my dream?

How many mountains, oceans, and seas will I cross?

I need to understand the voice

That was echoing so loud

I could barely unravel its words,

Though I knew where it was coming from...

The timing for this offer was perfect. My service year had just recently ended, and the job was in Lagos State, where I was born and raised. I could make the trip from Jos to Lagos for the interview if I didn't mind the idea of thirteen hours in a bus jostling over bad roads and staring at the endless forests. I could take the night bus, which would allow me to get some sleep for the least expensive fare.

A few days before my trip, I had a nightmare that felt so real that I knew something terrible was about to happen.

In my dream, I saw a dead man in purgatory. He appeared with a scar extending from the corner of his right eye to his lower jaw. His face was severely burned. The man was enraged. His shirt and pants had blood stains all over. He held a shotgun in one hand and a knife in the other. He moved around in a room occupied by two old men and a young woman.

They seemed innocuous as they stood motionless, quietly and helplessly watching the lunatic who'd possessed the room. He stared at the beautiful young lady and said, "I could do something with you."

Then, he turned to the two jittering old men as they begged him to spare their lives. Without listening he pointed his shotgun at one of them and shot him in the chest.

He moved closer to the older man who was still pleading for his life. Gently, he slowly drove his knife from mid-abdomen, through the xiphoid up into his chest while whispering into his ear, "It will soon be over."

As the man fell to the ground lifeless, he callously pulled his knife out from the still body and wiped his blade clean on the dead man's jacket. Just like butchers do on the feathers of a slaughtered chicken.

The floor was quickly painted in blood. The man showed no recognition of his actions as he got up and walked past the bodies of two innocent men he'd murdered in cold blood. I stood there, shocked out of my might, as I waited to be next in line. He walked towards and around me while ignoring the young woman for a moment.

I swear he can see me, I thought to myself.

I stood speechless, watching him as he walked back and forth and around me. When I turned to take a quick look away from him, I saw a child, about seven years old. She had been there all along, holding my left hand. She gave me a quiet nod as I stared at her reassuring eyes. I could hear a soft voice in my head. It was hers, telling me never to let go of her.

"As long as you hold on to me, you will be safe," she assured.

The killer continued to rage around the room. He was searching for something or maybe someone. I knew for sure he could not see me. However, as my fear of the murderer escalated, doubt started to creep inside me. I was losing awareness of the child holding on to my hand from the growing fear of the lunatic standing a few feet away from me. The child continued to seek my attention to distract me from my fear, but I was in more fear of the maniac than I trusted the child. She was my shield, but I doubted her protection.

Why is she protecting me? How long will she stand by my side? Will she be around till my predicament is over?

I continued to ask myself the wrong questions. The type of reasoning that further gave me away. As my faith withered, like a dying flower, the grip between us began to loosen. The killer instantly seemed to notice something ahead of him. I was unsure if I was letting go of the child or if my shield was letting go of me. Nevertheless, she shook her head in disapproval of my actions.

"There is time to fear, and there is time to cling tightly to faith. Faith cannot feed on the fear of the unclean, nor will fear ever be willing to accept the mighty shoulders of faith," she said to me.

Big words for a seven-year-old, I thought, but I was more bothered by the disappointment written on her face. I knew I ruined something so dear to both of us, the child and I.

The killer was desperate as he concentrated on validating his senses. I could not control my fear as I watched the little girl slowly start to withdraw from me - or maybe I was stepping away from her. Her face showed no expression still, but there was so much love in her eyes. She uttered no word, but I could still hear her voice inside my head.

"You give in to fear. You let go of your inheritance. You squandered all that was offered to you. I did all that I could to save you," the little girl said without a hint of anger in her tone.

Fingertip to fingertip, I had given myself away. I watched her slip away from me, knowing disaster was imminent. The young woman trembling at the corner of the room gazed at me with her mouth wide open. With a shotgun in one hand, a knife in the other, and a cold smile on his charred face, the dead man in Purgatory looked straight at me as I finally woke up.

I was initially worried about the nightmare, but eventually I decided to pay no attention to it. After all, it was only a dream, and nothing was going to change my mind about the trip to Lagos for my interview.

A few days later, I headed to the bus station.

It was past dusk when I climbed into the sixty-passenger luxury bus and slid my travel bag into the overhead space. I'd packed a few clothes and the papers I needed for my interview—every educational document I'd ever earned from primary school to my doctorate, as well as all my financial and family records. How strange, that I could sling my entire life's achievements into a small leather bag.

I settled into my seat, hoping whoever took the seat next to me wouldn't be a talker. Outside the window, I watched my friend blow kisses up to his girlfriend, who was sitting a few rows ahead of me. She was on her way to visit her parents in Lagos. They smiled at each other. I couldn't help but smile, too.

Then a man sat down beside me, taking a quick look at the bus driver, who was distracted by another passenger. The man squeezed his young daughter discreetly between us, which I thought must have meant he'd paid for only one seat.

I scooted myself to create a little more space for the little girl now nestled in next to me, then sank into my little corner as the bus pulled out of the station. I glanced up at my friend's girlfriend as she rested her head against the bus window, clearly exhausted. The woman directly across from her in the front row had two little girls with her, all three of them sharing two seats.

Some youngsters filled the back rows, most of them recent graduates like me who had just completed their community projects. Some of them were visiting family members, while others had job interviews in Lagos.

As some of them laughed and chatted, I closed my eyes and listened.

I listened to the woman with the two little girls in the first row as they talked about a wedding. As I listened in more detail, I was able to determine that her eldest daughter was getting married. It was the reason she had to pay for almost half of the baggage area below the bus. She laughed and went on about how long she'd waited for this moment. I could tell she was proud about spending so much money on her daughter's wedding.

The two little girls were the bride's little sisters. I thought the three of them must have been really entertaining, as the passengers in the first few rows couldn't stop laughing.

By midnight, more than half the passengers on the bus had fallen asleep. With the bus humming with steady speed beneath us, I knew the ride would be peaceful enough to sleep before my interview in the morning.

Have you ever felt like you live in
A different world in your mind?
You can smell it, see it, and feel it...
Every moment of your breath!
A million fragments of varying visions,
You can't quite explain it.
Even so, the urge is undeniable:
Never stop running!
It is your future without a doubt!

You keep chasing after yourself.
It looks as though it's thousands
Of years away from you.
The closer you get,
The more it feels like
You have taken a wrong turn
At one imperceptible point.
Alas, you're at a halt,
Pondering and seeking,
Where next to turn,
Peradventure, the time you could procure,
Or so you reckon.

As it seems toilsome to align
The pieces of your own puzzle,
You perceive for certain that time waits—
Time which has been indomitable.

Call it impatience;
I call it one life to fulfill—
A life I can't help but helplessly and patiently wait for,
Even when it's the most grueling thing to do.

I must have drifted off to sleep when the next thing I heard was someone outside the bus shouting.

"Stop! Stop!"

There was the murmur of sleepy questions from a few of us passengers. Then several gunshots.

The bus started to slow down, not quite coming to a halt. The noises got louder. I heard an angry voice ordering the driver to stop the bus, then the engine revving as the driver accelerated. He was going to crash his way through the pandemonium. My heart thudded against my ribs.

We must have been surrounded as bullets clanked off the frame of the bus and pinged off the windshield. Gunfire flew through the windows on either side of us. Bullets whirred over my head and struck the leather of the seat beside me with a sickly soft thump.

"Get on the floor!" I screamed, pushing the man and his daughter to the floor and shielding them with my body.

Finally, the bus rumbled to a halt. I wasn't sure if the driver was shot or if they had shot out the tires.

I heard the doors open. A spray of gunfire hit the forest around us, and men's voices were hurling threats after the bus conductor, who must have made a run for it before the gunmen got to us.

"If yu no come aut, we go find yu keel yu!" The angry voice announced in pidgin. Meaning *if you don't come out, we will find you and kill you!* They kept firing into the forest. God, how long would it go on? Now I was sure the bus driver had died.

Suddenly, all the noises stopped. The passengers underneath me remained motionless. *Had every passenger on the bus been killed?* I wasn't sure if I was dead or alive. I was too afraid to open my eyes. I might be the only one in a quiet new world.

Then, from outside the bus came a warning, "Get aut of de bus peepool! Ollof yu! If yu neva die, yu come down! If yu no come aut, we go keel yu!"

I'm still alive. I had to stop myself from screaming this out loud. I wagered that if they really wanted to kill every passenger, they wouldn't warn us about the consequences of not complying with their orders. So, I pulled myself up from the two motionless bodies beneath me, feeling them move slightly. They weren't dead, just too shocked to come out. I looked around the dark bus. Slowly my eyes adjusted as moonlight lit a route for me through the aisles.

First, I'd remove my wallet, in which I'd tucked 12,000 naira, worth about 100 US dollars. I slipped 1,500 naira into the back pocket of my pants and tucked my wallet with the rest of the money between the seat cushions. I knew they would want to find something they could take. I dropped my cell phone in the front pocket of my shirt, where they could easily locate it.

I was the first to find my way out of the bus, bracing my hands against the bus seats to move my shaking body steadily. If anyone else was alive, they weren't moving.

With each numb step, I stumbled over bodies. Wanting to arrive in Lagos before my interview looking polished, I'd put on a white button-down shirt, which was now splattered with blood. I didn't know if I'd been hit, but I didn't give it much consideration. I didn't feel any pain. In fact, I felt nothing.

I raised both arms above my head as I finally made my way out of the bus, where two men standing on the road were waiting to search me. I didn't look at their faces, afraid they would kill me if I were able to identify them. With my head down, I tried to gather as much information about my surroundings as I could.

There appeared to be about thirty of them, dressed in army-like uniforms with automatic machine guns in their hands. One of them was armed with what looked like a SWAT HK machine gun, while the other swung his AK 74 around as he prepared to search me.

"Where ya money? Where ya phone? Evrytin you 'ave!"

"In my pockets," I replied.

One of them took my cell phone while the other searched my pants pockets. They ordered me to move forward and lie flat in the middle of the road. With my forehead pressed to the cold, tarred ground, the chaos, the fear, and the uncertainty all ebbed. I grew slightly calmer as more passengers stepped off the bus. I listened as they begged for their lives, offering to give the gunmen all they had.

The bandits secured their ammunition with one hand, and searched passengers with the other. I could hear one of them, whom I assumed was the leader, warning anyone left alive on the bus to come down or be killed.

"We no wan keel anywun! We juss wan robb leave una, but ya driver dey play smaat! Na he put una for dis mess."

We didn't intend to kill anyone. We only planned to rob and leave but the driver caused the mess by trying to escape.

One of his men walked over to the driver, who was sitting in front of the bus. I was relieved to see he was still alive but looking too weak from excessive blood loss. A bullet had hit his right arm. He'd managed to tie his shirt over the wound, but he still had his left hand firmly placed over it. The man pointed his 9mm to the driver's forehead.

"Yu! I go keel yu! Na, you make us shoot keel all dis innocent peepool!"

"Abeg no keel me!" The driver begged for his life. "Na mistake, abeg forgive! I get wife and two children!"

Another of the robbers stepped in. "Leave am!" he said. "No keelam! Enof peepool don die already. We juss wan robb dem peepool. All dem dead peepool dey for him head."

I listened as they debated between themselves, ultimately not harming the driver any further.

Every so often, the bandits would shout at those of us lying in the road, warning us not to stare at them. From where I lay, a few feet from the bus, I subtly cocked my head to the side and continued to observe what was going on.

Two men at the front exit of the bus aggressively patted people down, taking whatever they found—mostly cash and phones. A few climbed onto the bus, yelling and waving their guns, tossing passengers out whether they were wounded or not. If someone was too slow in their shock to move quickly, the robbers screamed, "Move! Get on da ground! Put ya face down!"

I had wanted to believe that they wouldn't kill any more of us as long as they got what they wanted, but now I began to doubt this. A few were ruthless. I wanted to be as alert as possible and knew I needed a strategy, especially if I had to race off into the forest by the roadside.

On the bus, the bandits cut into passengers' bags, mutilating people's luggage completely. They scrutinized the packages in the overhead compartments and the bags in the storage area below the bus. Then they exited the bus and searched all of us again as we lay on the open road. *If they find the money that I hid away,* I thought with grim certainty, *my life will be over.*

"Mom didn't move!" The eldest of the two little girls traveling with the bride's mother began to weep uncontrollably.

"I tried to get her off the bus, but she didn't move!" In the corner of my eye, I could see the younger one had taken a shot to her right shoulder.

"My sister is bleeding!" cried the older one.

"Yu! Aw old yu be?" The leader asked.

"Seven," replied the elder.

"An' your sister?

"Five."

"Where una seedown inside de bus?"

"First row. By the door." She pointed.

The poor mother of the two had taken a stray bullet to the head and died instantly. I was able to take a good look at the leader while he questioned the little girl. He had black, frizzy hair and stood a skinny five and a half feet. His gun hung from his shoulder as he barked orders and signaled to two of his men,

"Go check for dem mama." To another, he commanded, "Yu! Tie the sister wound!"

One of them took a scarf off another passenger and tied it over the wound.

"Any woman wey dey carry pikin for here?" It was his way of asking *Is there any woman with a child among the passengers.*

When one woman stepped up, he ordered her to deliver the girls to a police station in Lagos—the same police that wouldn't show up when you needed them most. It had to have been over an hour since the robbery started.

"Make sure say yu carry dem go station or dem family in Lagos." He gave some money for transportation to the woman who volunteered to help the kids, cash he'd taken out from the pile of money they robbed from all of us.

This exchange had caused several other surviving passengers to look on.

"I wan make ollof una lay flat!" the leader said. "Put ya face for ground! If anywun try look up, na him keel himself!" *Lay flat with your faces to the ground. If anyone looks up, that person is responsible for his or her own death.*

A streak of liquid ran sideways toward me. I traced its source, coming from the crotch of a young man lying on the road next to me. He looked about my age, but he was trembling the entire time. Quietly, over and over, he repeated a name in a shaky tone.

"George," he whispered. "George."

His brother had died beside him on the bus.

"He no move."

He whispered as if he had to remind himself to try to believe it.

"He no move."

I tried to avoid his urine trailing toward me but realized I would compromise my stillness if I kept attempting to shift myself away, so I stayed put.

For all of us, the event had been traumatic. But I knew there were several whose lives would never be the same.

It grew quiet. We all lay obediently for a while. *Something has to break this up,* I thought. By now, three hours had passed. *Someone has got to come on this road and find us.* I wasn't sure how the cops would have been able to rescue us—the armed robbers owned far more powerful ammunition than what the Nigerian police carried.

It was still pitch-black. We remained on the road with our faces to the ground till two other buses came. The robbers didn't kill any of them but had taken their belongings. Then they finally left. The other bus drivers helped the wounded driver onto another bus.

"You for don stop," one told him. *You should have stopped*!

"Dem rob evrywun for awa bus but dem no kill anywun."

The other driver said to our driver, *"They robbed everyone on our buses but killed no one."*

As they rushed him to the nearest hospital, the rest of us were left stranded.

I found the father and daughter who had been sitting beside me, feeling a rush of relief to find they'd both survived unharmed. Other passengers bled profusely, and I knew there wasn't enough time to get them to the hospital. One of them was the five-year-old girl. Her shoulder had begun to bleed again as she sat between her crying sister and the woman who had volunteered to take them to Lagos.

The young man who'd urinated next to me wasn't injured but utterly confused and in shock. I grabbed his hand and placed it on the little girl's shoulder.

"Apply pressure over this scarf," I instructed him, "and keep her arm elevated, just like this, until I come back."

The little girl flinched as I gently brought up her arm to try and control the bleeding. I knelt in front of her.

"What's your name, darling?"

Again, she flinched.

"Rose," she answered softly.

I held her wrist. Her pulse was a little weaker than average but not too severe.

"Rose, you are doing great. I'm so proud of you." I tried to reassure her by looking straight into her eyes, letting her know she had my full attention. "This will hurt just a little, but I will stop your bleeding before we get you to the hospital, okay?"

She nodded.

I rushed into the bus, tore open the first aid kit, and ran back to Rose in the middle of the road. I rinsed her wound with saline and took a moment to make sure there was no severe damage to a major artery in her shoulder.

She was still breathing fine, and she responded to pain. These were good signs. With the young man's help, I applied a pressure bandage over the bullet wound and gave more bandages to the woman. I instructed her to keep the girl's arm elevated as much as possible and to add more bandages if the bleeding started again.

I moved on to help stabilize a few other victims. With a few more able-bodied passengers, we moved the wounded onto buses that had finally arrived to whisk them off to the nearest hospital.

Back on the bus, I found my wallet. The cash was still intact— enough to pay for several fares to Lagos. I was about to slide my wallet into my back pocket when I found the 1,500 naira I'd left for them to find. All of that death, all that heartbreak… and all I'd lost was a cell phone. My stomach turned.

People searched for their loved ones who didn't make it out of the bus. My friend's girlfriend, seated in the front row, had taken a bullet to her side. She didn't survive. A man who sat directly behind me took two shots to his back and another to his mouth.

There was blood everywhere.

Within seconds, our paralysis turned to pandemonium while everyone searched for their loved ones and belongings. I glanced into my overhead locker, but my bag was no longer there.

I rushed off the bus. I'd noticed some papers in the bush right across from the mid-row windows, so I walked into the forest while the moon faintly lit my way. I held up the first paper I came across: my veterinary degree certificate.

One after another, I found them all—the history of my life's documents so I could get this job in Lagos. Outside I found my bag ripped into pieces. I didn't bother to search further for my clothes or anything else.

As I walked away from the bush into the open space, I listened to the cries of agony. I reminded myself that I could have been dead.

Then, like one of the two little girls who had lost their mother, I exploded into uncontrollable tears.

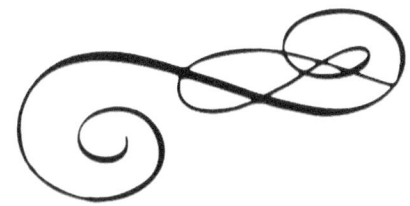

Chapter 9

NIGERIA: November 2007
A Cat with Nine Lives.

The smell of the meadow came from both sides of the narrow muddy road. The scent in the air was fresh and soothing, more comforting than the air-conditioner in my car.

Botany was never my strong suit but whatever they were, the grasses were quite tall, like they'd never been bothered by the cattle. The vegetation extended over several miles, entirely free of human interference.

I traveled this road with my driver once or twice every week, and each time the view was the same—lonely but peaceful. As far as I could see, the grasses looked the same height at a distance, while the feathery tips dangled to the dancing wind.

In anticipation of the wonderful moment every time we drove into *Igbesa*, I rolled down the car window so I could inhale the beautiful scent one more time.

I often longed for that brief period when I closed my eyes as the feathery edges of the tall plants brushed over my face. Our car struggled past the bushes, galloping in and out of potholes, but it was such a beautiful and soothing scene that I hardly ever noticed.

This moment was often too short, thanks to the smell of the neighboring farms, which gradually replaced the beautiful fragrance as we drove deeper towards our destination. The colorful butterflies, bees, and grasshoppers also slowly disappeared from sight and were replaced by poultry farms, large and small.

The glimpse of the first farm on this road often triggered a lull in my perception of the first few miles. I glanced at the gate from the front passenger side of the car, wondering how long my fate was tied to this part of my job.

Once I'd almost lost my life trying to secure this job - a dream job as anyone else in my shoes would call it. However, the time to move on to the next goal was fast approaching. I could feel it.

I wasn't exactly sure what was coming next. For me, this beautiful job was just another stepping stone to the big plan. I constantly reminded myself that every step I took and every decision I made were interconnected chain reactions. Everything I did was to get to that plan.

The large-scale farms in the country were as far as they could be from the cities. This made it harder to commute, knowing the roads were either bedraggled or muddy. Ironically, I often left the farms with a big grin on my face, holding substantial checks in one hand.

I didn't have to report to my boss earlier that day, which gave me more control of my time. In fact, it was an excellent opportunity to start my day earlier and end it sooner than my regular routine.

So, leaving Lagos for Igbesa was the best chance of getting hold of my clients. *Sango-Ota* was the last major city that connected beautiful *Igbesa* to the rest of the country.

The land was dry, colored red and looked barren, but it wasn't. There was such life in it, as it sprouted forth anything that fell on it. Red esparto pierced through the dry land, although they were not common in this part of the African continent. It was calm, peaceful and lonely despite bearing huge forest-sides as a shield.

The oldest and most honest hamlets are found inhabited by the poorest but happiest townsfolk, unaware of the changing world, or so it always seemed to me. The latter part of Sango-Ota and settled areas of Igbesa were not unusually congested, typical of most poverty-stricken locals in South- Western Nigeria.

Most families owned or worked on a farm. It was their source of pride. Many city dwellers preferred to travel to the little towns and villages between Sango Ota and Igbesa on farm days, which was on Fridays, to purchase food items at much cheaper rates compared to the city.

It was the end of what I would call a good day with my clients at Igbesa, and I was very much eager to head back to Lagos. We drove through the bushes and finally back to the highway, a well-tarred road. There were a few police roadblocks on the turnpike connecting the villages to the city.

This was no surprise because the highway was less than seventy kilometers from the *Republic of Benin* border, where auto dealers were notoriously known for smuggling used cars into Nigeria. The policemen routinely stopped cars for inspection, especially those that looked suspicious.

I noticed one of the cops signaled to us. He wanted us to slow down, but it didn't seem like my driver saw him. I'd been driving through these checkpoints for almost a year without any hassle whatsoever.

"*Baba! Baba!* Can you see the policeman?" I asked him as he continued to drive, pretending not to see the police ahead of him.

But Baba did not respond. He simply kept driving.

Baba was a much older man, probably in his late fifties. He was from the Yoruba tribe in the southwestern part of Nigeria. He had little education, so he often mixed *pidgin* with the Yoruba language when he spoke. I could understand him perfectly well because I'm also from the Yoruba tribe and fluent in pidgin. But Baba comprehended basic English, so I spoke or replied to him mostly in English to uphold professionalism on the job.

"They want us to stop!" I yelled at him, unsure if he'd heard me the first time. As we got closer to the checkpoint, another cop walked to the center of the road holding up a stop sign.

"They want you to stop!" I yelled again, almost sure he was up to something so unwarranted.

My driver did not respond. Instead, he stepped on the gas while zooming straight ahead like he'd been suddenly possessed. He wasn't going to stop. I had no idea what was going on in his mind.

"*Baba! Baba!* You need to stop! You will get us killed!" I pleaded with him to no avail.

"I no fit dokito! E ma binu! Dis men no look like police to me ooo! E be like say dem be army rubber!" Baba replied in Pidgin. *I'm sorry Doctor, I can't stop. These men do not look like police to me. I think they are armed robbers.*

"They are not armed robbers!"

I tried explaining to my driver that they were policemen doing routine checks. As a matter of fact, I had seen them several times whenever I journeyed through this road in the mornings. However, it was too late; the moment didn't give any room for such explanations.

Baba attempted to venture through the roadblock, which was countered by a few gunshots. The moment stood still for a few seconds, dead quiet like nothing had happened.

I suddenly saw myself outside of the car, walking through a group of people. No one seemed to notice me. About six armed policemen stood quietly, with guilt written all over their faces.

I looked down; it was my body in a sitting position, my head down with my chin tucked into my chest. I was not breathing, nor was I moving. There were several gunshots to my chest. My shirt was covered in blood.

My driver's body was a few feet from mine. I wasn't sure if he was still alive or not, but all attention was drawn to mine. I could hear voices in my head as I knelt before my body. The policemen held their waists in penitence, wishing they could turn back the time.

"*Chai!* Why didn't they just stop? This car looks relatively new, so they should have known that's why they were being stopped!" one of the policemen muttered in frustration.

Another replied, "We know the young man, he's the young doctor who visits all the farms at Igbesa, but we didn't know it was him in the car. He used to drive in a green Corolla. We've never seen him in this car."

"There was no reason why they shouldn't have stopped! They have no contrabands in the car," one of the policemen interjected. "Do you notice his driver looks new, too? Maybe it was the driver who refused to stop. You know how some of these drivers fear the police for no reason at all. We didn't have any reason to do this to the poor kid."

Why would your vision be the same
When I keep you out of my sight?
Why would your memories remain

169

If I keep you out of my mind?
Why do stones thrown in anger
Only hurt twice as much?

Staring at the sender
Only makes me feel worse.
I am empty inside,
So like a dead leaf, endlessly, I float.
No one could ask why,
'Cause I found myself in a blank world alone.

I wish that beating
heart,
In the world I so crave,
Could hear my plight,
As I drifted, waiting to be saved.
They say that hearts won't stay broken,
And I'm afraid
The bruise in my still heart will never heal.

I awoke from the nightmare. The policeman's voice still ringing in my ears. It had felt so real I had to touch my chest to be sure there were no bullet holes. Here I was, afraid to leave for work after a nightmare that left me too fearful of getting in my car. I wished there was someone who could explain this horrible dream to me. Calling my mom would be a bad idea.

"I've had enough difficulties in my short existence as it is," I said aloud, trying to soothe myself. "I'm not planning on living in fear, nor have any loved one live in fear for my life. After all, it was just a dream."

The truth was, deep down inside me, I knew my dreams usually meant caution, a sort of premonition of some imminent disaster that might happen to me. So instead, I called my mom and requested she prayed for me. I told her everything without sparing her any details.

I did not narrate my nightmare to my driver. He was relatively new. Instead, I insisted I wanted to drive myself to work.

"Dokito, se ewa?" Baba asked in Yoruba language. *Are you okay?*

"I'm okay, Baba. I would like to drive myself this morning. It's been a while since I drove myself."

"O da. But you no go send me home today, abi?" Baba asked. *You're not going to send me back home, right?*

Smiling, I replied, "No, Baba, I'm not sending you home. We are traveling to *Sagamu* today. I don't like driving interstate."

Hesitantly, he stepped into the front passenger seat and put on his seat belt. My company had just replaced my Corolla with a relatively newer one. I had been involved in a bad accident - the Corolla had rolled eight times off the expressway to a side ditch before it stopped. It was a miracle that it didn't go up in flames. Though I was able to crawl out of what was left of the car, I was severely wounded. The car was completely mangled beyond recognition, so the insurance company had to write it off.

After that, my boss wanted me to drive more exotic cars to boost the company image. He also offered me a modest driver's allowance, so I didn't have to drive myself during business hours.

I could read Baba's body language and facial expressions. He was very uncomfortable in the passenger seat, which was entirely understandable.

"Enjoy, Baba!" I said to him calmly. "Relax, just enjoy the ride. It's no big deal that I get to drive you sometimes."

I could see his smile from the corner of my eyes.

"You know, there are lots of things I need to discuss with you about this job, Baba," I continued. "I'm sure you are aware of the numerous trips we have to make to other states of the country." I paused for a few seconds to let him acknowledge my words.

"But, that's not the most difficult part of the job. Dealing with policemen can be frustrating at times. Once they know you work for a big company, they think it is their government-given right to extort you. I am happy that you are a wise and patient man, so please let's be careful with them anytime they stop us."

I was happy to see him lighten up with confidence at my words of affirmation to him. It was the response that I desired.

I gave him a little more insight into how to handle police situations he wasn't familiar with, especially when we traveled outside Lagos. Checkpoint requirements varied tremendously across the country's different states, and the police culture of brutality also differed from state to state.

"Baba, I know most of these policemen are very corrupt," I said. "However, there is no reason to fear them. If they should stop either one of us or both of us, we will do our best to cooperate with them."

All I needed him to do was listen, respect, and obey policemen whenever he came in contact with them, especially if this happened on the roads to our client destinations.

"Just have confidence in the fact that there is nothing to worry about," I added.

I hoped having this talk with him would help avert any tragedies for as long as it took to get over my fears and forget my nightmares.

I oversaw sales, research, and medical consultation for all clients in southwestern Nigeria, mostly the biggest farms in this part of the country to include all the farms that belonged to the then President of

Nigeria. I was quite good at my new job but much better at resolving medical and clinical issues for the big farms.

Soon I became *"the famous young doctor"* every farmer wanted to meet. Baba got more comfortable with the routines of our daily work. With the addition of new clients on my list, most of whom contacted me through referrals, the number of trips out of Lagos doubled—more than we could handle over the course of each week.

It'd been three months since my nightmare about getting shot by the policemen at the checkpoint. We successfully made several trips to other parts of the country without a single adverse incident.

One day, I received a call from the biggest farm in Sagamu, a very successful farmer who heard about me from a hatchery manager in Ibadan. There was a severe outbreak on his farm, and he'd found out that I could solve his problem.

We jumped in the car from Lagos, and off we went. Baba drove and I was in the front passenger side. The road to Sagamu wasn't new to us—as a matter of fact, we'd traveled this road at least once a week. I thought I could kill four birds with a stone since there were three other clients within a ten-mile radius of the new customer.

About fifteen minutes from our destination, we heard a loud noise from the back of the car.

Without thinking too much of where the sound came from, I calmly turned to my driver and said, "Do not step on the brake. Do not step on the brake."

Before I got a chance to make reassuring eye contact with him, the car began to spin out of control. Baba undoubtedly stepped on the brake.

I hadn't realized we were on a river spanned by a narrow bridge.

The car took a third spin before falling off the bridge backward. As the car fell into air and space, I turned my head, looking downwards from the passenger seat. In my heart, I experienced a suspended, peaceful moment while I turned my head forward with my eyes closed. The feeling was familiar. I'd been here before. My body remembered, from my recent nightmares and the accident that I'd lost my first car to - and barely survived - a few months before.

Sometimes, time stands still. Your life lies before you, so tangible you can almost touch it, but gone at the slightest breath. I could not hear any sound except for the tranquility that had taken over during this fall.

I did not make any attempt to struggle, nor did I panic as my driver did. I wasn't exactly sure if I accepted the fact that this was how my life would end, or maybe I instantly acknowledged that this was coming. I felt shielded as if I was being protected from something. Whatever it was, it was tender and gentle, limpid and calming.

Eventually, I opened my eyes. I woke up covered in fumes. The car was engulfed in smoke. I slowly looked around and noticed shrubs around the car. The car was upside down, but I couldn't see much. I would find out later that the roof of the car had hit the slopey abutment of the bridge on its way down. The abutment knocked the car over to the side, so that it landed on the bushy land from where it had rolled several times before coming to a stop just by the river.

I felt squished in the car and had no room to move my body. I hit the car door a few times, to find my way out, but it was stuck. I was trapped.

I screamed for help, but it was louder in my head. I felt drowsy. My movements slowed down. I muttered a slow and quiet "help" and hit the car door about three more times before falling back into darkness. As I blacked out, I wondered if anyone had seen our car roll off the bridge. Would anyone come to help us?

I'm not sure how long I had been unconscious, but I started to hear voices that seemed like they were coming from a distance.

"I found his ID!"

"He's a doctor!" another mentioned.

"He's probably related to Professor Ayoade! See his last name!" another voice interrupted the first two.

"The driver. I think we should send him to emergency first. He looks to be in better condition."

Slowly, I opened both eyes. I saw one of the young men trying his best to get a response from me. I wasn't sure how long I'd laid there, unable to move. There must have been twenty-eight people that came to our rescue. Most of them stood and watched in pity while about six young men tried to keep me alive.

The scene was identical to my dreams, except that I wasn't shot by some unscrupulous policeman or kneeling next to my dead body. I was alive, and my rescuers heard me when I responded.

"Ayoade. I'm 'Deji Ayoade."

"Can you remember any number we could call? We couldn't find your phone, but we found your ID in your wallet."

I called out a number, which turned out to be the direct number to the logistics manager of my company.

My rescuers were a group of medical students on field exercise from the Sagamu Teaching Hospital to other parts of the state. They had seen our car spin off the bridge. Somehow, they rescued my driver and me before the smoke from the car could kill us.

The ambulance arrived on time but could only accommodate one patient at a time. My condition must have been horrifying, because they didn't think I was going to make it. They decided to save my driver first, hoping that that way at least one of us would live.

Although my vision was still blurred, I could hear the students requesting that the two policemen there take me to the ER, because there may not be an ambulance for another hour.

"It might be too late before they come back for him. The hospital is about 20-25 minutes from here," said one of the students.

"We will take him in the car," the policemen offered.

A police station wagon pulled over next to me. I was still lying on the side of the road, unable to move any part of my body.

"Hey, doc! Can you still hear me? We are going to get you to the hospital."

"Stop! Stop!" I screamed. "Don't touch me! Please, wait! It must be in unison. I'll count to three."

The young man who turned out to be a third-year medical student responded reassuringly, "We know, doc. We are medical students. We rescued you from the crash. We know exactly what to do."

The policemen scurried into the front seats of the station wagon while I lay in the back seat, watching them with my peripheral vision.

Looking back, I still couldn't trust Nigerian police, even in a near-death condition. They could have given up on my chance for survival, but they didn't. How ironic, that the same police that shot me to death in my nightmare helped save my life in real life.

"I hate tragedies like these. Can you imagine what a kid like him must have been through to become a doctor, only to end up dead, or worse useless from an accident due to bad roads?"

The policeman who spoke seemed frustrated. I didn't share his confusion, nor did I blame my hapless accident on bad roads. I thought about how an entire generation of the Ayoade family was almost wiped off the surface of the earth from a single road accident. I thought about how my father never drove a car for the rest of his life following multiple shocking, inexplicable accidents that he had barely survived. I imagined how my life could have ended from the previous year's bus attack that claimed the lives of so many and how I had lost count of the car accidents I'd been involved in ever since I started driving a year and a half before.

My family would get to know about this accident only because my admission to the hospital was imminent, and I thought I'd be there for a while. There had been many accidents that I never told them about. The insurance company would replace my car three times in eighteen months, because it was so much cheaper than trying to fix them.

It then made me mull over the eventual fate of every male child born into the Ayoade family, as much as I pondered on the origin of my forefathers. Is there a generational curse in my family, a sort of anathema, or could the cycle of accidents be mere coincidences?

I thought about the safety of my brothers. Why are these accidents happening no matter how much I tried to avoid them? What can I do? What must I do? How do I make these tragedies stop?

I could only continue to ask myself these questions because I was still breathing, still alive. I felt haunted, especially in moments when I could perceive such horrid events before they happened. It then made me wonder what my father was going through during his desperate years. Nonetheless, aside from praying to God for life, I had no clue what else to do about such premonitions.

The policeman sitting on the passenger side continued to rant about his frustrations with the government and the bad roads. They weren't acting like typical Nigerian policemen at this moment: they sincerely empathized, just like my family members would do for me.

I have no alternate lives;
There is just this one season,
A generation of existence.
It's one in which I spend my time
In an absolute fritter.
I have a colossal mind
But cannot bring it to life.

There's only one reason—
As if my hands are bound
By a mortal sin, and I attest that I'm fine.
And how—why—am I always three?
There are so many thoughts
And nothing's done,
Like twinkling stars fading in and out.
Ideas, like a river, flow,
With nowhere to call home.

The agonies of living lie in the regret of the past.
Oh, that I may hang these shirts and buy a new one,
And how it haunts me so to realize
You've been squandering your time.
Everything is by grace,
Not by power or might,
And my productivity is only a proclivity,
Not veracity.

I deserve no pardon but clemency.
It's getting bad… verily, he works hard.
I wish I could work now, that it would work out
And burn all these shirts up!
The man of this morning is another—
Another tomorrow evening, even this night.
How my life is like a mirage!

There are so many worries
Of the past and the future times,
But how to make today materialize is unrealized.

So, what do I do now?
With these sour comments and whining,
Heaven, wake me from these
Nightmares and make me what I ought to be.

I count on your chance
So much—I need to be found
By you so enrich me.
I just hope, in you, somehow—anyhow—
And above all, my faith, I believe in you.

When I arrived at the ER, I realized that I had suffered temporary paralysis of my entire body. Nurses from the emergency room ran helter-skelter. One of them came up to me. She happened to be the wife of the professor who bore my last name. I stared at her name tag, "*AYOADE*," engraved in bold letters.

"Everyone here thinks you are my son," she said, smiling at me. "But I have no doubt we are related somehow."

She ordered one of the younger nurses to remove my clothes. With a pair of scissors, she hurriedly cut through my shirt and pants. Completely stripped to my underwear, she rinsed my body as generously as she could with water. I later discovered my driver suffered a chemical burn, and they had assumed I had as well.

I was wheeled over to trauma, where I silently began to panic. I wondered if I had multiple fractures that I couldn't feel.

"Maybe my spine is fractured? Maybe I'm paralyzed from the neck down?" I thought aloud to myself.

Questions raced through my mind as I silently watched the emergency team responding to more accident victims brought into the emergency room. The team was still busy attending to my driver. I began to move my head and arms. I could feel my entire upper body, but I couldn't tell if my waist down was the same.

After dozing off for over an hour, I woke up, not remembering if I was sedated or not. Across from me were my sister, aunt, boss, and the logistics officer staring at me from the feet of the bed.

I looked back at them and turned to my sister. "I need you to pinch my leg."

"What?"

I guess no one knew for sure if I sustained a spinal injury or not, so my sister hesitated.

"Pinch my legs! And my feet! As hard as you can!" I yelled at her, frustrated.

She trembled as she obeyed my command. With a sigh of relief, I took a deep breath.

"I can feel it," I announced. She let out a sigh of relief as well.

"Okay," I continued, taking a breath, "Can you pinch both at the same time, please?"

My aunt joined my sister this time. I never thought I would be so happy about pain at some point in my life.

"Good!" I said. "At least, we can rule out paralysis."

I thought my face was disfigured, judging from how they stared at my face, so I requested a mirror. Again, my sister hesitated, but I was adamant.

"After all, it's my face," I retorted as she handed the mirror to me.

I had a neck collar on from a mild neck fracture, my eyes were bloodshot, and my face, and chest, severely bruised.

"It's not that bad! You all stare at me like I'm the Frankenstein monster," I said, looking to ease the strain in the air.

"Son, it's not your face," my boss replied. "It's just hard to believe anyone could survive what just happened to you and Baba. When you see your driver and what's left of your car, you will understand." He shook his head. "You are one hell of a fighter, boy," he said. "A cat with nine lives.".

Three days later, I was discharged from the hospital. The doctors could not explain the rapid healing in my body, but most affected parts were completely healed except my neck, which would now be in a collar for a month.

After the accident, I became single-minded about my applications for research grants and scholarships abroad. I'd been halfway through veterinary school before I realized that the bad dreams had always correlated frequently and were stronger when I was in danger. Even when I hired a new driver and got a new car, the nightmares and upsets continued.

Cops threatened to kill me when I confronted them for taking bribes on the street. Once, on an empty road, a woman rear-ended my vehicle. When I met her in the road to examine the damage, it was clear she'd been perfectly sober. She couldn't explain why she'd hit me.

I tried to take extra precautions, to make sense of it to avert another disaster. But no matter how cautious I tried to be, the longer I stayed in Nigeria, the more I felt I was putting myself in harm's way. I became more and more sure: it was time for me to move on.

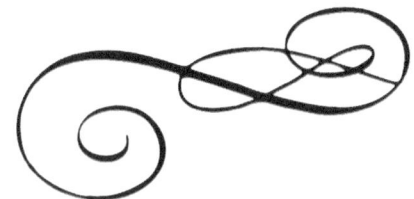

Chapter 10

NIGERIA: February 2008
One Last Hug from Father.

Three years since my induction into veterinary practice, my relationship with my dad had become far better than it ever was before.

I loved him dearly, and I was determined to care for him. I had learned to love both of my parents separately since they avoided talking about each other. My mom still struggled to forgive my dad for the things he had done to her.

My father shared my belief that the time was coming for me to leave. In our most candid exchanges, he confided in me that he owed a lot of people quite a lot of money. He believed some former business partners would kill him on sight if they crossed paths.

My siblings and I offered to help him, but he refused, stating they were his problems, not ours. He'd spent his early years taking risks that damaged all of us, but now my dad did everything he could to not involve his family with the problems he had gotten himself into. To keep his family safe, he decided to stay away from us altogether.

Whenever he called, he never disclosed his location. However, he always kept in touch with me.

One day, before my accident in Sagamu, I received a call from my dad.

"I'm sick." He said, coughing into the phone.

I had only one response.

"What do you need?"

In my childhood, my father had always been the one handing out money to help whoever needed it. Now, as each cough drained the energy from his voice, I wanted to be the one to help him. I sent him all the money he needed, but it was two weeks later when he called again. The cough was worse still.

"Where are you, Dad? I have to come get you! Your cough has gotten worse!"

"I'm sorry. I can't tell you, son. I'm seeing a good doctor here. All I need is more money to continue my treatment."

"Did your doctor tell you why you're coughing non-stop? If he did, he must have told you that your illness is much worse than you think. You need serious treatment right away, Dad."

He didn't give a reasonable answer, so I knew he wasn't seeing a doctor. My father was self-medicating. He'd been doing so since I was old enough to understand illnesses and treatments.

"Dad, I'm sorry I can't send you any more money. You haven't been to the hospital. I know you haven't! I will get you to the hospital, but I can't if you don't let me."

"I'm in Abuja," Dad finally admitted. "I can't even get to Lagos without worrying about someone trying to kill me."

"What difference does it make, Dad? Would you rather not take a chance on your life? If you stay back, what you have inside you might get worse."

It had been almost two years since my father had stepped into his house. He'd been more or less a fugitive as some of his business partners were searching for him because he owed them so much money.

"Dad, I will send some money for your transportation to Lagos," I said, even though I knew he was probably hiding somewhere in Lagos. "We have to know what's behind the coughing so you can get the right treatment. The type of cough I'm hearing right now will not stop unless you get the right treatment." I assured him.

I tried to make him as uncomfortable as I could, because I knew my father. He never yielded to fear. I have no memory of him ever visiting the hospital for any treatment. Any attempts to make him do so always failed, which would take many years away from him.

My dad believed it was unwise to look up too much medical information about one's illness, certainly not enough to know how it might end one's life. He didn't believe in medical diagnostics.

Every chance I got, I sought to explain how important it was for him to get examined routinely and get the help he needed before it was too late. On a few occasions, I asked him how he could be proud of me as a doctor if he wouldn't see one for himself.

"Those tests only create fear in you," he often said. "You start to drown in fear while the results are often not accurate. Fear is what kills you eventually, not the disease if there was one in the first place. Don't ever try to know why, when, or how you will die."

This was an age-old argument between us. Once, he scolded me for getting an HIV test done during premed. He thought it wasn't a smart thing to do.

Sometimes it's tough to convey an emotional story through poetry without jeopardizing the integrity of what makes it a poem. I hated reading or writing poems about my father. His life was a sad song: short and dark and more profound than a thousand-page book.

Although I knew my dad to be lionhearted, I also knew he was not completely without fear. I came to know this during the moments that I am about to narrate, listening to my father as he gave me his last words of wisdom:

Did you know, son,
That living fires get scared?
They grow legs
And make haste while being chased.
Oh, son, by circumstance's pranks.
Who knows his stand?
Who knows his fate?
Strong bows break
When bent by strong hands.
So now you see why we have to fear...

Fear? Why fear?
Fear the fall of mighty men.
Fear the fall of righteous men.
Fear the fall of able men.
All ridiculed, most miserable—
Their stead.

Son, that's the end:
When the weak oppose the strong
And the dogs beat the lions—
When material withstands ethereal,
And darkness breaks boundaries with light.

The fetters never loose.
Spider webs are good
Enough to entwine.
Long you'll tarry in blue.
You'll think you're two.
The race—this race is but doom.
Delicate world,
Weak hearts.
Fragile souls wait to be swallowed.
There's confusion all day long,
But grace is so strong.

So, humbly be bold,
And let those shoulders hold.
For we don't know who goes
By treating life like clothes
'Cause truly, it wears out, becoming old.
Men are waiting vipers,
Venom spat about.
But, watch—don't sleep.
Watch on this steep.

Weeks later, I walked into LUTH, where my dad had been admitted for a few days.

I found my sister in the hallway talking to the resident doctor in charge of his case. My dad was taking a nap. My sister never left his bedside until three days before, when she'd visited me at the hospital in Sagamu following my accident. I'd warned everyone not to tell my father about it.

"He is beginning to forget things," my sister said. "His naps are much calmer and longer than usual. Sometimes I thought he wasn't breathing. I heard him mention his late brothers' names a few times in his sleep. Then he continues to talk to a few dead family members. I mean, most of these guys died thirty-one years ago. I had to wake him up a few times because I worried he might die in his sleep."

Visibly unsettled, my sister continued, "By the way, his results are back. He's been concealing his CT scan results. He wanted to show them to only you."

"That's fine. I'll go talk to him."

"He's been asking for you for days now. We told him you traveled. I'm sure you know what to say. I think he really wants to talk to you, so you should wake him up if he's still sleeping."

"Okay, sis."

When I arrived by my dad's bedside, his eyes were closed, and it was hard to tell if he was breathing or not. I moved closer to him and placed the back of my palm underneath his nose, so I could feel the warmth of his breath. He was breathing.

I took a step backward, and tears filled my eyes as I watched him swallowed up by the hospital bed, quietly asleep. It was the weakest and most vulnerable that I had ever seen my dad.

I tried to pull myself together, sat next to him, and gently whispered, "Daddy."

As soon as my dad opened his eyes, he smiled, held my hand but didn't try to sit up.

He said, "I have so much to tell you, Ramon. I'm glad you finally made it."

"I'm glad to be here with you too, Dad," I replied. "Everything that I am about to tell you today, keep it in your

left hand and hold on tight to it. Never, never forget or let go. You will need to remember them from time to time."

"I'm all ears, Dad." I moved closer to him so that he had my full attention, though he was still lying in bed.

"Good. Now listen, a tongue bears no bone. If you feel pain in your tongue, something has gotten in there that doesn't belong," he began.

"If you have no idea how it got there, you can be damn sure the enemy has gotten a hold of you," my dad continued. "So, tell me, what would you do? Leave the bone lodged in your tongue causing you such unbearable pain, or do all you can to remove it?"

I sat listening, trying to discern his message for me. A few years before all this, he'd found a fish bone lodged in his tongue for some time without knowing. Now, in his hospital bed, he told me, "A tongue bears no bone." Like Alhaja, my dad sometimes told stories in parables.

I wondered if he was referring to himself. Did he mean his present condition?

My father continued, "Okay, let's assume you remove the bone successfully, completely relieved of this unbearable pain. Yet, it is not the time to sit back like nothing had happened. In life, you have to ponder, you have to meditate on why and how a bone that long found its way completely embedded in your tongue without you knowing it. Then you will appreciate the war you have just won and understand that the battle yet is far from over."

Finally, I was beginning to understand my father's words. He knew my life was now much more comfortable, better than it had ever been since I was born. I was spending a lot of time in Europe, advancing quickly on my job and having the most fun any young man my age could ever wish for. What more could a lad want?

I knew my achievements were premature, just like my dad's, maybe too early for my age at this time.

"When a man feels indestructible, he acts like an immortal. However, he paves a way to an early grave with his name engraved boldly on it," my father continued. "Son, take your worries to no one but God. Trust no man except God. Take lessons from my story. Men will come. They will eat your food and drink your wine when life's good. They will even share your woman if you let them. On the other hand, when your pocket runs dry, they will flee from you like anyone would from a plague at the sight of you. They will take the closest and shortest turn possible to avoid you.

"You have suddenly grown long spikes on your skin without knowing it. Not because you don't want to, but you just can't see the thorns. You and your family would probably be the only ones blinded by them. Beware, they can make you feel like you are a walking bad luck, a leper, or worse, make you believe it."

I continued to listen intently to my father. I was lost in the world of his words. I saw them. I breathed them. They would be his last words to me, but I didn't want to think about it, let alone believe the truth.

"Learn from my gullible mistakes, Ramon," he said. "They weren't supposed to be my biggest mistakes because I already knew where I fell. The things that I have done to get back up defied my faith and my belief. I turned my back to the ones I believe in, deceiving myself that I was only protecting myself and my family. I found reasons for taking an unusual turn. A wrong turn.

"I found more excuses for staying on this path. What I have done cannot be undone, for there are no more right turns for me, nor can I go back in time. It was a one-way road that I embarked on. Maybe I didn't know what I got myself into, but I received my warnings."

This time, my father finally awoke memories that had remained cloudy to me for many years. I was beginning to understand my dad's life better. How the events that took place in our house were his decisions. How his decisions had changed the course of our lives as a family. Why they had occurred, the price to pay, and the consequences that later befell us as a family.

"You see, son, I have no excuses for my mistakes," my father said. "Things will only get worse from wherever I am. I ate the forbidden fruit, and there's a lifetime price to pay for it. Remember the story Grandma told you about choices and changing things? Well, I had mine.

"I made the wrong decisions by listening to bad friends. I followed a very dark path, and it did change everything for the better for a moment, yet led to a lifetime of pain, unfortunately." He took a deep breath which was rather forced and incomplete so that he had to take a few more short breaths. "Grandma did not leave for Grandpa's house because she got tired of us. She saw the path I began to take since the housewarming party. She knew I was acting out of fear of what the wicked might do to my family and me. I denied my fears but fortified myself through desperate means."

I sat there quietly, absorbed in his words as my father continued to unveil the details that had been cloudy to me for years.

"She warned me for as long as she could. She made clear the repercussions of my actions. The path that I led ended in nothing good but destruction. Sadly, she mentioned you'd all share the cost of my belligerence. She could not bear the pain any further, watching her son destroy himself and for her not to be able to do anything about it. I guess she was right. Most days, I wished I had listened to her. I wish I had listened to all of you. So, she left. Eventually, you all left."

He turned his head towards me, away from the hospital ceiling he'd been staring at.

"Remember what you said as a kid? *If Alhaja ever leaves, everything leaves with her?* Everything indeed left with her. My home came crashing down because the pillar that held it together left. She left because of me."

Here I was, sitting with my father on a hospital bed. He'd been talking to me for the past hour, and only then seemed to recognize something was different about my face.

"I haven't seen you in days!" he said suddenly. "What happened to your face?"

Surprised about my father's sudden change of topic, I thought about asking if he knew we'd been talking for a while, but I decided to save the question for his doctor. I still had a few bruises here and there, but I knew what to say if he asked what had happened to my face. I had hidden my neck collar in the car before walking into the hospital.

"Did you get into an accident?"

"I'm okay, Dad. Just a mild collision. It wasn't that bad."

I didn't want to worry him. I had never even seen him admitted to the hospital, let alone confined to a hospital bed.

He'd shrunken to about half of his weight and stature, much worse than his appearance during the tough years. His eyes, palms, feet, and skin looked greenish- yellow. His abdomen was distended with fluid. I could easily palpate his liver from where I sat, listening to him. His words didn't sound like they used to. He'd become soft-spoken, too weak and too frail to talk or walk. He was only 52.

My father reached underneath his pillow.

"I have something to show you. The CT scan results came back. I wanted you to see it before any of the doctors come over here."

I knew my father still had his reservations about diagnostics. Unfortunately, CT scans couldn't lie.

I held out the film near the open window to get a good read of the images. It was hard to believe what I saw, but I managed to contain myself.

The sudden changes in conversation, forgetting things, it all made sense. There were tumors everywhere.

My father must have been harboring these for years.

The tumor had grown into his lungs, covering a little more than half of both lungs. They had metastasized to his ribs, bone marrow, liver, and brain.

It explained my father's gradual loss of memory, drastic weight loss, and constant cough. It also explained the ascites and severe weakness.

"What do you see? Is it bad? Whatever it is, it must stay between us."

Dad continued to ask several questions while I stood by the window gazing at his CT scan result dumbfounded.

I scanned the rest of the report. There it was—*small cell carcinoma*, signed by the hospital's chief oncologist.

"Dad," I asked, trying to hide my reaction, "Did the doctors ever take any biopsy from you?

"Yes, they took a biopsy of my liver."

"I'll be right back. I need to talk to one of the doctors."

I walked down the hallway, past my sister and the resident doctor, without acknowledging them. My sister must have asked what happened or where I was heading, but I was in too much of a hurry to respond.

"Please, can you tell me how to get to the chief oncologist's office?" I asked the receptionist.

Locating the professor's office didn't take much time.

"How may I help you, young man?" an older man wearing eyeglasses asked from behind his desk after inviting me into his office. He must have been in his mid-sixties.

"I'm Mr. Ayoade's son."

"Oh, the doctor! Your father talked a lot about you. In fact, he wanted you around before we break any news to him. I supposed you already saw his CT scan result?"

"How long does he have, sir?" I interjected, ignoring the old professor's questions.

It was unusual for professors in his position to be so friendly, but he was to me. Maybe he was relieved that he wouldn't have to break the bad news to the patient himself now that I was around.

"To be honest, son, I'm not sure how long."

He pulled his eyeglasses, held them in one hand and looked me straight in the eye.

"I can tell you a day, a week, but he might last a month. Nevertheless, it's atrocious. He's got very few days left. Treating small cell carcinoma at this stage is impossible. I'm really sorry about your father."

Looking down at my dad's report in my hands, I remembered standing in the living room with him six years before, telling him he ought to see a doctor when he had complained to me about chest pain.

Slowly, I pushed my chair back from across the professor, where I sat listening to him. I couldn't look at him as I left his office.

I wish I forced him to the hospital. I wish I knew it was cancer. It was most likely still benign when he complained to me. We could have done something.

Thought after thought followed me down the hallway. He could have survived if he had been to the hospital back then, as the tumor was probably in the early stages. Although I wasn't going to admit it, I knew there was little I could have done to change my dad's mind when he was much stronger, but it didn't stop the guilt.

I was back in the hallway where my sister was still waiting. This time, they were sitting in a chair, still chatting. *The resident must be interested in my sister*, I thought. I walked past them one more time to my father's bedside, not uttering a word.

"Dad, it's not a good report."

My dad sat up on his bed, ready to take the news, whatever it was, like he was expecting what I had to say. I brought myself to sit next to him, closer than I did before heading to the professor's office.

"Go on, son. Tell me exactly what it is."

"You've got lung cancer, Dad."

"Okay?" He anticipated what I had to say next.

I took a moment to deliver the worst of the news. "It's spread to other parts of your body."

I managed to control my emotions. The last thing I needed to do near him was to break down and cry. He thought I was much stronger than that, so I continued.

"Is it treatable?" he asked.

"No, Dad, but we can pray to God for a miracle. Remember how you tell us God answers prayers if we trust in Him? It's all we've got left."

The truth was, I sincerely believed in my heart that my father could make it, although the tests proved he had only days left.

He'd always been a fighter. The strongest man I'd ever known. I expected a long rough road, but somehow, I believed in miracles. I thought he would somehow survive it.

My father leaned back. His face was without hope, but I was going to do whatever I could to keep my father alive.

"Daddy, I will do whatever it takes to get as much help as we can. Please, don't give up."

He turned towards me. "I know you will, Ramon. I know."

All your life,

You wished for the painless rest.

Time showed no mercy,

For you squandered all chances.

Tomorrow,

You wished to make things right.

Your days came shorter than you planned,

For your fate wasn't entirely in your hands.

Once a lion,

The world could hear you.

You wished to roar one more time.

With your days numbered,

All hope was gone…

If my father didn't want anyone to know about what we had just discussed, this time, it was not because he desired to keep it a secret. He wished to end all the pain he believed he'd subjected his family to over many years.

But it was too late. All my siblings already knew something was eating my father up from the inside. It was killing him slowly. He'd been in continuous pain for months. It would be impossible for me to deny them the truth. They all had the right to know what was going on with Dad.

"Please, don't tell anyone what you have just said. I need your help to get me home. The doctors can't do anything for me here. When I die, it must be in my house, on my bed. I need to go home. It's been a long time."

"Anything you want, Dad."

It was the one promise to my father I would ever break. I had to tell my siblings. Our father was dying.

He looked tired again, ready to go back to sleep.

"I'll be around for your discharge paperwork. We should be able to go home tomorrow."

"Good. Thank you."

I walked past the hallway to an open space outside the building where my father was admitted. My sister had taken a walk with the resident. They were standing by a rail. She ran towards me as soon as she had me in sight. I tried to look at her face while I talked, but my eyes were cloudy with tears.

Soon tears began to roll uncontrollably down my face. I looked down, trying to hide my tears because I couldn't bear for my sister to watch me cry like a baby. I was his baby. I was Dad's baby. I cried just like a child would when they lose a loved one. The emotions I had tried to conceal were finally letting loose right in front of my sister.

"Daddy may not make it. His cancer is untreatable," I mumbled, but my sister fully heard me. "God, he's only fifty-two!" I gasped in disbelief that my father could soon be gone, forever.

My sister froze, not able to say a word. I turned away from her, holding on to the railing with my face down as my tears wet the flowers below.

"We need to let others know," I sniffed. "He didn't want me to tell any one of you guys, but this is when he needs us the most. He could leave any moment, Biola. Every moment with him counts. I'll start the discharge process."

My sister remained where she stood, speechless. I might have been my father's favorite, but she was the closest to him, being his only daughter. I stepped towards her and gave her a hug.

We held on to each other for as long as we could while her tears wet my shoulders. She had always been the strongest among us, but her father was dying, too.

Smile—

The many hours of life are but rose flowers;

Every single day is a blossom that withers.

But it's hard to understand the certainty of death,

Even though his cold hands are ever-present.

Life is short but looks long.

Life is too short to sluggishly live on.

Yes, smile—

For every rising sun begins in God's might.

And do not remember your sorrows,

But borrow those experiences for tomorrow.

Register the lessons of the mistakes,

And then open every letter in hope, not fear.

Please, smile—

'Cause if we consider the past,

The bitterness, and offenses,

We will never live for a better task,

As the sun will never set on our profound sense.

The best thing to do, my dear, is to forge ahead.

Now, smile—

There's nothing as easy to carry as a light heart,

For troubles and problems are a part of every life,

And what makes a man is his courage in spite

To pick every good part and emerge standing.

So, come on, smile—it's never ever hard.

A week later, I woke to my phone ringing.

It was about 1:00 in the morning. My sister had been staying with my dad at home since his discharge from the hospital. I reached for my phone with my eyes shut in the dark. Finally, I felt it in my hand right next to my bed on the floor.

"Hello?" I said, still wondering who the hell called my phone in the middle of the night.

A sob came over the phone. It was my sister's voice.

"Daddy stopped breathing."

I fell off my bed as my sister broke the news that I fervently prayed to God never to receive anytime soon.

"I was lying next to him. He made a sound like he was about to puke, then a big smile came over his face. I held him and shook him several times, but he had stopped breathing. He's still got a smile on his face!"

My sister was crying louder and louder as she spoke.

"Don't tell me he's dead!" I cried, struggling to gather myself in my dark room. "He can't be dead, right? He's smiling!"

I drove almost thirty miles to my father's house. My dad was just talking to me two days ago. He probably knew it was his last chance to tell me all he wanted to. As I drove in what seemed like the longest trip I had ever made in my life, I tried to replay our last conversation.

"You are not planning on relocating to Europe, are you?" he asked.

"No, Dad. It's just for work."

"Good. Don't settle down there. You will travel the world, but your future is not in Europe."

He always encouraged me to travel the world as a professional, which started quite early in my career. However, this was the first time he sounded most confident as he stared into my eyes on his dying bed.

"You're exceptional at what you do, Ramon. You should consider moving to the U.S. You are destined for greatness over there. Your future is in the U.S."

My father's words were unbelievable. He was certain about his visions. But before this moment, he had no idea of my exit plans from Nigeria to the U.S. I'd been quietly working on them for months.

"I know life's good for you right now," he said. "You have an excellent job. I also know you've had several accidents you didn't tell anyone about. Ramon, if only you could see the greatness in your future. I can see your light. It shines farther than you could ever comprehend. You must not suffer the same fate as the rest of us. You seem to be doing well right now, but there's nothing much for you here in Nigeria. You must leave everything behind. You will have a long life, but you will have to leave this place, this country. It's no longer safe for you here."

I knew these were not just empty words.

I began to understand: my life had been filled with pain, and as a boy in Nigeria, I had been taught to endure it. Now, the lesson my father had to share in his final days was very different: if life is difficult, we have to make a change. If our path is blocked, we don't continue on that same path, but find another.

"It is no longer safe for you here," he said.

I stared at him silently.

"Go," he said. "Start your life in America."

This was the last conversation we had before he died.

One more time,
I looked out my lair
With tears streaming down my face.
My eagle glides through the air,

Forcing its way through the thick,
Dark trace up into the night sky.
I'd just left a chapter of my dream To turn a new page
Where I could become a better story.
I cry out for him—
If only my father had a breath left in him,
This moment could be cherished more.
If only he weren't lying six feet under,
I'd get one last hug.

PART 2:

America

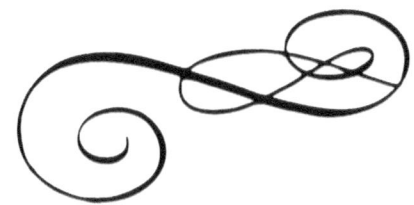

Chapter 11

BALTIMORE, MD: November 2008

A Missing Piece.

Immediately after my father passed away, it was as if he was blessing my journey.

One week after he died, I received my first graduate scholarship letter from the London School of Hygiene and Tropical Medicine in the U.K. to study Public Health in Developing Countries. So, a week later, when another scholarship letter arrived from the Heller Graduate School of Social Policy and Management at Brandeis University in Massachusetts to offer me a spot in their International Health Policy and Management program, I was convinced that my father's spirit had a role to play in it. I'd only applied to Brandeis a few months before, and it was the only American graduate school I applied to.

America had been my dream. The decision was easy.

It was just two days before my flight when I told my mother and siblings that I was leaving because I was afraid if I'd revealed it any sooner, some event in our family would jinx the opportunity. I was also trying to hold off on making any of them sad. Instead, they were supportive, exhilarated.

"It's about time!" my sister cried.

I left Nigeria on July the 4th, 2008—U.S. Independence Day, which I didn't notice as significant until later—after resigning from my job. It had been five months since my father died.

I stared out of my flight window: it was dark, and I could see nothing. I was thousands of feet up in the air, finally heading to the right destination. I was twenty-eight years old.

Here I was, leaving all the comfort behind and possibly meandering back to where I was years ago, just before my college days. As I drifted into vivid thoughts about my father on the plane, all I could remember were his last words. Just like a child, if you'd asked me to make a wish, all I desired at that moment was one last hug from my father.

As I walked through Logan Airport in Boston, I told myself: *This is the land where I will make all my dreams come true.*

It felt like the beginning of my biggest accomplishment in life. I was thankful, elated, but only briefly. I already knew I had a lot of work ahead of me.

I was the first international student to arrive for summer school at Brandeis University. Even with the aid of my scholarship that covered half my tuition, I couldn't afford what remained. I faced a somewhat complicated decision: for the past eleven years—and really, for my whole life—I'd been investing in my education, but now, finally, in the United States, I had to start thinking more practically about my future. I had to ask myself, *Did I come to America to just get a graduate degree or build a new life here?*

When I thought of it that way, the answer became clear. Since my childhood, I had dreamed of creating a life that was better than what

I'd experienced when I was young. I'd only ever known struggle. Now, I wanted to begin to learn what it could feel like to thrive.

But it wouldn't be easy. At first, the culture shock thrilled me—the energy of the United States was so upbeat and optimistic, just like I'd seen in the movies when I was a kid. I went to a baseball game at Fenway Park and then walked the streets, taking in all the events and the whirl of activities around me, the bars and pubs, people of different colors from all different places. I observed all the different hair textures, the tattoos, non-traditional sex orientations, the way people here spoke—fascinating and straight to the point, but also extremely sensitive to words and the minute details in gestures.

Sometimes, my American friends would defend me from someone's words or actions that I hadn't even realized were offensive. Other times, it was a mean gesture from someone I had not quite noticed, but my friends did and would explain to me much later on what it implied.

I figured quickly that I still had a lot to learn. The society seemed very individualistic, yet everyone spoke the same language and acted similar to each other, which was very uncommon where I came from.

It was after the first couple of months that the magic started to wear off.

I realized that establishing a new life, even if it was in the country I'd always dreamed of, wasn't easy. First, I became aware that American English is relatively different from the British English I'd grown up speaking in Nigeria. I was astonished the first time I heard Americans refer to *trousers* as *pants*, which to me had always meant *underpants* or *rubbish*. I came to summer school to take English courses in the American context.

But that was nothing compared to the biggest way reality contradicted my earlier expectations.

I had assumed that I would be able to secure financial assistance for graduate school in addition to the partial scholarship the school awarded me, but I was wrong. I learned I wasn't eligible for any U.S. government loan because I was only a foreign student, and I needed a citizen or permanent resident with great credit to co-apply with me and help me secure a private loan. I had never even heard of a credit score. America was full of concepts and regulations that were totally new to me.

My godmother had passed away two years after I finished veterinary school. Now her elder sister, who lived in Maryland, called me in Boston. Until she called, I hadn't given a thought to the fact that she lived in the U.S.

My late godmother's elder sister, whom we often referred to as *Mummy*, had offered that I stayed with her until I settled down. It is not uncommon to call older women in the family *Mummy* in my culture, especially if they are old enough to be your mother or too old to be called aunty. She had been alternating between the U.S. and Nigeria for many years as a resident of both countries.

Her mom had called her from Nigeria after I departed and demanded that she helped me.

"Mummy told me you cared for her just like my sister cared for you while in school," she said.

She wanted to help me figure things out quickly in the U.S. but didn't think schooling that far away from her would help. So, she advised me to get a transfer. As disinclined as I was to the idea, it was a better option considering that I could take the U.S. Veterinary Board while in graduate school as well as maintain my status in the U.S. as a student. More importantly, I wouldn't have to worry about food and accommodation and be within a network system of information and direction on the alternatives available to me.

If I stayed in Massachusetts, I wouldn't have enough money to pay the difference between my scholarship and the rest of my tuition and living expenses. Worse still, I didn't know anyone who could co-sign with me to get a student loan since I wasn't an American resident.

So after summer school in Waltham, MA, I decided to transfer to another graduate program in Maryland. It wasn't a school that I liked - nor did I like the course I was offered - but it was the best option for me, considering that I needed to achieve more than just a graduate degree.

Due to the transfer, I was responsible for the full tuition this time, which I really couldn't afford without financial support. I couldn't secure a new scholarship due to the time factor between school transfers. Although I had a veterinary degree, it was nearly impossible to find a job without a green card or U.S. citizenship. I had to begin my search for a job as fast as I could.

This period taught what it really means to be a black immigrant in the U.S., especially one with a non-American accent. Even as educated as I was, finding work was incredibly difficult. When I started in a butcher's shop as a meat cutter, it was initially incomprehensible to me that I was actually working there. How could I go from all that I had achieved so far and debased myself to a position where my imaginations for my future would never take me?

After two weeks in the butcher's shop, the day came when I almost lost a finger, and that was the moment I knew it was time to stop. I didn't waste any time. I left without waiting to get paid for the two weeks of work. I realized how much I had allowed my desperation to get to me. The pressures from trying to contribute to the house expenses and possibly send some change back home to my family in Nigeria. There was no doubt that I was trying to do too much too fast, and I was putting myself in dangerous situations as a result.

It got worse. I went on to work at a local restaurant where I cooked and cleaned for $6 an hour, but the owner only paid for 10 hours for every 12 hours I worked. When he made it a habit to keep cheating me out of my paycheck, I moved on to sales and pharmacy technician positions. I worked part-time in both stores while taking my graduate classes and studying for the veterinary board.

Despite all that was going on, the most shocking moment occurred one day when an elderly woman, about eighty years of age, pulled over by the drop-off window to pick up her medications.

After handing over her pills to her, she laid them on the front passenger seat, looked me in the eye, and in a very contemptible tone said, "You African monkey!"

At first, I thought I misheard her, so I asked, "Sorry, what did you say?"

"You African monkey!" She repeated, but louder this time.

I still couldn't believe my ears, completely flabbergasted. It took a moment to pull myself together as I couldn't comprehend why anyone would say something like that to a fellow human. Then I leaned in to speak through the drive-thru intercom.

"Why did you say that?" I asked her.

I had seen this woman at the pharmacy before and couldn't understand what I could have done to provoke her to speak to me like that.

"Because you African monkeys keep coming here, taking jobs away from our sons," she responded.

She was African American. The past few years of my life passed swiftly through my mind. It was bad enough that I was on a job that I was far too qualified to do and walked four miles each day to work there. Now I had to deal with someone who insulted me and tried to make me feel small when all I was trying to do was help her.

But after a moment, I felt sorry for her. I realized then that to have dreams, goals, and aspirations, but more importantly, to be able to pursue them is in fact a blessing. To this woman, the position of a pharmacy technician was something she wanted for her sons, when I had only taken on that job to survive graduate school.

"Why not have your son study pharmacy and take the exams?" I asked her. "I'm sure he would get the job. I'm only passing through."

I watched her force her car into drive, but before she could take off, I hurried to lift the sleeve of my white coat. Through the intercom, I spoke to her again.

"Do you see this?" I asked her, pointing to the skin on my arm. Startled, she turned to look at me. "Isn't this the same as yours? Before you call someone 'African monkey,' you should look at your own skin and see it's the same."

When I turned back, the Pharmacist, other technicians, and customers that witnessed what had just happened were still frozen, utter disappointment written on their faces, and the anger brewing inside them was palpable. I tried to regain my composure but struggled to return my focus to the customers that were waiting to be attended, so I excused myself for a few minutes and headed to the restroom.

When run-ins like these happened, I wondered whether I'd been fooled about the promise of America. Why were some people so unkind and unwelcoming? The only memory I had of how we treated Americans while growing up in Nigeria, irrespective of their skin colors, was love, singing, dancing, and happiness to have them around us. *Why would someone I feel that way about treat me the way this woman had just treated me?* I thought to myself, trying to understand the depth of hatred in this woman's heart.

I knew racism was a major issue in the U.S., but that I would experience such hatred from a woman old enough to be my grandmother, who shared the same skin as I, was beyond belief.

There was one thing about my skin that experiences like these taught me: it had to be thicker. I had to be smarter. I needed to finish school then find a great job to finally work my way to a position where dealing with people like that woman would be more bearable. In the meantime, I would live with the constant reminder to treat everyone as an individual. It wasn't the first of such experiences, and it sure wasn't going to be the last.

Those first few months after I arrived in the United States, interactions like these were especially difficult because I had no one— no friends, no social life. I spent my time in school, studying for the veterinary board, working two jobs, and at choir rehearsals in church.

Fortunately, Toyin, Mummy's son, arrived from Alabama. He'd lived in Nigeria for many years, so he understood the difference in cultures and showed me the ropes. He explained that Americans could often misinterpret things if I didn't put it the American way and helped me get a better grasp of what was acceptable and what was not.

One day, my godmother's sister persuaded me to accompany her to a wedding in Baltimore.

"Sorry, Mummy, I really don't feel like going anywhere," I said from my mattress.

I had a lot on my mind, and I'd have rather stayed in my room, complete my class assignment, and then return to medical texts to continue my study for boards.

Mummy wanted me and Toyin to tag along to the wedding in Baltimore, about thirty miles from Hyattsville where we lived, but I wasn't interested. She finally convinced Toyin, who tried to cajole me on her behalf.

"Hey, brother!" Toyin said. "What's going on? Let's go with her. You know she won't give up unless we go with her."

"I already told her I don't feel like going anywhere," I said. "I have some school work to finish up. Besides, I should be thinking about how to pay my tuition, not partying like I don't have more pressing issues."

"You've had your head buried in those books all day. It's a good way to take a break, don't you think?"

He was right. I'd been studying a few texts all day while I had been on the computer for almost six hours. My cousin was Mummy's only child. Although born in the U.S., he was raised in Nigeria until he turned eighteen when he returned to join the United States Navy.

I relented.

"You're right," I said. "What time do we leave?"

"6:00 p.m. It's a night wedding."

"Okay. I'll get dressed up. After all, staying at home won't pay my tuition," I said with a smirk for my troubles.

As we arrived at the wedding venue, it dawned on me how long it'd been since I went to a party. I've been absorbed by all the academic demands of my life at the time, complicated by financial hardship. Thank God for Mummy, who provided food and shelter. It would have been worse without her.

The wedding decorations were beautiful. The colors were alluring, and they matched the guest attires, which were also tailored to various African designs. The lights gleamed across, reflecting over the colorful hall. The ladies looked gorgeous in their dresses while familiar music played.

A wave of comforting nostalgia washed over me. It had been several months since I attended a Nigerian party or listened to Nigerian music. As I expected, dollars soon started to rain and fly around the bride and groom while a trusted party helped the couple pick the bills up as they fell to the ground. It was a very common part of Nigerian culture for guests on the dance floor to spray cash over the other celebrants as they danced.

After the bride and groom had danced, all the women were called out to catch the bridal bouquet. I couldn't help but watch all the women in their beautiful clothes shoving each other out of the way as they each fought to possess the bouquet. The moment further ignited into uncontrollable excitement when the music began to play.

The DJ easily got most of the young ladies out of their seats. Like a lion seeking its prey, I tried to decide which of the women I'd like to dance with. It had been a long time since I had a good time, so I was going to leave all my stress on the dance floor.

"Hey, guy! What are you doing sitting there?" Toyin asked, coming up to the table. "If I do remember a few things about you, you are a great dancer."

"I am still a great dancer, Toyin," I responded without turning my gaze from the dance floor.

"So, what are you waiting for?"

"To decide which of the ladies I will dance with," I answered, gesturing to the beautiful ladies without taking my eyes off them.

"I don't think you are aware of everyone at your table," Toyin said, lowering his voice. "You need to turn back but be smart about it."

My chair was slightly repositioned so that my side and my back faced away from the center table. I could see my cousin from the corner of my eye , but I did not notice one or two people now sitting behind me. In fact, I'd had no clue when they arrived.

I turned my head in the opposite direction to meet the gaze of a beautiful young lady. With a smile on my face, I opened my mouth.

"Hi!"

"Hi!" she replied, but I couldn't tell if she smiled underneath her reflective eyeglasses. She didn't seem shy, nor did she sound rude, so I continued.

"Would you like to dance?" I asked.

"Sure."

Moving my chair out of the way, I led her to the dance floor, where we danced for about fifteen minutes, after which the MC decided to stop the music for the cake cutting. We returned to the table, where we laughed and joked about different dance moves on the floor.

"You should have warned me you were a good dancer."

"You should have warned me you were a better dancer," I responded with a smile.

There was no doubt she was a little more reserved than I was, so she had to step out of her cocoon to catch up with my dance moves.

"It's been a while since I danced, so I really enjoyed that. I needed it so badly," I continued.

"Really? You must be busy. It's been a while for me as well, but it's not because I'm busy. I'm just not the dancing type."

I'd always had an attraction for quick-witted ladies. She was friendly, like we'd known each other for ages. The party was beginning to slow down, but the music was still deafening. It was harder to make out what we were trying to say to each other, so I asked if she wanted to step out of the hall.

"You know, we could probably hear each other better if we were outside," I suggested, leaning my head forward toward her and almost yelling into her ear.

"That's right," she yelled back into my ear.

We got up almost simultaneously while I let her lead the way out of the hall.

"So, I'm 'Deji."

"*Tolu*," she replied.

"I guess it's been a little over an hour."

"Over an hour?" she asked, puzzled.

"Yes, since we met… without knowing each other's names."

"Oh! Yes, it is," she responded to my cheap attempt to amuse her.

Tolu's accent sounded like a typical New Yorker's, but there was more to her. She seemed so elegant. There was a lot of courtesy and discipline in her demeanor, but she was still lovely and friendly.

She told me she studied criminal justice in undergrad and administration of security and justice in graduate school. She worked as a child protective specialist for the City of New York, so we had an interesting exchange of information. She was a good listener, and very thoughtful in her responses. I liked her instantly.

Toyin, Mummy, and the rest of her friends at the table walked out the exit door while we stood on the patio talking about work and academia. My cousin later told me we had been talking for over an hour and the party was coming to an end. Tolu and I walked a few inches sideways from everyone else while we concluded our conversation.

"I don't have friends around except my classmates, so if you don't mind, I'd like to talk to you again," I asked, suddenly nervous she would say no.

"Sure! I left my phone at home, but I can give you my cell number."

"Got it. I'll store your name as *Prettie*," I said with a smile. "That way, I know it's you."

She didn't make any comment about that, and her face remained as difficult to read as it had before.

"It's really nice meeting you, 'Deji."

"Same here! Safe trip!" I waved.

My cousin teased me a few times before we got back home. He liked Tolu. He thought she was an excellent catch if I was really interested in her. Surprisingly, I hadn't actually given it such a thought. I enjoyed my conversation with her, I would have loved to be friends with her, but I wasn't planning on asking her out on a date. I had far bigger problems to tend to.

I had my school financial issues, I had exams to write. I enjoyed the diversion the party afforded me, but I wasn't ready to commit to any more distractions, especially since Tolu lived four hours away from me. Mummy was excited when she witnessed my meeting with Tolu at the wedding party.

"You know, Tolu's mom is my friend," Mummy said. "We went to college together in the seventies, here in Maryland. I was around when she had Tolu at the Baltimore Hospital. We used to call her *the miracle child* because she was only five months into gestation when her mother went into labor. We didn't think Tolu was going to make it."

"Wow! How did the doctors do it? Wow!" I exclaimed.

"You know the most stunning part of the story was following her delivery. All the doctors and nurses thought she was stillborn. They left her on a surgical tray in the hallway while they tried to save her mother's life. As one of the nurses ran through the hall to get more surgical materials, she noticed the stillborn baby they were about to take away had moved and then opened her eyes."

"Five-month-old? Opened her eyes?" I asked, still shocked.

"Yes," Mummy said. "And after a closer look, the nurse ran back to the doctors screaming, 'The baby is alive!' That was how she was saved. Otherwise, she could have been incinerated or buried alive."

I was amazed by Tolu's story as my aunt recounted her birth. Just a few hours ago, I was standing next to this lovely young lady enjoying every conversation without any clue about what she'd been through as a baby.

"'Deji, I know you like Tolu, and I think she likes you too. I watched both of you while you talked, and I sensed a connection between you two. If you know for sure you aren't interested in her, please don't ask her out on a date for any reason. I'll kill you before you break her heart. Just saying."

Tolu meant a lot to Mummy despite not being her biological child. I completely understood her.

"I won't try anything stupid, mummy," I said to her. "I'm not like that. I just want to be friends with her. I don't know her that much. We just met, so don't start insinuating."

Falling in love was probably the last on my list at that moment. I was so focused on my career and trying to settle down in the U.S. without any interest in dating or searching for a girlfriend. In fact, I totally forgot about calling Tolu until I received a call from her a week after we met.

"I'm sorry I broke my first promise. I've been busy with schoolwork."

"That's fine. I understand. I thought so. That's why I called."

Sometimes, some days, life asks you questions that you have no clue how to answer.

You can only explain the time that passed but find it impossible to completely understand why your life had taken such a course. You are eager to know what's next, though you tirelessly struggle with how your desperation was usually tossed ashore, only to live with what's bestowed upon you. This often takes you on a very different path.

Faith, however, is a good thing to have as the only evidence to what you consider success is based entirely on your experience, that which you couldn't change. Then you pause and sometimes ponder whether your life would have been better off if your life had gone your way. That which is tangible follows time, and in time, you will find what you are destined for. Somehow, in the end, it always makes sense, or we try to make sense of it, as we hope for at least a crumble of our dreams to be realized at some point.

Only if I'd known then, Tolu was godsent—my rescuer in disguise.

She was the one who would give my life the meaning it'd longed for, and I had almost walked right past it. The one meant to resolve all my struggles was on the other side of the line, and I didn't know it. The one who would love me unconditionally no matter what, and I almost didn't give us a chance.

When life grows challenging, sometimes it's easiest to blame the past and examine all the ways it led us to this point, but sometimes we don't know how we are being prepared for what's next in our lives.

I knew I would never settle for a relationship out of desperation to make life in America easier. I wanted to fall in love again. I needed to be loved as well. How long it might take was the least of my worries.

When I met Tolu, I realized my father was right about my future being tied to the U.S. In her, I found a savior. She came into my life like the answer to a prayer I didn't even realize I had spent my whole life asking.

Sitting by the window,
I see splashes of water falling.
In between them were blocks of hail,
Which shattered and melted away
As they touched the earth.

Once again, I feel my heart rebirthed,
And all I want is to see new reasons,
With each passing day,
Why I feel this way about you.

219

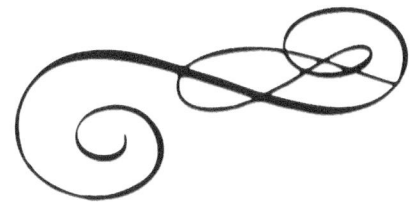

Chapter 12

NEW YORK CITY, NY: 2009
A Friend.

At first, I worried about entering into a meaningful relationship with Tolu. She lived in New York City, and I was in Maryland. I wondered if the logistics made sense. Since I was a little boy, I'd made a lot of commitments to my family and right then, I was on the brink of fulfilling them. I wasn't sure about a relationship.

My responsibility was to secure an income to bring my mom and siblings to America and establish a home for us. I'd been sending them money whenever they needed help or if I had a little something extra than I needed for myself.

Thinking about the promises I made to them and what my father said on his deathbed kept me going. He was clear: *There's nothing for you here in Nigeria. You have to leave for America.* As frustrated as I was during some of those early moments in the U.S., my family was my driving force.

Those commitments were why I didn't think a relationship would be wise. But Tolu was unlike anyone else I'd ever met.

I was working, going to school, sending money back home, paying tuition, preparing to pay for my board exams. For a long time, my resources had been drained—both financially and emotionally. But Tolu needed nothing from me. Her life was simple. She had her own strength; she didn't need anyone. She was supporting herself with her career, with no interest in adding stress to my life with a list of needs or demands.

All she wanted from me was my friendship. And when we visited each other, I heard something I hadn't heard for a very long time: the sound of my own laughter. I had a friend with whom I felt safe sharing my problems.

And for the first time in my life, I was the one leaning on somebody.

I'd tried to do so many things in my life that should have worked out but never did. I realized that my relationship with Tolu was different from everything else.

My experiences were hard. But our relationship was easy. She had quickly filled a lifelong void that I'd lived with for so long I hadn't even been aware it was there. What I'd worried would be an enormous distraction turned out to be a blessing: for instance, when I ran out of money for tuition and risked losing my student status, Tolu co-signed my student loans and sponsored my veterinary board fees. She cared unconditionally.

Still, I couldn't bring myself to make it permanent. I didn't want to put her in a position where she would feel obligated to sponsor my permanent residency or question that I had an ulterior motive.

In June 2009, seven months after our romance began, I knew it was time.

After going out with friends, I waited until we were back home and alone. When she noticed my sudden silence, she knew something was wrong and asked what it was. I stared into her eyes and held her hands in mine.

"As consoling as it is to know the things we do not want happen to us more than a few times as blessings in disguise," I said, "we foolishly wait too long to acknowledge those blessings more often than not. I had been madly in love once. I'm not sure how it influenced me emotionally, but it was hard to experience moments beautiful enough for me to hold on to. I promised myself never to fall in love with someone who does not feel the same way.

"When we decided to be together," I continued, "I wasn't sure how meeting you would translate into something tangible in my future. However, I do know that I really want to be in love with someone who is in love with me just the same. I might have assumptions about how you feel about me that I shouldn't. Who knows? Whichever way, I know you love me so much. I don't need words to know how unconditional your love for me has been. Sometimes I try to convince myself how you must be an angel, but then I see clearly how foolish I've been. Tolu, you are the woman that I have been searching for all my life."

Tolu's eyes filled with tears, but I still had more to say, so I told her, "I might have made many wrong decisions in the past. I might have paid the ultimate price for being ambitious and always wanting more, but the biggest mistake I will ever make is if I don't ask you to marry me today, right this moment."

Tolu stood motionless, tears rolling down her face, her hands in mine, and all she could do was to draw me closer and kiss me.

I recall the first time I set eyes on you,
I heard the sound of my laughter.
For a moment,

My heart did not believe it,
But my mind reminded me otherwise,
As I tried to make sense of it.

Lonely times passed by...
Though they weren't troubled times,
Especially with a radio nearby,
Playing such a beautiful song.
Several wishes,
With wonderful imaginations
Filled my thoughts.

How I wish to be by your side always.
Howbeit, you will always be with me,
In my thoughts,
In my imagination,
In my joy,
In my sorrow,
In my heart,
And in every breath.
Just you, only you.

Just when I thought I'd finally found something new and positive in my life, I received a shocking phone call from my brother, Abey, about my dad's sister, Aunty Modina. She was the one who had come to our rescue when my family almost died of starvation while I was in high school.

"Aunty Modina is gone!" He said to me.

"Gone? Where? What do you mean gone?" I asked, hoping it wasn't what I was thinking.

"She died in an accident yesterday," Abey told me in a low, despairing tone.

I was silent for a few seconds, pulled the phone away from my ears, and my arms hung on my sides in frustration.

"We've barely gotten over Daddy's death, and now his sister is gone?" I said to myself, feeling lost,

My brother heard me. I could hear him talking again, so I slowly put the phone back to my ears and found a chair to sit on in Mummy's living room as Abey narrated how the accident happened.

"She was on a bus from Lagos heading to Abuja when the driver lost control from over-speeding. She'd been flung out of the bus to the middle of the highway. You know how two-way roads aren't usually marked properly here? Observers noticed her still confused and in shock from the incident as she tried to make her way out of the middle of the road. Unaware of the current accident, a trailer from the opposite side of the highway ran her over like a truck would run over a stray animal."

"What? A trailer again? Just like her siblings?" I confirmed.

"Yes, just like her siblings in '77," Abey answered.

"Aunty Tola just had a baby," Abey continued. "She was heading down to Abuja to help her. Ramon, what was left of her body was grisly, her lifeless body completely unidentifiable. As hard as it was for every one of us to admit that she had gone in such a horrifying way, her dress, which was inseparable from her body tissues, was confirmed by her husband. The transport company log confirmed her identity as well." Abey stopped talking just when I desperately wished he would.

While I could not come to terms with the dreadful news I had just received, I didn't shed a tear until three days later.

Alone in the apartment, I completely broke down and wailed for as long as it took to feel somewhat unburdened. I finally allowed myself to grieve for the first time in three days. I was exhausted, helpless, and choked with too many unanswered questions.

Aunty Modina was survived by her husband and six children, besides the rest of us, her extended family. She was the only one killed in the accident.

Alhaja had lost her only surviving child to this tragedy; her only consolation would be her grandchildren and great-grandchildren. This gruesome incident proved to me that no curse was plaguing only the men born into the Ayoade family. There was simply a force - a blood-thirsty baleful spirit - evil, dark, and wicked, thriving on the blood of my father's entire lineage, men and women, and only my dad ever came close to unveiling it. Heeding my father's last words was one of the smartest decisions I ever made.

Darkness, light; denial clarity!
That's what happens
When you finally understand life isn't entirely
What you believed it not to be.
Wildebeests will always flock together, so would Zebras,
Pondering about it is a complete waste of time.
There isn't much you can do about it…

While my aunt's death took months for me to come to terms with, so recently after my father's, Tolu and I knew my program was fast coming to an end. My chances of securing either a veterinary residency spot or a relatively good job were getting slimmer without permanent residency in the U.S.

Marrying a U.S. citizen would change that.

I was beginning to receive a few attractive job offers from both Nigeria and multinational health research organizations that wanted to station me in Africa, mostly in Nigeria. We both agreed it would be easier to manage distance within the U.S. than between continents. Most importantly, I never wanted to leave the woman I was so in love with, nor did I wish to return to Nigeria.

We always talked about a very elaborate wedding and waiting another five years before having kids as if we had complete control of fate and time. However, we would have to choose between an elaborate wedding and the future of our love for each other.

One day, Tolu called from New York. She said, "Let's do it. I'll do it."

She sounded like a scientist who finally came to a decision after a very long, hard thought over a finding.

Confused, I replied, "Do what?"

"Get married."

"What? Married? No! We are not ready. I don't even have a job!"

"Well," Tolu said reasonably, "One way or the other, one of these companies will sponsor you, but then think about it; they own you afterward. Regardless, I know you will never stay in the U.S. illegally. I'd rather be the one who helped my future husband realize his dreams rather than anyone else."

She had valid concerns. But I wanted everything done right, especially at the right time. I didn't want to rush things.

"You mean you would sacrifice your dream wedding for me?" I asked, still surprised at how much Tolu loved and trusted me.

"No, I will sacrifice it for us," she corrected. "If the only reason we are not planning our wedding right now is because of our finances, then we can always have a big wedding whenever we are ready. Right now, we need to think about our future, and a simple registry will make our lives better."

"How do you think your family will respond to a simple courthouse wedding?" I asked. "You know how some immigrants marry Americans just for papers, only to leave after getting what they want?" Her family had experienced this before.

"How could you trust me so much to sacrifice that much for me?" I asked her. I would ask my sister the same question before she made such a life-changing decision.

"It won't matter, 'Deji," she said. "I would have done it for love. What could be a better reason? If things somehow don't work out for any reason between us, at least I would have known what it actually feels like to be in love with someone who loved me back. You are the most honest and sincere man I've ever met. Well, that's after my dad."

She tried to ease the tension, which worked because I chuckled briefly before sinking back into how fortunate I was to find a woman who loved me with everything.

"You know this will bring many challenges as well. We will be married, but you'll still be in your family house while I'll be all over the place searching for a job. Eventually, both of us are going to hate not living together."

I tried to put things in perspective for her.

"Well, no pain, no gain," she said. "You know that, right? Let's face each challenge, one at a time. We get what we need to establish a foundation for ourselves first. We use what we have to create options for ourselves. Eventually, we'll make the best decisions and try our best to make things work better for us. Slowly but surely, dear. It will be very challenging, but we'll be okay."

At that moment, I fell on my knees, praying to God never to take her love away from me. Dreams or no dreams, it was at that moment that I knew I would be empty without Tolu. She was *the one*; and knowing this would always remain my saving grace during tough times.

When Tolu made the announcement to her family, most were hesitant, while others were supportive. Their fear was understandable.

In the end, Tolu stood by her decision to marry me, and I assured her family that only time would tell. In September 2009, we got married in New York City.

After the registry wedding, we hired an immigration lawyer in New York to file for my status change from student to permanent resident in the U.S. I returned to Maryland to graduate school. With Tolu and my church to support me, I concluded my graduate program and the third out of the four steps of my veterinary boards.

If man could understand
That Love is the greatest gift,
If he would always take a stance
For virtuousness to win,
Then he would fathom Love.

If Love is more than just a feeling
Straight from the heart,
And if we write and sing about Love
As if it is a craft,
Then trust me, Love is beauteous.

If physical intimacy alone doesn't account for
Love, and you oppose vanity for Love,
If your Love is pure,
Then what more?
Your Love is true.

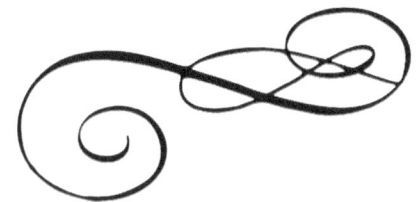

CHARLESTON, SC: 2010
The Guilt.

> *Dear wife,*
> *Forgive me for the things*
> *I have done that made you cry...*
> *Forgive me for how long it took*
> *To understand what Love means...*

In January 2010, my green card arrived. Tolu still lived with her family while I hunted aggressively for a better job in Maryland. With the recession hitting the country hard, these were challenging times for anyone looking for a job. Tolu and I often traveled monthly to spend time with each other.

A week after the green card arrived, Tolu visited to spend the weekend with me, and we decided it was best that I left Maryland to live temporarily with my close friend Sam in Charleston, South Carolina.

Sam had been a source of brotherly support ever since I'd connected with him in 2002 at a cybercafé while at university. Since we met, we'd fueled each other's dream to live in America—"One day, I'm gonna marry a girl from New York!" I used to half-jokingly brag to him—but Sam won the U.S. green card lottery and made it to the United States six months before I did.

Now aware of my problem securing employment, he invited me to join him in Charleston, where I could live rent-free until I found a job. He was persistent about my relocation to Charleston since graduation, primarily because my cousin and aunt had left for Nigeria. It had been over six months, and it didn't seem like they would be back anytime soon.

"You know, you don't have to take on this financial load. It's unnecessary," Sam had complained. "Why not move the household goods to the storage and come down? I live here alone, my job pays well, so you don't have to worry about sharing bills with me. You would have done the same for me, 'Deji."

He was quite right about that, considering all that we went through together in college.

"At least, you won't have to worry about house rent, feeding, and the internet. It will help you focus on getting into residency or any other alternative you prefer."

Tolu agreed with Sam, pointing out it was a very kind gesture that I should consider.

"I think you should put all the stuff in the storage and leave for now until we can get our feet on the ground," she said. "There are no guarantees that Toyin and his mom will return soon."

"Well, judging by his responses last time we spoke, Toyin seems to like Nigeria. He didn't say anything about coming back soon, and his mom started a new business there. They both know I can't afford this apartment. They understand my situation."

"See, babe? That's why I think you should take Sam's offer. We can afford the expense for the monthly storage until they get back to the U.S., but with an apartment that expensive, we can't."

My wife was right. As a couple, we were beginning to run out of savings. Thank goodness Tolu still lived in her family house. We couldn't maintain an apartment in New York where she worked, nor could we continue to foot the bill for the apartment Mummy and my cousin left me.

We had two options given the circumstances. I could either secure a reasonably well-paid job in New York so we could get a place of our own, or she could leave her job to move in with me. That is, if I managed to secure a well-paid job anywhere else.

I tried to remind myself how these burdens could have been mine alone if we weren't married. Tolu didn't have to share such adventures with me, but she chose to. All the same, we would be facing my biggest fear in months to come.

We hinged on Sam's offer, so Mummy and Toyin's property went into storage until they returned to the U.S.. En route to South Carolina, I attended three residency interviews with three prestigious veterinary institutions. I had no other plans but to volunteer with the American Red Cross once I settled in Charleston.

When I arrived in Charleston, a company expressed an interest in me after I'd communicated with the hiring manager by email. As soon as he called and heard how I sounded, he froze, stuttered, and hung up. That was the last I heard from that company.

I had hoped that people in the South would be hospitable and warm, but I found some people to be anything but.

A few times, when someone met me for the second time in Charleston, they would apologize for how they had treated me during our first encounter. Most of them often confessed that they had never met an African before.

Thinking about how much my wife sacrificed for me, it was time to fasten my pants tight and be the husband I'd always wanted to be.

Everything about this transition was a struggle, and then came the biggest curveball of my life: Tolu called to say she might be pregnant two weeks after I left Maryland.

"That can't be," I said, trying not to panic. "You're on pills, aren't you?"

"Yes, I am, but I think I'm pregnant. It's been a week past my cycle. My cycle's pretty consistent."

"It's okay, babe," I said, trying to reassure her. "I don't think you are. It's only been two weeks since I left. If it helps, you should get a pregnancy test."

It was one of the longest hours of my life, from when my wife departed to purchase the pregnancy test kit to when she finally got the result.

"It's positive," she said.

I simply could not believe it. "It can't be," I said stubbornly. "I don't trust over-the-counter supplies. You should go to the clinic tomorrow. We can get a definitive result."

I was making the greatest mistake any man could.

Instead of jumping around in excitement, I did all I could to convince my wife she couldn't have been pregnant. I should have been supportive of whatever she thought might have been happening to her body. Instead, I made my wife feel like the pregnancy was the worst mistake ever. After all, we were married.

"I will if you want me to, but what happens if the result's the same?" Tolu asked. "I know we didn't plan for this, but what if this is it?"

"I don't know what to say," I responded. "It's not just right. All I know is that we can't afford to have a baby now." I became even more assertive than my initial reaction to the news.

As much as I tried to calm down and control my emotions, the desperate and possibly over-ambitious little boy in me reacted otherwise. My wife, who was also shocked about the pregnancy, handled the news better than I did, especially considering that she was the one carrying a baby inside her.

I began to tag many reasons to the needs of both of us, but in fact, I was more worried about my future as I revisited my childhood, desperate that I must shield my children from it. I felt like I had just reached a roadblock in my dreams. I didn't ask my wife how she felt about the pregnancy.

It was all about me and not her; I know now that was how I must have sounded.

Reflecting on the circumstances then, I wondered how my wife managed to remain calm, knowing I never inquired if she wanted the baby or not. In my attempts to decide for both of us, I began to sound more selfish than ever, considering how selfless I had considered myself.

"Remember children are gifts from God, even when they show up unplanned," Tolu said.

"You're right about that, but we planned not to have one," I argued. "Not just yet. If your tests came out positive, it is your fault. It means you didn't take your pills at some point."

"I won't play defensive," Tolu responded, remaining far calmer than I felt, "Because it's possible that I'd forget. It won't change the fact that I might be pregnant. What would you want us to do if it's positive tomorrow?"

If Tolu knew how rough it was for my family and me, how tough it was for us to survive, she may have understood the source of my unkind words. I wished I had told her the rest of my story, but it was deliberate. For a child raised in the U.S., I thought it was wise to slowly unfurl many parts of my terrible childhood as it might be hard for her to process.

"But we're not God. He gives, and he takes. He will make way for our baby and us. He will provide for us."

"Our baby?" I asked, suddenly accusatory. "It makes me wonder if you had all this planned out without my concession."

I knew instantly after I said it that I sounded like a man I didn't recognize. I'd never experienced this part of me ever, and the worst part was that I didn't take a moment to pause and seriously rethink my words. I didn't consider how my behavior might force her to make drastic decisions, a decision that might likely damage our brief marriage.

"If the results turn out positive," I said, "I don't think we should keep it." The words came out as assertive as they could possibly sound.

"You sure that's what you want? If that's what you want, I'll do it," Tolu said, but I knew she hadn't taken the time to think through a decision yet.

She thought she could keep me happy by going through with my decision, so she told me what I wanted to hear. She would later turn the tables around on me, which was fair; after all, I didn't give us a chance to decide together or consider her thoughts and feelings.

"This is for us. You know we aren't ready. You should ask the doctor what our options are."

When I look back at this moment, I realize that I couldn't have been crueler. I refused to be even a little sensitive to my wife's state of heart.

"I'd like to go to bed now. I'll let you know the outcome tomorrow. If it turns out positive, I'll speak to the doctor like you want me to."

It dawned on me later that my wife had expected a different reaction from me. Despite the fact that we weren't ready, I should have been excited for us for the moment, or I could have been more mature with the way I handled myself. If she could lay everything on the line for me, I should have been able to do better.

I always thought I knew the man in the mirror,
And that's why I still saw a sheep,
Even when I turned into a wolf.

But you have,
And that's why you chose me.
How was I to know
I could turn on one of mine someday?

Beneath my innocence
Thrive my greatest fears.
Like the easy drag of the water by the riverbank,
I never comprehend how much danger.

My callousness haunts me,
And like heroin gushing through veins,
My greatest desire is to have your forgiveness.

"Hey, doc!" Sam said as he walked into the living room. "What's up? You look down in the dumps." I barely heard him, wondering what I was to do about my situation. I felt confused. It wasn't only about the news or how poorly I handled it, but how I had treated Tolu. The one who loved me like no one ever did. She sacrificed everything for me. The least I could do was to make her happy.

I felt like a beast, so much that I knew for sure if she were standing next to me, I couldn't look at her face out of shame.

"Tolu is pregnant, and I think she will keep the baby," I said to Sam.

My head was on the laptop, eyes closed in disappointment with myself. Sam was sitting on one of the living room couches, just where I could see him with the corner of my eye, trying to take off his shoes.

"I thought you guys were holding off on having kids for now," he asked as he leaned back on the sofa so that I would have his full attention. "Did you discuss with her, see what she wants?".

This time, my elbows were on my laptop while my face rested on both of my hands.

"I don't think I did," I admitted. "I freaked out! All I did was tell her what I wanted. I told her to confirm with her physician at the clinic tomorrow."

"Oh, so you guys still need a confirmation?" Sam asked, waving his hand. "In that case, you should relax and hope it was a false-positive result. However, my advice to you is that you both need to talk about this if it turns out positive. If she wants to keep the child, you might have to be more careful about how you handle the situation. She is your wife. Remember that, 'Deji ."

"You know, she said *our baby*."

I divulged the little piece of information to Sam in a much lower tone, as if there was a third ear in the apartment. I pulled my legs out from beneath the dining table and adjusted my chair so that I now faced him, though from a few feet away with my arms extended out in frustration.

"See? I know exactly where this is going," I said. "Those two words gave her away. I will be lying if I don't admit I was deeply touched by those words, too. As premature as it sounds, she's already emotionally attached to what the possibility might be. I know for sure she will keep the baby. I'm not sure what to do, Sam."

Suddenly, I wasn't sure if everything was about to change. I could barely support myself, but my wife wanted to keep a pregnancy. Definitely not sure if I was ready to be a father, not with all the challenges on my table. I had so much to catch up with.

"I've never been worried about responsibilities before, and you know that yourself, Sam. However, the thought that this will be a life commitment concerns me. I'm not sure of the things I will have to give up to be a good father and husband at the same time. What will happen to everything else? My mother and my siblings are still in Nigeria. They desperately need help. Will everything change for the worse?" I asked, all my concerns coming to the surface.

"A lot of commitment comes with raising children," I said. "I'm unshaken about our marriage. I'll always be in love with Tolu. I'm sure about us raising kids together eventually. Still, I'm not sure if I'm ready to have one yet."

Sam listened intently as I continued to ramble on in frustration. Not to my closest friend did I ever disclose my genuine fears, and yet here I was.

Sometimes, I thought I didn't thoroughly understand the source of my fears. I had my own demons locked away somewhere inside me. Now that some of them were coming out, I sure didn't know how to face them.

"I think I understand how you feel, 'Deji." Sam said. "Unfortunately, this wasn't planned, but you still have to make the best out of it. You always do. Make sure you do the right thing," he said as he got up.

"Just know that this too shall pass," Sam continued. "Be careful not to ruin anything before it does. It will work out just fine. Somehow it always does for you."

He patted me on the shoulder as he walked into the bedroom.

After a sleepless night, I waited impatiently for Tolu's call the following day. The tests took longer than we expected, but she finally called late in the afternoon.

"So, how was it? How did it go? Did you get a confirmation?" I couldn't wait to receive the news. Tolu must have noticed my hasty tone.

"Yes, I did," she said, sounding apprehensive.

"So?"

"I'm sorry, 'Deji. I can't abort this pregnancy. It came out positive. I'm almost three weeks pregnant," my wife said as she burst into tears over the phone.

There was no use for persistence in convincing her, but I'd tried. It was her body, so it didn't matter what I insisted on. The final decision was hers.

"I know you don't want a child right now, but we will be okay without your help. I thought you should know, whatever your decision is," she continued as she sniveled on the other side of the phone.

It had just dawned on me that I was about to be cut off from my family. I'd been awful to Tolu. I had pushed her all the way to the wall. She had nowhere else to turn but to confront me. It was time for her to push back.

Although she was emotional about the new development between us, she sounded calm but sad, sorry but assertive about her decision. As she spoke over the phone, I realized that she was devastated about how I had reacted to the pregnancy.

She had never been much of an arguer, but she knew when to fight back. The only reason Tolu had continued to bear the pain I would subject her to through the following week was that she was still madly in love with me.

I was fast losing respect for myself, considering the promises I'd made to Alhaja and myself: *Never will I allow myself to be referred to as a man who is just like the rest of them.*

I should have taken a trip into
your world,
Then I probably could understand
you more.
You have built for yourself a
castle of fear
So weak, a gentle breeze it
couldn't bear.

I caused you so much pain,
But we can start all over again.
If every pain that I put you
through
Remains alive in you,
Then every trial,
Would be mine.

I have empty shoulders to lean
on—
Would you let me be the one?
I have listened to so many songs,
And I have waited for so long,
But I choose to believe in this
Love,
And in it, I want to live
Forevermore.

It had been almost two weeks since we confirmed the pregnancy. It was enough time to reflect on what I could have done better since the advent of the pregnancy news. I thought those actions didn't define me. That wasn't 'Deji. Typically, I would resolve to the best solution from a few options that I would have come up with, except that it was now *us*.

After weighing in on my choices, I decided to write my wife a letter.

I needed her forgiveness, but the best way to do so couldn't be over the phone. I couldn't fly to New York to see her, but I imagined her reading my words would be like sitting next to her. I'd always been a man of my word.

I knew it was wrong for me to let such an occurrence bring the worst out of me. Besides, that was going to be just one of the many unexpected surprises that would follow suit. It was time for me to be the man I thought I was.

I would beg for my wife's forgiveness, and I would finally explain the source of my fear to her. How I didn't want any of my children to experience my childhood. How I'd foolishly thought to bring a child into this world during this time might slow us down. The thought that it might shatter our plans and dreams for the future, especially a befitting wedding that I wanted to surprise my wife with. I was wrong about all of it. I was only a coward. She was right.

Children come from God, and he has plans for them, I said to myself. *I'll leave all to God for direction, but I'll never leave her, nor will I abandon our child. We will live together as one family. We will grow in love while facing the life before us together.*

I assured my wife that I was ready.

I would turn down residency offers from three prestigious hospitals in the following six months to move to New York. I couldn't secure the kind of job we had hoped for, at least not one competitive enough for my wife to quit her job and relocate to be with me. Unfortunately, I never received any residency or job offer from New York.

My wife was due in less than three months. We finally rented a one-bedroom apartment in New York with the money we had saved up for over nine months and moved in together. It was better to remain in New York since Tolu could easily spend as much time as she wanted with her family. It would also help save costs with babysitting when she returned to work.

Never marry for Love,
Marry for friendship.
Never sleep a night,
Heart heavy with malice;
It's a complete waste of emotion.

Never make Love
Just because you can,
Make love for the bond it brings.

You can count the friends you've missed,
But reminisce more on the good times you've shared—
Somehow, you will always find them
In this life or the next.

Dwelling in your past
Is like holding on to a map
That only sets you back on your path
But can't guide you toward your future.

If you're to hold on to your past,
Let it guide your future.
Unavoidable situations are unfortunate,

So we believe.
To have perfect control of one's future
Can be more destructive.
Fate is an element to believe in
And a good excuse not to have ambition.

I hate to admit it,
But it's true:
No man would triumph,
Without the sacrifice of another.
The philosophy of good only comes from bad,
Success from failure,
And a cathedral from crumbs of destruction.

Although Tolu had forgiven my past behavior before my arrival in New York, I hadn't earned it. We had never talked about my initial reaction to the pregnancy news - it was as if such an occurrence never transpired between us.

It was in the past, but I still lived with guilt, especially while watching videos of my baby kicking in her womb. I was tortured by my childish behaviors, especially when I'd already thought myself a man.

I looked back at how much I was starting to resemble my father, the man I never wanted to be like—the man who never wanted me to be like him. Treating my wife the way that I did was callous and almost unforgivable. My attempt to further analyze my strange reaction only fetched more excuses that I hated to think about, nor did I know how to go about forgiving myself. I simply hated myself, and I would silently bear the burden of my sin against my wife for a long time.

As I strived to make up for the past, convinced that my words alone were no longer deserving of her love or that I didn't deserve how much she loved me still, I waited for time to heal me while showing her that I indeed live for her and the baby.

The one-bedroom apartment we moved into was in Far Rockaway, NY, only about nine miles from her family house in Saint Albans. The apartment and its location wouldn't have been our first choice a year before, but it was where we lived.

As it turned out, it was always safer to expect unforeseen disappointments in life. They usually come with the package.

For all that, it was a good place to start. The apartment complex was built in the 50s, so they were brick buildings, secured and well maintained. Our building was right next to the beach, so my favorite part of living in Far Rockaway was taking a walk on the boardwalk with my wife.

The boardwalk continued over a three-mile distance. Stretching past the railings were the beach sand and the constant surfers. The evenings and weekends were often beautiful to watch as friends and families came by to have picnics. Even more beautiful were the winters when the sea was entirely painted white across several nautical miles with nothing whatsoever to stain the view, not even the ships.

We had two other neighbors on the same floor, a couple with two teenage sons and an older woman probably in her mid-fifties, who lived alone with a quiet Schnauzer. From the bedroom and living room windows, we could view the endless expanse of the blue ocean during a quiet day and listen to the soothing sound of waves at night while in bed with the window opened.

It was only a matter of ten weeks before Tolu took to bed. She was entitled to three-month maternity leave, unpaid. She tried to garner hours so her paycheck would keep coming, but it would only last an additional month of pay from the three months away from work. All the same, I wasn't worried. Mentally, I made a promise: I would make things work financially, even if I had to walk from dawn to dusk, one company door to the next, to secure any reputable source of income.

It was no longer a matter of pride, nor was I going to accept any residency offer. I figured this was another milestone and was no longer about my own survival. It was about building our family's future. My decision baffled Tolu at first, but she later realized it wasn't just for them and me alone but for my family back in Nigeria.

Tolu could not fathom the rationale behind my career decision to take a break from veterinary practice other than the fact that I had no offers from New York.

"The reason I didn't accept any of the residency offers was not entirely because they were outside New York. I want to take a break from veterinary practice," I admitted to my wife.

Finally, I thought I had found a concrete reason for my decision, but it wasn't good enough for my wife. She knew there was more.

"You what?" she asked, shocked at what was going on in my head. "So, what's the point in wasting all that time, effort, and money on the boards when you knew you wouldn't practice?" she asked, attempting to make sense of a decision she thought was outrageous.

Veterinary medicine was all I knew, and I'd find myself driving my life in one direction while it was obvious that my path kept heading in a different one. I wanted to stop trying to force things to happen, pause, and allow more clarity on all that I could possibly do with my life, not just medicine. I thought, *If I don't change, I will be holding my life back and miss all that's in store for me.*

My perspective had to change because everything happening in my life kept changing. Deep down, I knew I needed to allow things to happen and exercise less control over what had to be. I needed to make a decision that would not only stand to benefit me, Tolu, and the baby but also my mom and siblings that were still in Nigeria. Although, most importantly, I was desperate for all the time that I could muster to rid myself of my guilt.

"I can still practice," I assured her. "Besides, I can do many other things with my academic background and experience. Veterinary practice is only one of them. If the time ever comes when I feel like going back to it, I can, and I will. As I said, I'm only taking a break."

I tried to defend my surprising decision.

"This is the time for me to do everything right for my family and my future," I said. "I will not live a miserable life, Tolu, not even with all the money in the world. I have a bigger purpose out there, and I know that I won't get to it by restricting myself to only what I know or getting stuck in a clinic."

"But how did you just come to the realization after so many years of schooling?" Tolu asked.

"Well, the only constant thing in life is change. A lot has happened since I graduated from vet school. I've learned new lessons, and I can assure you that I can see with much more clarity now than I did six years ago when I graduated. I just need you to trust me. Everything will turn out just fine."

Yet, since my childhood, I'd been committed to one main principle. As a new immigrant in America now about to have a child in this country, I asked myself, *What can I contribute to a country that I need so much from?* I knew there was plenty I could do with my background, and maybe I was still being haunted by my upbringing, but I'd grown convinced my purpose was bigger. I had to be out there. I had to touch people's lives.

I had to save people's lives.

247

I believed America could provide me with that opportunity. Imagining what life in America could be like had given me hope and determination that got me through my years of struggle in Nigeria. Despite the interpersonal and cultural challenges I experienced when I arrived here, my life had become easier. Feeling loved unconditionally by someone I was in love with lifted my burdens.

Also, it might seem small to someone who grew up in the U.S., but here most things *worked*—from power supply to water supply to basic amenities like food, shelter, and clothing.

Most importantly, the laws, rules, and regulations were by far better enforced. You could simply pay for a service and expect good service, and if the service was not rendered, the law was there to take care of it. In Nigeria, people, especially the rich, got away with the most heinous crimes. For me, these differences were everything, and in return for what this country promised me, I would commit everything I had to it.

After spending a total of six months in Charleston, earnestly searching for a job in public health research and international health, my disappointments continued. The ones I qualified for required security clearance that permanent residents couldn't secure. In other words, most open jobs that suited my profile required U.S. citizenship, which I couldn't apply for until three years later.

I also knew that because the U.S. had been a beacon for me since I was a child in Nigeria, serving this country would help the whole world. I began to contemplate joining the U.S. military, although I hadn't been eligible in the past because I wasn't a permanent resident. But through marriage, this was no longer an obstacle.

I'd done some research to find that there were two ways you could join the U.S. military. If you were coming straight out of high school with a diploma, you enlisted and started at the lowest rank. On the other hand, if you had already completed a college education, you could use your academic degree and professional experience for the president to commission you as a military officer appointed by him. But to commission, you had to be an American citizen.

If I really wanted to be in the military, the only viable option for me was to enlist, naturalize, and then commission. It seemed like a terribly unwise step to relegate myself to a high-school diploma job and then fight my way back up to just below where I was before I came to the U.S.

But despite the quest for the American dream, I understood the real journey was my pursuit of happiness. If I would proudly call myself an American in the future and relocate my family to the U.S., there had to be a way to prove my devotion and loyalty to the U.S.

It felt right to serve and commit in some sort of way, but I couldn't quite figure out how to do it on time. All I knew was that it hadn't always and only been about money for me.

Despite my fervent desire for my family to be comfortable, I sought personal satisfaction with my life. To serve humanity in return for my life. Whichever way I dreaded compromising a happy life with my wife and child, the best thing I later came to realize was the void in my life that needed to be filled to make me whole. My family became the source of my strength with which I could face my demons eventually.

Tolu had a 2005 Nissan Altima sedan that we shared. Every morning, after dropping her off at work, I headed back home, cleaned the house, and cooked before going out to hunt for jobs since we would both be tired by the time we returned home. I went from one sales store to the next, assuring them that I didn't need a salary. I would work on commission. Once it was 5:00 p.m. I would return to pick up my wife from the office.

Tolu wondered why I wanted to name our first child after my father when I wasn't sure of the gender of the baby. My wife had accidentally found out what we were having. One of the nurses mistakenly declared the sex of the baby to her during one of her ultrasounds. It happened before my arrival in New York.

The nurse apologized to her, but she secretly wanted to know, so she didn't make a fuss about it. However, I pleaded with her not to tell me until the child was born. I wanted to know what it felt like to wait nine months for such a gift.

"You know, that's a masculine name. What if the baby were to be a girl?" she often asked.

"It won't make any difference. Just because it was my dad's name doesn't mean it's for boys alone. It's not a common name if that makes you feel better," I would add.

I've learned never to lie to the woman of my dreams.
What really matters is that you're real,
And not what you want to be—
Life might deny you a deal.

I've learned to listen to my heart-call
And not my head-toll—
To seize the world
Before it seizes me.
Beware of fate!

I've learned to make choices that fulfill dreams.
You may never comprehend faith,
But you know your dreams.
Your dreams may be your fate,
So why let go?

I've learned not to be a dreamer
Who makes a good lover when it's darker
But cannot be depended on
As soon as the morning comes.

The much-awaited moment finally arrived.

It was about 4:00 in the morning, the month of October 2010. I sensed the bed empty next to me. Slowly, I opened my eyes: my wife wasn't there. I propped myself up with my hands and looked around the bedroom, searching for her.

The contractions had been more consistent in the past few days, but the baby wasn't supposed to be due to arrive until the following week. It was the third consecutive night I'd woken up in the middle of the night to find her kneeling on the carpet behind the laptop, googling for more information on signs of labor.

"Are you okay? The contractions again?" I asked as quietly as I could. She nodded in affirmation without turning her gaze from the computer.

"It's probably still Braxton Hicks," I said while trying to get off the bed. Then, I noticed the grimace on her face. It was that of pain.

"I don't think so," she said. "It's different this time. The pain started from my back and then to my abdomen. It won't go away no matter how much I try to relax or move around." Tolu was obviously in a lot of pain.

I knelt next to her, attempting to take a glance at what she had up on the laptop screen.

"See what they say? Contractions are painful and at regular close intervals, increase when you walk, last longer, and feel stronger as they continue. I've tried to walk around, I even tried to go back to sleep, but it's not working," she said.

I noticed she had my wristwatch in one hand, so she'd been monitoring the interval between each contraction.

"I think we should go to the hospital," I suggested.

"Not yet. Let's give it a little more time; maybe it might stop. I don't want us darting off to the hospital only to be sent back like we'd been the last three times."

She was right; we'd been turned back three times in two weeks already.

"The baby is not ready to come out," they had said. "You are only about two centimeters dilated, Mrs. Ayoade," they assured us on three occasions. However, the doctor stripped her membranes on the last visit.

"Okay, come to bed then. I can give you a little massage. Let's see if it helps," I offered, still not exactly sure the baby might arrive a week early from the due date.

Clearly, those were early signs of labor, but the baby wasn't quite ready at that moment. I tried various supportive care techniques to help manage the pain the best way I could.

Her contractions continued for another two hours. I looked at the souvenir on the room dresser, a table clock I had brought from Nigeria more than two years before. It was a few minutes past 6:00 in the morning. I could no longer hear the ticking sounds of the clock, masked by my wife's struggle with the growing pain from the contractions in her womb.

They had become more regular, closer together, stronger, and steady. I grabbed my phone, called her obstetrician, and notified her we would be heading to the hospital. She trusted my judgment, so she didn't try to ask questions.

"Tolu is ready," I announced to her as confidently as I could while grasping the maternity hospital bag from my wife's closet. It's been packed with all the essential items that we needed for the childbirth about three months before.

"I'll be back in a minute, babe," I said as I hurried out of the apartment door. I needed to drive the car around from the parking lot to the front of the seven-story apartment complex.

If how much time we spent with someone
Was a measure of our thoughts about them,
Then twenty-four hours a day
Would be as trivial as the star I can't see
Every night up in the sky,
As to the wishes of my heart.

If I had thought of those years to come
With holidays, woods, snow, children,
Grandchildren, and gray hairs,
And in between those years,
We would share moments of laughter and tears,
Then my life couldn't be without you.

If I dreamt of memories with you,
Walking side by side, hand in hand, eyes to eyes,
And never part,
Then that moment is now.

Moments I would call right back
After an argument to tell you I adore you;
Moments you would cry on my shoulder
And smile back at my humor;
Moments I would watch you fall asleep on my chest
And feel the warmth of your breath on my neck.

Queen, tu es la belle vie que je cherche.
If Love is the greatest
Gift to share and treasure,
It lives within you.

If Love is faith
That dream will come true,
Then you are real.

And if Love is so beautiful
It can't be described,
Then amour tu es.

"Mrs. Ayoade, do you want an epidural? It will help with the pain," the anesthesiologist told my wife at the hospital.

"Not yet," Tolu said, grimacing. "I think I can still handle it."

My wife wanted to experience natural childbirth, so she'd told me she would hold on for as long as she could and, if possible, avoid the epidural. However, her pain was getting out of control.

We had been in the hospital for another three hours. Her aunt and I were there with her and the rest of her family members on the phone. I hadn't notified my family yet, wanting to wait until the baby was born.

We were in one of the labor rooms at the North Shore-LIJ Medical Group at Flushing, NY. My wife's obstetrician had arrived. She was in and out from time to time, checking on my wife's progress. She confirmed that the baby was ready, but it might take a few hours.

She infused a drug in her intravenous line and ruptured her membranes to further induce the labor since she was adequately dilated and the baby's head was fully engaged. It was almost noon, and her contractions were so close that she didn't have much rest between the pains from the contractions.

"Hey, babe, you sure you don't want an epidural?" I asked her while pointing to the readings on the tocodynamometer machine next to her. "Your contractions are really close now."

"Yes, I think I'll get one now," she finally gave in.

I ran out of the labor room to find one of the nurses who brought the anesthesiologist back. In less than thirty minutes, the procedure was completed, and my wife felt much better.

Two hours later, our baby girl arrived.

I had the umbilical scissors ready to cut the umbilical following the clamping of the cord. The baby was handed to Tolu while my wife's aunt picked up the phone to start calling every family member available.

It was October 2010. We named her after my dad, *Lani.*

Throughout my life, I'd known my dad's demons—but my last year working in Lagos was the best time I ever had with him. I thought we had so much time ahead for us to make our best memories. When he died so young, I felt deprived of so much I'd always wanted to do with him as a child. I didn't think I made enough memories with him; at least that was what it felt like losing him at 52 years of age.

As I gazed at the new life in my arms, I remembered the words Alhaja had told me when I was a child: *I've seen all your father's good qualities in each one of you boys.* Now, every time I would speak the name "Lani", I would live by Alhaja's wisdom. For the rest of my life, my child would be a reminder of my father's words to me: *Go to America.*

Lani was the promise of a better future. Her name would not only remind me of the best things about my dad, but she would also be my constant reminder of the kind of man I wanted to be.

I continued to stare at the new life in disbelief of what I could have done to her. She was part of me. She came from me. My blood.

My flesh. My joy. My pain. My sorrow and everything that I was, she was part of. Words couldn't capture how disgusted I felt when I remembered how I hadn't wanted her, and the foolish decision my wife stopped me from making.

How could I have known my wife had lived with the fear that she could never bear a child in her lifetime? As a five-month preterm baby with fetal epidermis, she had been exposed to numerous radiations in an attempt to save her life. Hence, her pediatrician had told her mother that she might never be able to bear children as a woman.

I could overhear the conversations over the phone about how doctors could only tell us what they know, but only God has the last say. What my wife had mentioned to me once so casually turned out to be bigger than I had ever imagined. Although I knew my wife had completely forgiven my blunder, I didn't expect her to forget so quickly, so I left for a moment of isolation to ask for God's forgiveness.

My wife was discharged the following day, but Lani was kept in the hospital for another day because she was mildly jaundiced, a common occurrence in babies born to parents of different blood groups. Both Lani and Tolu headed to my wife's family house upon Lani's discharge.

It is common in my culture for both mother and baby to be cared for by older and more experienced women in the family for the first few weeks following childbirth. They are then left to cater for themselves afterward. My wife and daughter spent four weeks in the family house, enough time for her to learn new things a mother must know to nurture a newborn baby.

After my relocation to New York, I had promised my wife that we would take the baby home in a new car when our baby arrived. What she imagined was only a dream from a man without a job became a reality when they saw a new car parked in front of the family house the night our daughter was to be taken home.

Tolu and I, New York registry, 2009.

From left: Tolu's aunt, Me, Tolu, Tolu's uncle, and Tolu's baby nephew, Tobi.

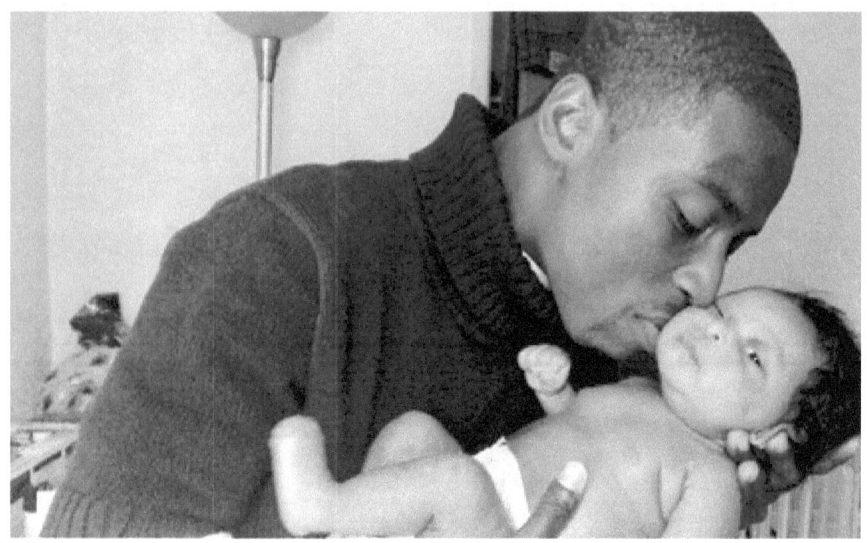

Lani and I, 2010.

Tolu and I, Lani's naming ceremony, 2010.

From Left: Sam, Tolu, and I. Lani's naming ceremony, 2010.

PART 3:

U.S. Navy & U.S. Air Force

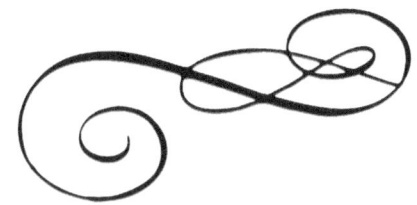

Chapter 14

NEW YORK CITY, NY: April 2011

Anchors Aweigh.

W hen Tolu was seven months pregnant with Lani, as we were getting settled in our apartment in New York, I received a call from a Navy Health Professions Recruiting Officer, who had seen my resume online.

"Hello, doc! This is *Lt. Grober!*"

He sounded like he knew me in person. For a second, I thought he could be a friend that I didn't remember, but I had no lieutenant friend whatsoever in the U.S. military.

"I'm a Healthcare Professions Officer Recruiter with the U.S. Navy," he said, as if he could sense my confusion. "I saw your resume online and thought I should give you a call."

"Oh, I see. Okay?"

"From your resume, you are really more than qualified to commission into the military. The U.S. Navy could use someone with your training and experience," he continued.

I had been quietly researching the military and the commissioning requirements while in Charleston, but U.S. citizenship was a requirement, so I hadn't bothered to follow up with more information.

"I don't think I'm qualified to commission due to the citizenship requirements," I informed him, trying to save him some time. "I'm a permanent resident with a green card," I continued.

"I see. Would you be interested in commissioning if we were able to secure a waiver for that?"

"I think I might," I responded without much confidence.

I imagined what the response of my wife would be, who didn't have the slightest knowledge of my desire to join the military. Still, based on my research, I didn't think it was possible to get a waiver for citizenship to commission as a military officer, so I encouraged the lieutenant.

"Good!" he said, sounding more excited than I expected. "You can email all your documents to me. I will email them to the central office, see what they can do for us."

"Sure!" I responded. "You will get them within the hour."

I always wanted to be in the military, but I didn't know how to ever communicate that idea to Tolu. I dreaded being away from her and the baby as much as I knew she did. My mother would later tell me that my father had always wished I could join the military in the U.S. after college. Of course, he'd never told me so himself.

"I received a call from a military officer, a health profession recruiting officer," I said to Tolu after picking her up from work.

It came out casually, as I took a left turn onto the highway towards our apartment exit. My gaze alternated between the roads and my wife's face, attempting to discern the expression I'd expected following the news.

"What did they want?" she asked in a very disapproving tone.

"Well, he said he saw my resume online and thought I could make an excellent officer in the U.S. Navy," I responded, still taking alternating glances at her body language.

"I don't think it's a good idea. Everything about the military worries me. Don't tell me you are considering it, 'Deji?" she asked, as if she expected the worst. Her eyes gave her away.

"To be honest, babe, it's not as bad as you think or see on TV. You can read up about the U.S. military. People make good careers out of the military. I would be lying to you if I told you that I hadn't considered it ever since I moved to the U.S."

"Wow! Are you serious? I mean, have you thought about being away from us? The same reason you have turned down other opportunities?"

"Yes, I have, but this is different," I said, trying hard to explain. "Joining the military doesn't automatically imply that I'll always be away from my family. It mostly depends on my job. You have to look at it from the perspective of being in service to this country, its people and most importantly, my family. I'll be able to use my expertise where it's most needed, meaningful, and rewarding."

"How?" Tolu asked. "This doesn't sound like the military that I know. You've never even talked about the military!"

"That's because I don't think I qualify to commission into the U.S military. I need to be a U.S. citizen."

"So, the recruiter thinks otherwise?"

"I think he believes my resume could earn a waiver, but I don't think any resume is impressive enough for the military to waive the citizenship requirement for commissioning."

"So, it's not possible?"

"It is," I said. "I can decide to go in enlisted. Currently, the U.S. military will naturalize permanent residents in military service as soon as they complete initial military training. In fact, many are able to do so during basic training. So, as an enlisted recruit with citizenship, I can secure the necessary security clearances and then apply for commissioning. It won't be overnight, but it's an alternate route if I really want to be in the service of this nation."

"Did he tell you all this?"

It was clear from her tone that Tolu thought I had gone crazy to even consider the military. It was all out of her respect for me and her concern for our family.

"No," I admitted. "I researched all about it a few months ago after moving to Sam's place. If I really want to be in the military, the only viable option for me is to enlist, naturalize, and then commission— in that order."

"You're a doctor," she told me. "Why would you demote yourself from being a practicing physician to enlist and be treated like a kid with all the other 18-year-olds?"

"I know it seems unwise to relegate myself to a high-school diploma job after everything, but you also have to remember that your past accomplishments can hold back from what's in store for your future, if you let your pride stop you from starting over when you need to," I said as jokingly as I could.

"But you're not seriously considering enlisting if he came back to tell you the waiver was denied?"

"Honestly, I'm not sure, babe. All I know is that, right now, this moment, all I care about is you and our baby's arrival."

"Really, 'Deji?"

Now she seemed anxious, and I was ready to end the conversation. The last thing that I needed at the moment was a stressed out, seven-months pregnant wife.

"I don't think you should worry about it," I said. "He will come back to tell me how sorry he is for getting my hopes up and all that, and it will all end there. Let's focus on the sales job I accepted. They are starting me on eight hours a day for three days a week."

I tried to distract my wife, who seemed disappointed. She wasn't quite sad, but she wasn't too happy either. I knew it was only because she genuinely cared about my happiness. She would spend many hours fact-finding all that was researchable about the U.S. Navy in the following weeks.

In the meantime, I focused on my immediate sales job. We had only one car, so whenever our schedule conflicted, I asked a co-worker for a ride or hopped on public transport, so Tolu could have the car to herself.

After five weeks selling for Sears, my sales were so impressive that my wife couldn't believe it. What we had expected to be supplemental income would be worth much more. My departmental head decided to increase my hours because she thought I made quite an impression on her boss.

"Not even the guys that have been here for over three years make such impressive sales," she said.

Soon, finances weren't so much of an issue. We lived according to our means, and we could afford the things we needed. I spent quality time with my wife because my hours were very flexible. We made new friends and spent a lot of time with my wife's family. Life with my wife was more beautiful than it ever was when I was alone.

How could I ever imagine the life I had tried my best to run away from would turn out to be the spring that my soul needed to fill the vacuum inside me that I'd borne for years? My wife and my unborn child completed me. They gave meaning to my life, and finally, I knew what it truly meant to be loved. I knew I had them even if I lost everything else. What I needed found me.

The warmest day of my life,
I stood by your side
And held you in my hands.
When you looked into my eyes,
I couldn't help but wish to tell you
How much I wanted to share my dreams with you.

Times change,
The truth unfurls.
I never felt in so much of a hurry,
For there was so much to bury.

Many promises have been kept in my heart,
And so little hope has been left alive,
But I know for sure,
In you, my dreams will survive.

"Have you heard back from the recruiter?" Tolu asked.

It was a Saturday evening, and we were taking a stroll on the boardwalk. It had also been two weeks since I told her about the Navy recruiter.

"Oh, yes. He called exactly after one week."

"You didn't tell me. What did he say?"

"You hated the idea, so I didn't want to bother you. Besides, it was as expected. Remember I told you there isn't a waiver for citizenship requirement?"

"Did he say if there were other options?"

"Exactly what I told you. I have to enlist to be naturalized. Then I can commission in-service. Why the sudden interest anyway?"

"Well, I want you to be happy," she said.

"I'm happy, Tolu."

"Seriously, 'Deji." Tolu tugged at my hand. "I read up about the Navy. It's not as bad as I thought at all. In fact, I believe you will do amazingly well. You have so much potential, and I know you're burning to do much more than you are doing right now. I know how much you're sacrificing just so you can make everyone happy. I will be a terrible wife to sit back and watch such an enormous potential go to waste. I can't let you sacrifice that much for what's already yours."

I was at a loss for words.

Amazed at her encouragement, I stopped walking to face her and asked, "Are you saying it's okay if I enlist?"

"Sure, if you want it," Tolu said. She looked straight into my eyes so that I could see she meant it.

"Slow but steady wins the race. It will be a very low start for you, but if it makes you happy!" Tolu continued.

Still surprised, I paused to listen to her.

"Lani and I are not going anywhere," Tolu said. "After all, we'll be back together after your training. Also, I read a few articles on enlisting to officer accession."

"Ok?" I prompted her to continue as I listened, still holding hands and looking into each other's eyes.

"I read from people's comments on some military sites how it will become much easier to commission after about two years since you would have met all the requirements," she continued. "Besides, it will make it faster to move your family down here."

I was surprised at how much she had learned about the military in such a short time. These were ideas that I would have had a tough time conveying to her on my own.

"It's very encouraging when you consider what's in store for the future," Tolu said, "So starting from scratch is a noble path if this is really what you want." She concluded with a small smile, prompting us to continue with our walk.

Tolu had come to see what was really behind my desire: to commit to a path that I believed I would find my purpose and fulfilment. In the process, to give back to the U.S. through service.

It was also for my family back in Nigeria, still scattered and working to scrape by. My mom struggled to manage her personal business without my father's direction, while my siblings worked to make ends meet despite their academic qualifications.

Tolu knew I was trying to find a way to help them, but I could only help if I was a U.S. citizen, and I could only become a citizen if I were to either wait three years or enlist and receive my citizenship immediately. Though many years have passed, my memories of Nigeria were clear, and I knew life there could be short. There wasn't time to waste.

"Okay then. I'll call the officer recruiter, see if he could refer me to a local recruiter." I said, still surprised at her reaction.

"Very well," she said. "Your future is so bright, 'Deji, you'll see."

"Thanks, babe," I said, and then added seriously, "Thank you. For everything."

A month after Lani was born, the recruiter called me. It was November, and they finally had a departure date for me to ship out to training.

"Congratulations, Ayoade! We got you April 2011!"

The recruiter sounded more excited than usual over the phone. I had been in the Delayed Entry Program for only three months, and I was expected to be delayed for up to a year. Securing a waiver for an early departure date for my job rating as a hospital corpsman was unexpected good news.

I had five months left to spend with Tolu and Lani before leaving for Navy boot camp, and I was planning to make the most of every second of it. I requested fewer hours from my sales job to care for the little one after Tolu returned to work.

In five months, I spent more time with Lani than my wife was able to. I was with her most hours of the day and night. Even so little, Lani recognized my face, my arms, my touch, my voice. It was a glorious feeling, to be known and loved by my child.

"You're as maternal as I could ever be," Tolu often told me.

Initially, I thought maybe it was the guilt, but I realized in no time that the man who panicked at the thought of having a child was long gone. As I looked into the mirror every now and then, I reminded myself to strive to be better than the man my grandmother and my father wished me to be.

Tolu and I knew there was a high possibility of me being away from her and Lani for a very long time. She knew there was also a possibility that I would make very little money, and that I'd use much of it to finally actualize my family's immigration.

Everything I'd worked for since childhood was on the line, and now I was responsible for a child. I believed that this was my one chance to get citizenship earlier and bring my family here, but I also knew that nothing was promised to us. Not making it through training was not an option.

When I finally arrived at Navy boot camp, it was clear this wouldn't be easy.

The first thing I noticed at Navy boot camp was how hard it was to understand the instructor's commands - I simply wasn't familiar with the words.

Even in the movies, I'd never heard these turns of phrase before. Most of the American kids seemed to understand the instructor's commands and expectations easily. Sometimes, it wasn't what the instructor yelled about; it was the context in which it was implied. Sometimes I had no clue what he meant until I watched someone else respond to the orders.

I knew I had to find a way to figure this out; otherwise, I might be perceived as slow.

On the second day of the eight-week training, the senior chief for my division stormed into the hall, where most of the recruits awaited instruction as usual.

"Who is Ramon Ayoade?"

He yelled my last name as a three- syllable word, "hey-YO-dee" instead of four, "eye-awe-AH-day." Still, I responded quickly, frantically thinking back to the past twenty-four hours for what I possibly could have done wrong.

"I am, senior chief!"

"You?"

He seemed utterly surprised.

"Follow me!" he yelled again as I scurried behind him into his office, where there were about five other chiefs waiting for us.

"You have a doctorate and master's degrees?" he asked brusquely.

I had never thought that my degrees would be noteworthy here. America always reminded me of my academic achievements, which to me were simply things I did in the past. In fact, I never even made it to my graduation ceremonies except for my veterinary induction ceremony - my academic certificates were all mailed out to me.

The way Americans responded to academic qualifications showed how much this country valued education, but I'd never been one driven by past accomplishments. I was simply happy to be doing something new and hoping my plans for a better future for not just me, but my entire family, would come together.

"Yes, I do, senior chief," I said, standing at attention and staring at the "X" mark on the board straight ahead of me.

It was one of many rules trainees had to adhere to. Just like in movies, you didn't look the instructors in the eye when they were talking or yelling at you.

In most cases, it was the latter.

"What the hell are you doing here then? Didn't you know you could have commissioned?"

His instant frustration was understandable as I was nearly twice the age of an average recruit.

"I knew, senior chief. I am not a U.S. citizen yet. I'm still a permanent resident."

"Oh, I get it now."

He took a step back from where he had been interrogating me like he wanted to size me up. I noticed the reaction of a few others out of the corner of my eye. They knew that sometimes foreign college graduates with undergraduate degrees enlisted in the U.S. military for citizenship, but my case was a first for them, given my background profile.

"You know you can start working on your commissioning as soon as you secure your citizenship from here, right?"

"Yes, senior chief," I replied.

I was surprised to discover that behind that tough demeanor required for a military instructor, there was a genuine care for trainees and their future in the military. Through that unforgiving exterior, there was a caring human being who wanted us to succeed.

"Make sure you follow up with your naturalization process while you are here," he said. "I will personally see to it that you get the information you need. You are dismissed now."

"Aye, aye, senior chief!"

I turned on my heel so that the office door was directly in front of me, opened the door and marched out of the office.

Although I did not get any sort of special treatment for the new intel about my education, I felt that the chiefs and the other recruits were a little more respectful and understanding towards me from that point on. But I had to assume that more was expected of me, especially academically. Never in my civilian life had I been aware that I could run a mile and half in nine minutes, or max out the sit-ups and push-ups requirement for my age.

The eight weeks of training felt much longer for one reason: my struggle with swimming proficiency. The Navy Seals eventually figured that I was a *sinker*, which meant that I was one of the very few students that couldn't float no matter what, mostly due to my body frame.

As easy as the training seemed, being a sinker made some of the required routines harder than they really were. It took almost five weeks for me to pass my swimming qualifications after rigorous training. Despite that, I felt I was born ready for the military. A year later, I would be running a mile in five minutes thirty-two seconds.

While in Navy boot camp, we were allowed to make phone calls during the fourth week of training, so I'd told Tolu that I wouldn't get the chance to see them before heading to Texas unless it was an emergency. She had been able to deal with my absence thanks to her family. She'd been spending a lot more time with them, especially during the weekends, while I made sure to write to her every week about my training progress.

My chief made good on his promise. At the end of the eight-week boot camp training, I stood among the other recruits grasping my citizenship certificate. There were seven of us altogether from five different nationalities.

As Lee Greenwood's "God Bless the U.S.A" video played on the big screen, my eyes grew wet. I held back tears with difficulty, recalling every single moment of my childhood when I'd promised my family, *One day, I will become an American citizen.*

I was thirty-one years of age, holding my U.S. citizenship certificate in one hand while I clenched the other very tightly to remind myself that I wasn't dreaming anymore. This was real. Finally, this was real.

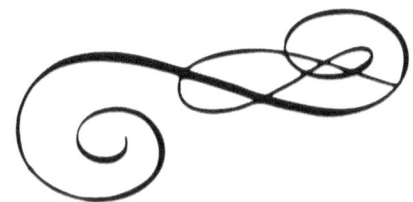

Chapter 15

SAN DIEGO, CA: September 2011
What Will Be, Will Be.

After graduation from naval training, my next stop was the Navy Medicine Education and Training Command in Fort Sam Houston, TX. By military orders, I had to report to training the day after graduation. The training at Fort Sam Houston lasted almost four months.

While in Texas, I tried to skype with Tolu and Lani every night, but there were several moments during this period that were nearly unbearable. I watched my daughter utter her first word *Daddy* and take her first step over Skype. My wife texted me that Lani had crawled to the laptop as soon as they arrived home and began to call out *Daddy! Daddy!*

When I called back after training, Lani had dozed off in front of the laptop while waiting for me to come online. Even though she couldn't express herself with words, I knew moments like that must have been disappointing for her. They were indescribably heartbreaking for me.

At the end of corps school, I had the highest GPA in my class, which entitled me to pick my next command before everyone else. I picked the Naval Medical Center San Diego (NMCSD), which was the headquarters of Navy Medicine West. Navy Medicine West cuts through the military treatment facilities and dental facilities in the Northern and Southern West Coast, Hawaii, Japan, and Guam. I would be stationed there for another three years, and train and deploy with the Marines as a combat medic during that time.

I applied for two weeks of leave en route to San Diego, CA, to go back home to New York. It was the last day of September 2011, and I had been away from my family for almost six months.

I arrived home just in time for my Lani's first birthday. She started walking at only ten months old and was now quite vocal, using a few precise words. She had no trouble remembering who I was when I finally held her in my arms for the first time in half a year. She knew I was the same Daddy from all our Skype calls.

I did my best to conceal my background from most sailors I worked with, especially the instructors and my superiors. Silence was my default. Unless I was spoken to, I didn't say much while in the Navy. I could imagine what they must have thought about me: How could someone in his right senses go through the rigor of medical school only to enlist in the military as a hospital corpsman? He must be stupid! But there was so much that I could do in the military with all that I had. I didn't expect anyone else to understand my decisions.

News traveled fast in the military, though. A few weeks after I began to work in the internal medicine ward, I quickly became the nurses' and instructors' favorite because of my flawless invasive techniques. I started instructing new medics both on the medical wards and in combat medic training.

Once, a new patient was due to be medicated. I looked at the medications to be administered and realized instantly she had been prescribed two medications that should not be taken at the same time. I notified the nurse, who looked up the drug information materials and was shocked to realize that I was right.

"How did you know what just by looking at the medication?" she asked in obvious surprise.

I smiled and told her I had a little medical experience, trying to brush it off.

Later, a few doctors showed up to my table to thank me, but they addressed me as a doctor instead of as a petty officer—they had heard about what happened and looked up my background. Sometimes events like these gave me away, but I was good at avoiding both necessary and unnecessary attention.

My time in the Navy opened my eyes to what it actually means to be an American on the one hand, and what it takes to be truly patriotic on the other. Many times I asked myself if my decision to enlist in the Navy was a wise one, but I knew it was the right choice. The Navy not only provided citizenship, security clearance, and life experience for me - I was also able to fulfill my childhood promises to my mother and siblings by relocating most of them to the U.S.

A year and ten months after I joined the Navy, my mom, sister, and my sister's baby boy boarded a plane to join me in America. They landed in New York City on February 21, 2013—the day before my thirty- third birthday and exactly five years after my father had died.

Because I was on duty in San Diego, Tolu welcomed them at the airport. She told me how explosively excited they both were, that my mom couldn't stop saying prayers of thanks all the way out of the airport.

The spell broke after they stepped out of JFK. The New York they saw for the first time looked nothing like what they had seen in the movies. In fact, my mom compared New York to one of the cities in Lagos known for its littered roads and congestion.

It was a month and a half later when I arrived in New York for a ten-day break—and just shy of five years since I'd last seen them—when the two of them saw me for the first time. They embraced me so tight and for so long that I could hardly breathe. Then my mom pulled back and gazed at me.

"Twenty-five years ago, you said you were going to make this happen," Mom said, with tears running down her cheeks. "And you did."

"I said I would do what?" I asked.

"You said one day you would become an American citizen and bring me to the U.S. You promised a better future for all of us, and you fulfilled it," Mom explained. "Remember when you won the American green card lottery while in college, but you never got called for an interview?

"Yes, I remember," I said. "God! How could I forget such a trying time?"

"Well, I thought that disappointment would probably change you," Mom said. "I thought you would give up."

"Mom, you of all people should know the word *give up* isn't in my dictionary," I laughed. "Still, that was a very difficult time for a kid my age at the time. I think those were some of the times that Alhaja's words helped me pull through my struggles."

"Really? Which?" my mom asked, anxious to know which of Alhaja's words stuck with me for that long.

"Alhaja said during tough times, you need to know that men can only slow you down, but they will never be able to change what will be," I said. "*Que sera, sera.* Our destiny is up to us." Alhaja never used the words *Que sera sera, but the spirit of the words was the same.* "I figured I couldn't give up on myself," I continued. "It's up to me."

Then, my sister introduced me to my nephew for the first time. I had always looked forward to being there when my little sister got married - my *only* sister, now a wife and a mother. I'd missed all of it. As I stared into the eyes of her one-year-old son and watched the way Lani took him in, I saw that this child wasn't a stranger to us. He was one of us. And I'd have gone through everything all over again just to assure him that he'd have a good life in this country.

"'Deji, what you have accomplished, comes with great determination and God's favor," Mom said. "Achievements like these are easier to watch on TV, but take so much more to realize. Most mothers could only dream of this for as long as they live."

It was a blessing to have a mother who reminded me of the past and what to be grateful for. In my mind, I always had more work to do. I always had to start a new task, if not several, a constant distraction that blinded me from the little things worth appreciating. She reminded me of those things.

For the next four months, my mother and sister lived with Tolu and Lani in our apartment in Queens, before moving to Maryland to be closer to my godmother's sister and her family. After my mom and sister secured their papers to work in this country, they both found jobs as healthcare aides.

Knowing we were all living in the same nation, governed by the same provisions and protections, I felt a peace in my heart that I had hoped for since childhood. But in no time, it grew clear there were times when I wouldn't be able to protect them.

One day, my mom called me. As we talked, I could tell she had a lot on her mind, so I asked, "what happened, Mom? You sound a little down."

She hesitated at first, then she asked the question that had clearly been plaguing her.

"How did you deal with racism when you got here?"

I paused for a few seconds and then said, "Tell me what happened, Mom."

"Ever since Biola and I moved to Maryland, it's been hard for us, especially because of our accent. I never knew how one sounded could be a problem," she said, utterly disheartened. "At first, it was hard to understand the African Americans when they spoke, maybe a little less for the white folks, but enough to know when they both mocked me." My mom didn't understand why they made fun of how she sounded. "I still don't know why they treat me that way while I do my best to understand them. I didn't think there was anything wrong about how they sounded."

"I went to Baltimore yesterday for a job interview in a hospital," she continued. "Biola and I are beginning to worry about rent and have been looking for a job since we got here." She took a breath before continuing, and I knew this was what had upset her.

"When I arrived at the interview," Mom said, "The first interviewer was a Black lady. After passing the assessment, she gave me her short interview. She seemed happy for me and sent me to the next stage: a hands-on assessment and an interview. When I walked into the room, I saw a middle-aged white lady in a white ward coat. She might have been a nurse." My mom tried to recall. "She told me to sit on the chair across the room and use the table in front of the chair for my assessment. Ramon, I answered all her questions and followed every instruction she gave. I thought it all went well until after it was over, and she told me to go back outside and wait for my result." My mom continued. "Later, another lady came outside to tell me my results."

Mom paused, and I could hear in her voice how much this affected her. I wanted to reach through the phone and comfort her, but I knew I couldn't.

"She said my results weren't good," Mom continued. "I asked why, and she said the second interviewer made the final decision not to hire me. She said I didn't follow her instructions the way she directed. I did!"

I didn't say anything, instead letting Mom finish.

"I was so obviously disappointed that the Black lady who interviewed me earlier called me on my way out and asked what had happened. I explained my interview outcome to her. She seemed very angry, and she agreed that I'd answered all the questions correctly! She said to me, *What that woman did to you is not right. She treated you that way because you are African, and she could tell you're a new immigrant.*" "I was so disappointed about how I was treated, Ramon," Mom said. I could hear the disappointment and hurt in her voice. "After attending training in Baltimore for weeks, I had been through tremendous stress trying to get to Baltimore every day, only for someone to disqualify me because of how I sounded and my skin color."

I stayed quiet on the phone. I didn't know how to comfort her - there was simply no way to protect her and my sister from the racial prejudice in this country. It hurt me just to hear it in her voice.

As my mom and Biola began to experience racial prejudice here, I realized how much intolerance I'd grown used to. After that run-in with the elderly woman at the pharmacy, I'd begun to stay silent or simply play dumb whenever someone behaved rudely or with ignorance. I'd learned that arguing with someone who was convinced they knew better was a complete waste of my time and emotions. I knew most people had never been outside the town they were born, and they just weren't interested in listening to anything contrary to what they believed in.

But to hear about the moments my loved ones experienced this hurt me much deeper than it had done when I'd had those encounters first-hand. As a child, I'd promised that I'd bring them here. Now that they were here, I couldn't control how others treated them.

"I'm sorry you had to experience that, Mom," I said, wishing I could make it better.

I explained to her how such things can happen from time to time, but also pointed out that she would have to treat people that treated her that way as individuals, and not assume any stereotype. Afterall, we had both experienced racism from folks of various races and had been helped by the same. People were often good and bad in equal measure.

We all struggled to integrate into our new worlds. After my transfer to San Diego, the Navy had moved me from one unit to the next, and I'd already been away from Tolu for almost three years. She was back in New York to keep her job and remain close to her family.

Tolu and Lani visited me in San Diego twice when she could take some time off from her job. Eventually, Tolu would resign from her job in New York, so they could join me. She could no longer bear the misery of being separated from me for most of our time together as a couple. They finally moved to San Diego.

Despite my struggles and despite barely seeing my family, I managed to do exceptionally well, so it took my leadership by surprise when I decided that I was going to start working on commissioning into the Air Force.

The decision was tough, but the reason was simple: after having been apart for so long, Tolu and I decided we must do whatever we could to stay together. I didn't want to miss as much time as I'd missed with my family after Lani was born, and our decision was confirmed just weeks later when we learned that Tolu was pregnant with our second child in April 2013.

I've come to realize
That hastening can be childlike.
Patience has become a rare virtue.
Excellence is the purest beauty.

I've come to realize that
The beginning of a man's future
Starts from the moment
He understands the need to be part of the world
And strives to make the best out of it.

I've come to realize that
In my destiny,
Lies my fate and the earth's hereafter.
And in my journey
Across the deserts and the seas,
I overcame the tides, storms, and whirlwinds
'Cause my faith could move the massif.

I've come to realize that,
Not only could destiny be discerned,
It could also be a bright and beautiful reflection
Of your muse and dreams.

The words you say and what you believe,
Each step you take, and the path you tread
Will make who you become.
Even though it may not be
On the near side of your knowing,
Your faith can see you through if you let it.

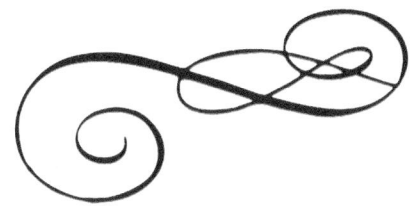

Chapter 16

SAN DIEGO, CA: November 2013
A Dying Tree at My Door.

> *I lie awake on a Saturday morning,*
> *Completely numb.*
> *I can't tell how far I've gone this time.*
> *I feel like a bag of sorrow,*
> *Seeking a heart to spill.*
> *I feel like a bunch of floating cloud,*
> *Tied up,*
> *And I can't tell if heaven is listening anymore.*
>
> *Something is eating me up,*
> *Bit by bit;*
> *I can only feel the pain in my heart,*
> *But I can't tell where it's coming from.*
> *The desire to break away*
> *Aches badly in my soul.*

287

A voice says, "Suicide's a perfect way out,"
But I don't even want to think of a way out,
'Cause I'm scared that if I leave,
I might end up someplace worse.

Not long after Tolu and Lani joined me in San Diego, we confirmed the baby was going to be a boy in July 2013. As we celebrated the news with friends and family, my nightmares began to return.

I had not had them since I left Nigeria, but now it was frequent, always the same nightmare, and it would continue for weeks like I was being haunted by something or someone.

The first time I had this nightmare, it began with a shrill, loud, startling scream. Bewildered and curious, looked for the source of the blood-curdling sound. The scream came from me.

I willed my heart to be still with each wobbly step I took. I felt my lungs tighten and clutched my chest. I struggled for breath, unexpectedly overtaken by despair. My poor lungs desperately craved air. I could feel the raging pulse in my palms like I was holding my heart in my hands. The veins in my forehead were throbbing incessantly. It was as if I was watching and feeling every heartbeat. In choked desolation, a feeling of complete emptiness engulfed me.

A realization hit me all at once, the way they always do in dreams: I was covered in blood.

I gasped in disbelief, trying to make sense of everything, of anything. I was on my knees holding an *Arsenal F.C.* inscribed soccer ball in both hands, also smudged in blood. I felt a sinking certainty that everything that meant life to me, all that I held so dear, had been taken away from me.

Then it occurred to me.

"Where's my family? My wife? My daughter? Where are they?"

Mustering what was left of my strength, I howled in agony, waiting for someone to hear my cries, but no one responded. I heard no voices. A crowd seemed to be watching, but they were without faces. They stood so far away, distant from where I was kneeling, and paid no mind to my cries.

There was an SUV with the four doors flung open. It was covered with dirt and blood. The car was empty. No one was alive or dead.

My screams got louder. My cries were like a child in burning pain, loud, open-mouthed tears and snot I took no notice of. The pain was deeper than I could ever comprehend, with my tears dropping on the bloodied ball still in my hands. I knew it belonged to my daughter.

I'd been teaching her how to kick. She had just turned three. Her favorite thing was to pose for pictures with the ball rather than kicking it. I could still see her cheerfully clinging to the ball as we ran across the field, laughing as she bounced up and down on my shoulders. In the dream, I knew I had lost something so dear, so deep, but there were no faces except mine. I was watching a mirror version of myself in anguish.

"No! This isn't happening! No!"

"This isn't happening! Where's my family?"

"My wife! My little girl! What's happened to them?"

"There's blood everywhere!" I yowled as I looked around.

"Is this my family's blood on my hands? God! Please spare their lives! Whatever my sins are, they are innocent! Please, take my life in place of theirs."

Strangely, the more I screamed, the less I could hear myself. The more tears I shed, the quicker my cries faded. Suddenly, all the pain and noises locked inside me with no way out. The magnitude of what I was feeling was far more than I could bear. It began to squeeze the air out of my lungs.

I felt my pounding heart slowly coming to a halt. I was in a very dark place, completely lost. I longed for empathy, but I could find none. The cold grip of it took hold of me.

With one last attempt, completely disregarding any consequences, I strove to end the moment. Loudly, the word "God" was forced out of my lungs.

I could hear myself once again. I took one huge, gasping breath, and felt it bring life to me. Panting heavily, I refilled my lungs with air and suddenly became aware of my own body. I was completely waterlogged in my own sweat. I brought myself into a sitting position, heart pounding.

> *"Save me! Save me!"*
> *A dying tree at my door*
> *Cried out to me.*
> *"My leaves are falling,*
> *And the wind is coming.*
> *Save me! Save me!*
> *Lest I die..."*

"Wake up! Wake up! Are you alright?"

Tolu tried to pull me closer with one arm while reaching for the edge of the blanket with the other.

"Are you awake?" she continued to ask as she patted my face with the dry side of the bedsheet. I was shirtless, and my torso was dripping with sweat. I turned to her, not sure if I was still dreaming or not.

"A nightmare?" Tolu mumbled, voice muffled by my arms as I clung desperately to her. It didn't seem to her like I had any intention ever to let go. Although I was still struggling out of the fog of sleep, my wife's distressed concern was crystal clear as she struggled to speak, her face pressed hard against my beating heart.

I quickly pulled away from her. I suddenly needed to see my daughter. I pushed urgently off the soaked mattress and into my little girl's room next to ours.

There she was in her bed, innocently carried away in a sound, peaceful sleep. She was still wearing her favorite *Dora the Explorer* pajamas. I pulled her tiny, fragile little body off the bed, holding her tightly to my bare chest while kissing her all over. Her face became smeared with my sweat still pouring down my face.

My wife followed me into Lani's room, still puzzled. She asked again, "What happened? Did you have a nightmare? Are you okay?"

I could not bring myself to answer her questions. I stared at my wife in disbelief, and my little princess, still far gone in her sleep. Her chin relaxed comfortably on the side of my neck.

"I still have my family," I reassured myself.

My wife, fuzzy with sleep and still confused by my behavior, asked, "What did you say?"

I held Lani close, hugging her tighter than I ever had before. She had just turned three.

"I will be alright."

"What do you mean, you'll be alright? Please tell me what happened! What did you see in your dream?"

"I'm sorry, babe," I said, heartbeat finally slowing. "I can't talk about it right now."

My wife gently pulled away from me, held my head in both hands, and stared into my eyes.

"It's okay if you don't want to talk about it right now," she said, taking a few steps back towards Lani's bed. She leaned toward the edge of the bed while I cradled my daughter in my arms.

The truth was that I couldn't get myself to replay the horror that I saw in my dreams, which seemed like a lifetime of fear. Besides, my wife would eventually end up listening to the story about my nightmare a month later from a man I had never met before.

Brown leaves, brown leaves,
They drop on my field.
Sorrow, pain; sorrow, pain,
Like a gravid sparrow, nests in my brain.
Fragile heart, fragile heart,
Tell me, will I die?
My soul, my house,
What's become of my life?

The nightmare tormented me many nights, leaving me with uncontrollable angst in the mornings. I was beginning to lose faith as sorrow crept deeper into my soul. I didn't seek help because I didn't know how or where.

Despite the nightmares that plagued me, I knew I would sacrifice anything to hold my son in my arms. To hear his first cry, wrap his tiny fingers around my finger, and bless him with a father's kiss. I couldn't boast of such hope. I felt stuck in the middle of a stagnant solitude.

Behind every smile and kiss on my wife and beautiful daughter was an urgency to make plans for their future. So, in despair, I began to prepare for something terrible, although I had no accurate knowledge of the time or date. But like an oncoming train moving closer to its next stop, I felt something horrid coming closer with each passing day.

O', King Jotham!
Remember me, son!
I have wept a thousand times—
So much that no tears left are in my eyes.

Nine months passed,
The pain has amassed,
And the question in my heart lingers.

Hopeful? I tried.
I owe you my life.
Though I await your arrival,
I may not live to hold you in my hands.
I long for your cry when the sun falls back,
When the morning comes to rock you in my arms,
And when the silence calls to kiss you back to slumber.

How do I make up for wasted time?
For the wrong questions I asked?
The eerie feeling that I'm soon to be gone will not subside.

O', Jotham!
My Love, my life.
Your mother is radiant,
For your arrival is nigh.
In her cries, joy she will find,
For you shall be there to dry them away.

One Sunday morning in November 2013, I stood in a corner in my church.

It was a Sunday service. We'd been attending the church for almost four months. I remember visiting the same church once the previous year on an invitation from a friend. However, I wasn't a consistent churchgoer, mostly due to a clashing work schedule.

Surprisingly, my wife knew about the church before they moved to San Diego; it was one of the branches of the same church she'd been attending in New York. Just before my family moved to California, I was rotated from Internal Medicine to Clinical Investigation, which did not require my presence at work on Sundays. It felt good to be able to attend church on Sundays with my family, although my interest was beginning to dwindle since my nightmares had begun.

Although I was a volunteer usher, it did not change how cynical I could be when I wanted to, something that my nightmares had made much worse. Since the dreams had begun, I felt constantly filled with dread and questions.

This wasn't a good attitude for a man who considered himself a Christian, or worse, a Christian worker. I scanned through the church, the congregation, and my wife. *Same o' same o'*, I thought to myself. It had been a three-day crusade program and I had no expectations for any of my questions being answered.

There was a guest pastor, from Ghana, West Africa. I knew there was a three-day program that would supposedly end on this day, but I didn't care much for whom he was ministering. I wasn't familiar with him, nor did I know his name. As far as I was concerned, it was a routine Sunday service.

I showed visitors and members to their seats while the choir continued to minister on the rostrum. The church pastor walked in with two visitors. The usher leader quickly helped them to their respective seats. They joined the church in praise and worship after taking various positions. I scrutinized the two visitors from where I stood.

The man I thought was the guest pastor turned out to be the assistant pastor. Just like the saying, "the greatest things in life come in smaller unexpected packages," the guest pastor wasn't just a preacher. He was a prophet.

As he walked to the podium, I couldn't help but admire his sky-blue, sharp-looking West African attire, tailored to fit perfectly well on his frame. The rectangular-shaped buttons were made of silver metal. They matched his dangling pendant, which was a massive cross made of white gold. He started off with a worship song, and the choir joined him while his assistant played the guitar. He continued with the same worship song for over twenty minutes, and stopped abruptly just when I wished we could move on to something more interesting.

Suddenly, he said, "Toast to the maker of dreams, who gives the wisdom to believe, plan, and know. He smiles at accomplishments and honors the humility that follows, for yet, the greater is always yet to come."

"You are in this church as I speak," he said. "You had a dream about death. Someone died in your dream. You don't know who because you couldn't see any face. You were in so much agony, crying uncontrollably in your dream. Despite not knowing who died, you felt the loss so close and dark. As you continued to weep in devastation, you pounced up to life, but you did not feel any different. Your feelings were more real than ever. Your agony awakened with you. You were sweating and crying just like you were in your dream."

I turned towards the prophet; *Prophet Nkum,* he was called. Like a baby would to his father, I hurried towards him with my hands up, hoping desperately that his visions did not point to someone else.

This was the first time I felt no hesitation in believing everything was true about someone I'd just met for the first time in my life. I could feel some lightness replacing the heavy burden inside me as I acknowledged Prophet Nkum. He was talking about me.

The man just described a dream haunting me for weeks, like he was right in the nightmare with me. He was no ordinary man. I couldn't explain the things he saw any better than he did, considering no one knew about my dream, not even my wife. I'd been keeping all of it to myself, making plans for my family in secret, just in case something appalling happened to me.

As if I was about to be saved and delivered from my demons, I was finally standing before a man who had answers to questions I'd been craving answers to.

He continued, with a smile on his face, "Son, you did not lose anyone in your dreams. It was you who died. You were crying for your own quietus. However, this will not happen because God wanted me to take care of this right now."

I was relieved to know it wasn't any member of my family, but I also felt saved and cared for to know that God could use another man to answer my questions and protect me from the tragedy about to befall me and my family.

"Church! Look at this young man!"

He pointed towards me. I looked up from where I stood before him, waiting to do exactly as he commanded.

"Look at him! He was that little boy, motivated by extraordinary things in life. Thousands of miles away from his inspirations, but he never stopped dreaming of finding his way somehow. He was that boy with many gifts but wondered which would make him someday. He would give everything to reap a million gifts from just one gift, yet he's without a clue which path he's on. He was that little boy with the dream to move his family out of poverty. He dreamt of a new life for them, even on his toughest days as a child.

He sincerely cared for them in his heart, but reality would require more of him."

I couldn't have described my past, thoughts, or disposition any better than he had in just a few lines.

His words were real, powerful, and assuring. I was sure that there was nothing bogus about this man. I read about prophets in the Bible; I heard about a few I'd never met, people who knew things.

The Bible described their gifts. However, I never knew in my lifetime, God would be sending one my way. A man I'd never met in my life who knew everything about me, including my deepest thoughts and fears that I had never shared with anyone before. He knew the sources and understood the forces within me that I had desperately tried to understand for years.

He told me about how much God loves me. The plans God had for me. How glad he was that I came to church that very Sunday, because he wasn't sure what would have happened to me in the following few days if he hadn't gotten a chance to help redeem my life.

"You were supposed to die exactly eighteen days from today. News that would have come as a great shock to your friends and family, devastation to many clinging on to you for support. The dark feelings you've been having lately were genuine. You knew this was coming soon, although you didn't know when." Again, he knew things I had never shared before.

Prophet Nkum compared my situation to that of Joseph in the Holy Bible. He was destined for greatness. Such immeasurable greatness. However, his brothers would do anything to ensure his fate did not come to light, even if they had to kill him.

"In your case, son, every time a child with greatness is born into your family, they don't survive long enough. It was the same with your grandfather. And your father. He had many chances to redeem himself, but he allowed himself to be consumed by this world. The wicked ones whom you innocently don't know of live for this. They do not want anything extraordinary to come out of anyone from your family."

How can he be so exact? I asked myself.

Why my father had kept us away from his extended family was not only making more sense to me now but was certainly a matter of fact. Clearly, there was a sort of generational curse in my family.

My dad saw things he didn't share with anyone else. He always thought it unwise to be close to his extended family. He'd wanted me to leave Nigeria for good after all.

"However, God's made it clear to me they will not succeed in your case, you are special, and God's plan for you must be realized," he told me. "So, wipe your tears because this is it. This is where your torments end. You won't die, nor will your enemies who endeavor to harm you succeed."

I can't believe God sent a man to take away my misery, I thought to myself. Once again, tears filled my eyes. Suddenly, all the pain and agony I'd been struggling with for weeks felt so tangible inside me, but I knew soon it would be gone.

Pastor Nkum implored the church to pray with him for me. He apologized to them, stating he wouldn't be able to attend to anyone else that morning.

"God wants me to take care of this young man." He paused and turned sharply towards me. "What's your name?" he asked.

"'Deji. 'Deji Ayoade, sir," I replied.

"God wants me to take care of 'Deji and him alone this morning," Pastor Nkum continued. "It's of extreme importance. He is important to God, and it will consume the entire morning service today. Many more lives will depend on this man's life."

Pastor Nkum understood how desperately most church members wanted to see him before he departed later in the evening. He promised to spend a few more hours later in the day with the church before he left for his flight back to Ghana. He would be praying for each church member individually before leaving, to make up for all the time he spent with me in the morning service.

He began to pray for me. He requested an anointing oil, so the church's deacon brought a bottle of olive oil. He poured out some on his palms and laid his right hand on my head. He assured me there was no use to worry because God had restored my life.

"No evil plan against you will succeed," he said. "You know, your enemies are quite confident this time, all agog to hear the news of your untimely passing that was soon to occur. Unfortunately for them, they have only made you stronger and untouchable from now on."

He stared intently at me for a few seconds and said, "Look, 'Deji, there's so much about you that I can see this moment. Your journey. What you've been through. Where you came from. Where you are going. If only you knew who you are, you would talk and walk differently. You are beyond the ordinary. There's such greatness in you that I cannot describe. Today you are born anew. You cannot turn away from God. It's the only way you could lose your glory. Even so, don't throw away your beauty because only a few are chosen."

Am I to be called a coward if I walk away?
Heart in throat,
Hyperthermia,
Blood in the head.
Pandemonium is the word,
Dreams buried by the beach palm.

If I wasn't warned,
The sun would never shine
And the moon would swallow the stars.
You have become my daylight
And my compass in the desert.

It's so gloomy in my head.
"If only I knew the truth," I thought,
"I would keep the light
And live my dreams."

It is easy to want to be cynical and not believe in miracles. Like the doubting Thomas, this experience showed beyond a doubt how spiritually myopic I'd become. However, my faith had only gotten stronger after I spoke with Pastor Nkum.

Pastor Nkum stepped down from the podium and headed towards the church pastor's office. It was the end of the service. I ran after him. I was desperate to know how he knew so much about my life secrets, things that I'd never disclosed to anyone. As he settled into the church pastor's chair in the office, I followed after him and asked, "How do you know all these things?"

The Pastor was visibly exhausted. I knew I was infringing on his time at this point, but I had his attention and I needed to know.

"The truth is," I said, "I'm probably as skeptical as any man can get regarding religious prophecies. I apologize because no one had ever been so accurate about things that I had never told anyone else before. Straight from my nightmares to your mouth. I believe everything you said because you are true. You are a true prophet. For the first time, I know it. You were precise about everything you said. You hit the nail right on the head today despite us having no connection."

He smiled and told me, "Son, it is a gift that took me so long to turn into a great blessing for mankind. Once I found my place in God, I have not looked back. I travel the world to give back. Imagine if I weren't in your church today, or you didn't show up to church today, there would probably never be another chance for you. You know I can still see more. I see a lot about you as we speak. It is too big, too much to explain all of it in one sitting. You need to understand it. You need to believe in yourself and your gifts and don't look back when you do. Act accordingly, for if you do know who you are, again, you will talk and walk differently. I know you are already a doctor, but you will go back to school so that you can change your current specialty. You will not be practicing what you were already trained to do."

There it was again, as casually as it came out of his lips. He was again accurate because I was already processing my paperwork to compete for a position in the Air Force Officer Corps.

"There's a lot more, but Father told me to save you and

protect your life as it is the most important thing to do right now. I have to warn you, though, that you can still lose your glory if you turn away from God. So don't, for he has done a great thing for you," he said as he stood up, ready to leave. "You are very special to Him, and the kind of love He has for you is unusual. The best you can do is to stay by Him for the rest of your life, and you will see how great things open for you."

He leaned over from the other side of the table, held out his right hand, and shook my hand while he rested his left hand on my right shoulder.

"You see, back in church, I saw so many visions meant for so many other people. Although it is not at much expense to them or their future like yours is, they will have to wait because of you. I'm sure you understand what this means?"

I nodded in acknowledgment.

"Remember me when the time comes," he smiled and pressed on. "I look forward to your future as money matters will be the least of your worries. The world will know you. They will know your name," he said as he stepped out of the office.

I remained standing where I was, still stupefied to think of what I needed to give. I would have given every material thing I had in a heartbeat for such an experience. I finally understood my life like I never did before.

God answered my questions, including the ones that had been eating me up since childhood. Pastor Nkum made it clear he didn't want anything from me. Whatever I desired in my heart had to be for God and for my church.

Love is faith
That dreams will come true.
You have to believe to hope for love.
Love is a precious gift
To cherish and treasure.
So hold on to love when you find yours.
Love is wonderful,
Like the candlelight, only shines
brighter when shared.
Love is beautiful,
Like the horizon in the countryside.
Love is heaven,
Like the air around us, it is everywhere.
Love is you,
And God is Love.

He must have prayed for over 150 church members and healed many of us. He delivered prophecies to almost everyone he prayed for, no matter how small the contact time between him and the individual was.

"You are an usher, right?" he asked me, looking deep into my eyes.

"Yes, sir, I am," I replied.

"Son, you sincerely love God. You do love him."

Two weeks following the prophecy, my son arrived. His touch gave me the strength to finally forgive myself and set my soul free from the guilt that I'd borne for almost four years.

Almighty Alom:
Depth of the unknown,
Maze of eternal perspective,
Trumpet and sickle-selecting,
Hope of our beliefs.

O, Creator:
Holiest of holies,
Heavenly inhabitor,
Lord of host praises,
Daemon of my days.

All magnificence:
Meritorious munificence,
Sound of the seventh heavens,
Storm of the sixth caverns,
Muse of my creativity.

Supreme reality,
Kind of third diversity,
Mystique antique,
Cloud of thick mist,
Divinely inspiring.

Dynasty of peace,
Ancient sagacity uncease,
Booming thunder utterances,
White stallion rider,
Spirit of my insight.

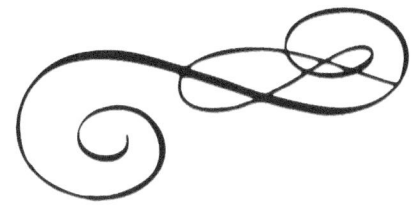

Chapter 17

SAN DIEGO, CA: July 2014
Farewell, Navy.

One day the Master Chief of Internal Medicine sent for me. He was new and had only been in charge for about two weeks. I worked as a hospital corpsman in a role similar to a nursing assistant. I loved working with the patients and supporting the nurses and physicians, but I knew that I had more to give with my training.

"Good day, master chief!" I said, knocking at his open office door. I tried to maintain my military bearing in front of the new boss by popping into an active stance.

"Oh, come in, HM3," he ordered firmly.

I marched towards his table and halted behind the empty chairs. HM3 rank denoted a third-class petty officer; master chief usually meant "master chief petty officer," the highest enlisted rank. However, in our rating, the official title is referred to as hospital corpsman third-class and master chief hospital corpsman, respectively.

"Have a seat."

He pointed to the chair across from him. In the Navy, we often referred to each other solely by rank.

"We have an opening at the North Island Branch Medical Clinic. I heard you had indicated interest to transfer out of Internal Medicine."

"That's affirmative, master chief," I replied as confidently as I could, resting my hands on my thighs. My head stayed centered, my shoulders drawn back, and my back straight. All part of a military bearing in the presence of a superior officer.

"I'm sorry we held on to you for a little longer than we should. I've heard a lot about you," he said. "Replacing someone like you will be tough. The matron and the nurse officers wished you could stay back here. They have only said remarkable things about you. How you once saved a four-hundred-pound choking patient and how you revived a seventy-year-old man in cardiac arrest by doing CPR before the Rapid Response Team arrived."

He paused to flip through a few papers in front of him. I thought they were my record documents.

"They mentioned how impeccable your intravenous procedures were even when everyone else on the ward tried and failed," he continued. "I also heard patients often ask for you by name or description. Your experience has been invaluable to Internal Medicine, especially to our patients. However, when it's time to move on to greater things, it is time."

"I can see you have completed more than required training for your job level, including the Tactical Combat Casualty Course. Quite impressive, HM3. Do you have any suggestions for me on how to make the ward more efficient?"

After putting forward a few tips to the boss, he signed off on my transfer paperwork to the branch clinic in Coronado.

"It's nice meeting you in person, doc! Good luck to you," he said.

As I marched out of his office, I thought he knew a lot more about me than just being a corpsman. *Perhaps my chain of command told him something,* I thought.

It took less than fifteen minutes to arrive at the door of the branch clinic in Coronado. As soon as I walked in, I reported to the receptionist, who was a rank below my rank.

"Good day. I'm HM3 Ayoade, reporting from Balboa Hospital," I said.

"Oh, I see. We've been expecting you. The senior chief mentioned you'd be here today. I'll get him."

The hospitalman walked away and returned after a few seconds with the senior chief, who oversaw the enlisted at the branch clinic.

"Good morning, senior chief," I said.

"Come with me, HM3."

He led me into an office, two rooms down the hallway from the receptionist.

"Can I have your paperwork?" he asked.

I handed over all the transfer documents I had with me. He signed off on some of them and called to the leading petty officer (LPO) of the branch, a first-class petty officer (HM1) who was two ranks above me.

"HM1, can you please take care of HM3's in-processing? Thank you," he said without waiting for a response.

I followed the HM1 to an office at the end of the hallway, where she handed over my documents to an HM2. It was a much bigger room. I remained close to the door of the office, which was the clinic in-processing office. The HM1 walked right past me, assuring me that HM2 would take care of me. As HM2 walked towards me and stopped right in front of me, we noticed the senior chief walking towards us from the hallway.

"I'm sorry, HM3. I have to send you back."

Puzzled, I asked, "Is there any problem, senior?"

The HM2 also had the same expression on her face.

"I don't think so. You are the guy with the doctorate degree, right? Some kind of crazy experience?" he asked, but I was a little hesitant to answer yes, so I nodded.

"They want you to report to the Directorate for Professional Education," he continued. "I don't know much about why but it's an order. You can stop the paperwork, HM2."

I walked out of the branch clinic without further questions after the senior chief lined through his signatures and initialed my transfer documents. All I knew about the Directorate for Professional Education was that they coordinated and managed all professional training and research for the Navy Medicine West, including Graduate Medical Education. I was still confused, but here I found myself standing at the door of another Senior Chief anyway.

"Come in, HM3," she said. She sounded much nicer and friendlier than I expected.

"Please, have a seat," she added, offering me one of the two seats opposite her. "I'm sure you are still wondering what's going on." She could read the confusion on my face.

"We received a call from someone about you. I can't tell you from whom. We know about your expertise, and God knows we could use your training and experience in this directorate." As she continued, she paused to acknowledge my anticipation for more information.

"We conduct training and research for Navy Medicine. The Navy doesn't have a veterinary medicine specialty, but the Army and the Air Force do. We usually have a veterinarian from the Army in our Clinical Investigation Department. However, he received orders to PCS from the Army, and we have no replacement for the next ten months," she said. Suddenly, it started to make sense to me. Although I wasn't a commissioned officer yet, this was how I finally found myself in my most fulfilling position to date.

I conducted medical research with the Navy medical doctors and researchers from various fields of medical science. They acknowledged the experience that I brought with me, which was a refreshing and validating change of pace. About thirteen months after my transfer to the new directorate, I had worked extensively on combat casualty care training with the Marines and various Navy special ops in preparation for combat deployments or special missions. I also trained and coordinated research in emergency care, hearing loss restoration for members recovering from explosion incidents from combat, and facilitated microvascular surgery techniques for graduate medical trainees. Later, the Navy's Clinical Investigations Department selected me to join the team working on an infectious disease medicine research project that I felt personally connected to.

At that time, our military had a lot of people returning home from all over the world with a particular strain of pneumonia that our antibiotics couldn't keep up with. Over time, the bacteria had evolved and mutated to resist the treatment, so it was the job of our research team to acquire samples of those strains and study the pathogenesis of the bacteria. We wanted to understand how they operated to the point where they eventually took over the lungs. From there, our mission was to develop an antibiotic formula to treat the resistant infection effectively.

The project engaged my passions and strengths. On a very personal level, it was also significantly full-circle: I was working to find a treatment for the United States to combat the illness that had almost taken my life as a child. At the conclusion of the project, the U.S. Navy awarded me a Navy-Marine Service Medal for groundbreaking research and a Military Outstanding Volunteer Service Medal for the hundreds of volunteer hours that I'd given to the community. During that time, I was promoted, and some of the work that I co-researched for the Navy was accepted for publication in highly reputable international scientific journals. I had my eye on commissioning, and it finally felt like it might be within my reach someday.

Although I have always been fortunate to serve under good leadership, the Clinical Investigation Department was the best thing that happened to me while in the US Navy. I tried applying for commissioning in the Navy, but the jobs that were available would still take me away from my family.

I had a decision to make: if I were thinking about leaving the Navy, I felt that now I had something meaningful to show for my time and service there. I'd shown what I could do, and my work had been useful to the Navy.

The administration's support was unabated despite my intention to leave the Navy for the Air Force. They told me it would be the Navy's loss, but that they understood my decision. They not only went out of their way to write a strong recommendation letter on my behalf, but they also coordinated with other directorate leaders to assist in building an impressive commissioning package. Later, an Air Force full-bird colonel who led my commissioning interview along with a captain said, *This is by far the most inspiring letter we've ever read about any applicant.*

It was hard to believe I'd have all that to my credit. I didn't wallow in any past accomplishments, or pay much attention to credits at all. To me, trusting how far humility could take me and devoting my best to everything I did, no matter how trivial, would always suffice.

There were discouragements and challenges as well, of course. I had less than two years left on my contract with the Navy. Most Air Force recruiters stated I was eligible for a commission, but they claimed to have never seen any active-duty enlisted Navy commissioned into Air Force while still on active-duty status. I also could not have a break in service. The senior recruiter that I sought to work with initially said it wasn't possible. I had to complete my contract with the Navy before I could apply.

I have followed the narrow path,
Away from the wide road.
In the valley,
I will find my purpose.
I may not know what awaits me
At the end of the broad road,
But no man could have two destinies.

How would I know the truth,
When my right could be wrong
Or my wrong could be right?
The ripples of my sin
Crawled to the edge of my destiny,
And all I could feel were the cracks in time
That I must get past.

The joy of life,
That this man may find his purpose here on Earth.
Like manna from heaven,
Fill my soul like living bread.
And like a balloon
So light, I want to swim into the sky.

With my eyes closed, I want to step into heaven's gate,
'Cause I know what could be in store.

The navy office in charge of processing my conditional release to apply for Air Force commissioning also had the same difficulty. They only had experience with Navy enlisted to Navy officer commissioning - not into a different branch, and especially not while still under service obligation to the Navy.

"It's never happened before," the Navy career counseling office mentioned. "No one's ever commissioned into another branch while still active duty enlisted."

Some particularly condescending people often said things like, "How could you be selected over those born, raised, and schooled their entire life in the U.S.?"

This was no time to be discouraged about my plans, though. At this point in my life, I finally came to learn that it wouldn't matter how much I struggled at every endeavor. As Alhaja used to say to me, *What will be will be.*

Throughout my pneumonia research, I worked with an infectious disease doctor who had been a nuclear commander in the Air Force before he went to medical school. So when the Air Force selected me for a very special duty - nuclear missile operations - the decision was a little easier, but I had to admit, I was puzzled. I understood that my medical qualifications were why I was selected for the pneumonia research, and I'd been anticipating another placement in a medical field.

But a job in nuclear missile operations? Why I'd been chosen for this job, I didn't have a clue. It was safe for me to assume that they'd never had an African immigrant on the job before. The responsibility would be highly sensitive, and the screening process, which would take place on both the national and international levels, would be incredibly rigorous.

To be considered for this role was equal parts overwhelming and an honor. But really: why me? My only conclusion was that they figured that the scientific training would come naturally to me. I didn't know. What I did know is that they didn't just throw people in there. This was a big job.

To prepare for such a job, I needed to pass several physicals.

On my medical physical appointment day at MEPS, I completed every test with good results until I arrived at the last medical station, where a physician would look through all my records to determine the final clearance. His approval would qualify me to proceed. When I showed up at his office, I found an elderly man in his late sixties or early seventies. He welcomed me, but didn't say much else. He flipped through my medical record on his table distractedly, like he had other things to do.

He ordered me to take off my shirt as he pulled up his stethoscope from around his neck to his ears. As he was listening to my heart and lungs, he suddenly paused.

"Have you ever had heart issues?" he asked, with more attention than before.

I told him never, and he returned to listen to my heart again. After he brought the stethoscope back to his neck, he reached for a form on which he scribbled a few things and handed it over to me. I held the paper in my hand and stared back at him, puzzled.

He explained, "You have a cardiac murmur."

"What?" I asked, shocked. "Cardiac murmur? I've been in the Navy going on four years. I've never had any heart issue, and the Navy never diagnosed me of any heart issue."

"Well, I know what I heard," the doctor said. "I've been doing this a long time." He sounded confident, almost dismissive, ready to move on to the next patient.

"Okay. So, what's the way forward? Am I DQ'd?

"No, not yet. That paper in your hand is a referral note to a cardiologist. They will do a bunch of tests and send the results down to me before I can decide on your qualification."

"Okay," I replied as I zipped up my jacket.

"We will let your recruiter know when the results come back. You may not have to come back." He said, indifferent to my obvious disappointment.

I walked out of his office and notified my recruiter of the new development, which was disheartening to both of us. We'd been through a lot already to secure a commissioning spot. For this to happen after all of that was upsetting.

I held my breath until I showed up at the cardiologist's office, where a bunch of new tests were carried out on my heart. They also released me and instructed me to follow up with the military doctor.

A week later, I received a call from the recruiter that the old doctor had disqualified me from commissioning into the Air Force.

The cardiologist had diagnosed a heart disorder whereby one of my heart valves didn't close properly, and the man had disqualified me.

This was a blow, but before I allowed myself to get depressed, I did what I'd always done and considered my other options.

I could always fight for a waiver or even return to the Navy, finish out my enlistment, and then get a job in medicine in the civilian world. After researching the heart issue, it turned out that it was, in fact, insignificant. There was nowhere in the Air Force's medical standards where disqualification had been directed for my case.

I expressed my frustration to the recruiter, who seemed to almost wave it off.

"This happens all the time at the processing station, especially with the old man," he said.

"So, there's a way forward?" I asked, excited at the prospect.

"We will have to send a request to the surgeon general, asking him to grant us a waiver for the MEPS disqualification."

"That's possible?"

"Yes, it is, doc. The physicians at the MEPS conduct the first-line assessments. The surgeon general's office conducts a more thorough review before making a final decision. The good news is that, if they grant the waiver, it overwrites the MEPS determination."

Relief flooded through me.

"Wow!" I said, sighing. "I guess there's still hope then. So, how long are we looking at?"

"To be honest with you, it takes time. If I send the package out in two days, we are looking at an average six-month wait time."

"Are you serious? You know I don't have much time left. I have to graduate from OTS before I turn thirty-five. That's less than a year, minus ten weeks OTS time."

"I know, doc, but that's all we can do. Try, and then pray. Who knows, you might be one of those rare ones that get quick responses from the surgeon general."

Three years long,
I had closed my ears to my song.
In deeper sadness,
I held my hands faceless.
Overboard I fell,
Promising I'd sink lifeless.
I count ten years behind,
And I had walked that far back, sometimes.

Like a picture
Painted in the middle of an ocean,
My thoughts seem boundless.
Like a paddle ball,
Searching for a place to fall,
I chased the vision in my head.
Like the moment between life and death,
When you accept the imminent,
I hope to not fall into an abyss of unfathomable depth.

The recruiter forwarded my package out to Washington D.C. I resolved to be patient and just hope for the best. However, three days later, I received a call from the recruiter.

"The waiver came back!" he said.

"What? I thought it would take…"

"Six months. I know!" he completed my statement. "I tell you, doc, you are a special one because they granted you the waiver. You're good to go. The surgeon general of the Air Force overturned the decision following further analysis of the cardiology result. It turns out the cardiologist confirmed that your case is normal and insignificant."

I couldn't be more thankful as things definitely seemed to be falling into place. It was a good sign, which was very uncommon for me in my three decades of existence. I knew something must be right about my current decisions.

"Thanks a lot for your help." I thanked my recruiter. "So when do I report back to MEPS? To reverse the initial decision."

"I will schedule your next visit and get back to you." The recruiter assured me. In my mind, I was going to avoid the old physician by all means.

Two days later, when I showed up to MEPS, I was sent over to a younger doctor just like I had wished.

"Welcome Mr. Ayoade," he welcomed me in a friendly tone. "I've been looking at your profile and don't seem to understand why you were disqualified." He said as he lifted his stethoscope to listen to my heartbeat. After listening to my heart sound a few times, he leaned back and sad, "I can't hear any murmur." Then he moved the stethoscope around my chest a few times again and said, "I see. I can hear it now, but it's pretty faint." He cleared me and wished me good luck with my flight physical.

For my flight physical, I was sent to Los Angeles Air Force Base as there was no military hospital conducting such specialized medical screening in San Diego. The tests took two days, but it was less cumbersome than what I had been through at the MEPS. My flight physical results came out fine and I was cleared to proceed to Officer Training School in Alabama.

As I left Los Angeles, I called my recruiter to inform him that I've been cleared to proceed to training. The next step is for us to secure a training date for the OTS at Alabama.

Just when I thought things were beginning to get better, the unexpected occurred.

The challenges never seemed to stop. As soon as I got past a roadblock, another would surface. My recruiter knew my thirty-fifth birthday was only seven months away and never told me about the training backlog at hand. When he finally opened up that he didn't know how long my wait was going to be, and that he had more than five batches of selectees before me waiting for dates, I decided to take things into my own hands.

I gave the Air Force office in charge of fixing training dates a call and explained my circumstances to them. Fortunately, whoever the lady was that picked up the phone couldn't be more understanding.

"HM2," she called me by my navy rank. "Do you know if your TS clearance is ready? It must be ready before I can send you out to training."

"I'm not sure. My final interview was two months ago, so I want to think it should be ready."

"Okay. I want you to hold on. I'm gonna go to the next building to confirm if it's ready or not. If it is, I might be able to help you."

"Okay. Thanks a lot," I responded as I held on to the phone close to my ear.

This time, I was ready for the worst results. I knew I had done all the best that I could to make things work. If it didn't work out, I wouldn't have any regrets.

After about ten minutes, the voice came over the phone.

"Congrats. I found you. Your TS is good. So, I have September 20th open and November after that. Which would you prefer?"

"Is September the earliest date you have?" I asked.

"I have August sixth for class 15-01, the first class of the fiscal year. It's only a week away, so I don't think you want to go for that. You need time to out-process from the Navy."

"I want it. I want the August class." I was as assertive as I could.

"What? Are you sure? That's going to be a lot of stress for you and your family."

"Don't worry, sarg! You've done all you could for me. It's up to me to not waste it."

"Okay, I'll call your recruiter and let him know you're all set.

He will take care of the paperwork."

"Thank you so much! I really appreciate your help."

As I hung up the phone, I took a deep sigh of relief, stepped out of the office building into the sunlight, and looked straight at the sky. I smiled and whispered "Thank You" like I was talking to someone up above. After sharing the good news of being selected into Air Force, I had not shared my recent challenges with anyone else, not even my wife. I wanted to do everything within my power to keep the news good, until otherwise.

Navy Boot Camp, Recruit Training Command – Great Lakes, Illinois.

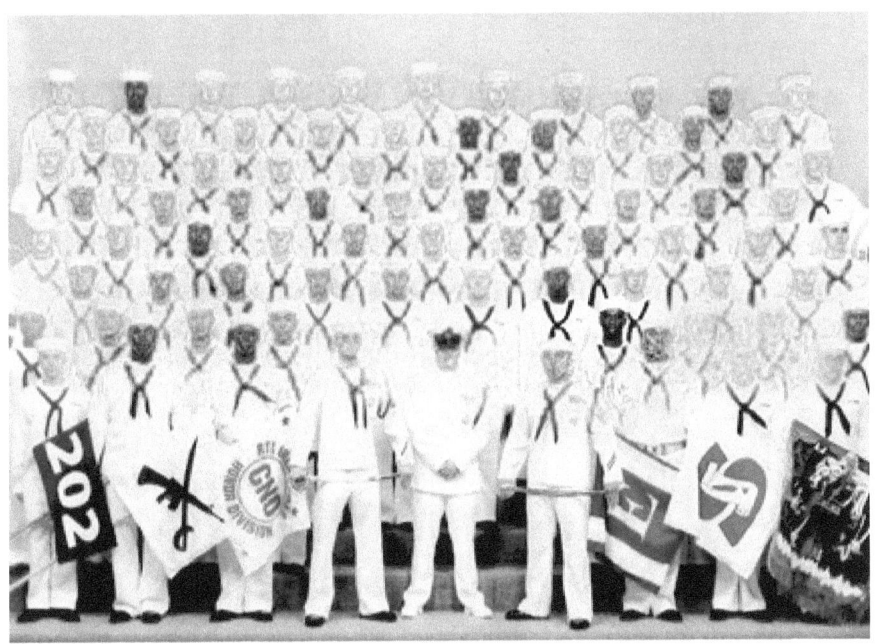

My graduating Class. Navy Boot Camp, Recruit Training Command – Great Lakes, Illinois.

Navy Boot Camp, Recruit Training Command – Great Lakes, Illinois.

Going-away celebration: Internal Medicine Nurses at the Naval Medical Center San Diego

Third-Class Petty Officer – Navy Service Dress Blue.

From Left: My mother-in-law, Tolu, and Lani, at my promotion ceremony to Second Class Petty Officer. We had also just found out our second child was going to be a boy, 2013.

Second Class Petty Officer – Navy Service Dress white.

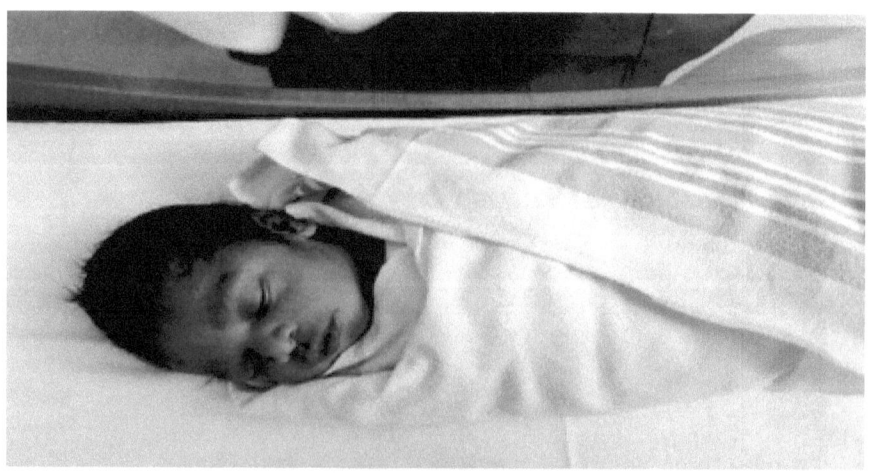

Mayowa's birth, 2013.

Mayowa's naming ceremony, 2013.

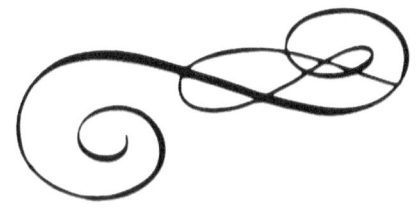

Chapter 18

MAXWELL AFB, AL: August 2014

A Different Beast.

> *Wake up from your slumber,*
> *And say no to lavished moments.*
> *Living a day as it comes*
> *Should be no man's cue.*
> *Each day is not free,*
> *Ten talents, but a hundred to reap.*
> *Wake up from your slumber,*
> *And say no to lavished moments.*

After out-processing and moving my family back to New York, I departed to Alabama for training, all in one week. All that didn't leave me enough time to gather the study materials I'd need for the first test administered to trainees at the Air Force Officer Training School. I tried to prepare for the training but didn't have time. The

Air Force Officer Training School is where the Air Force trains a few chosen college graduates from across the U.S. to become military leaders. Those who survive and excel will be commissioned by the President of the U.S. on graduation.

After arriving unprepared at the Officer Training School, I observed some of my classmates discussing a few things about the materials we had to know before showing up to training. I had no clue what they were talking about, so I asked them. They looked at me surprised, and one of them asked, "Are you here for the 15-01 class?" I replied, "yes," and immediately they all felt sorry for me. Later, one of them asked if my recruiter gave me some materials to study while waiting for training. I said he must have sent me some links to a few materials, but I didn't have the time to look at them because I had a week to get ready for this training which I spent out-processing from the Navy and relocating my family back to East Coast. Immediately, an older-looking trainee, who seemed to be prior Air Force enlisted, interjected, "You are really going to have a rough time here. It's not as easy as you think without preparation." He was right. I did underestimate Air Force training for the simple reason that I was coming from a Navy background, which I assumed was considerably more onerous than that of the Air Force. Although they are both branches of the U.S. military, what I hadn't anticipated was that they were very different in almost every way, a lesson I was about to learn the hard way.

After all the chaos of the first day of training, a lot of screaming and yelling, I realized that I was halfway lost like I hadn't been in military training before. Not that everything about the beginning phase of the training was tough, I hated being clueless in whatever I was doing.

After a few days, we took our first written test, and I failed the initial forty-question examination on Air Force culture. At first, it was hard to believe I'd just failed a test, but then it showed that I was far from prepared for this training. What made my predicament worrisome was that most students passed this test—a red flag to instructors, as it showed that I didn't know the most basic things about the branch I was entering. I worried about the first impression I'd made. Then I straightened up and considered what my father would advise me to do: take control. That night, I began to spend more time reading through the materials. A few days later, I tested again and passed.

Out of the eighty-six trainees in my Air Force Officer Training School Class, I might have been the oldest, but I hid it well. I was undeniably in better shape than most that I trained with, so I was able to blend in.

When it came to my skin, however, it was different.

I was the only person of color in my training squadron and the only student selected for nuclear and missile operations. There was no way to hide my skin color and my accent when I opened my mouth to speak, and it appeared to make me look very different from the other trainees.

Because of this, I knew all eyes would be on me. As training got underway, I felt a greater pressure to perform exceptionally well.

Air Force was nothing like the Navy. The culture, structure, and tradition were completely different, and the training was nothing like the eight-week Navy boot camp that I had attended three years before. The Officer Training School was designed to build leaders that would lead the Air Force through wars, and I was determined to learn that as fast as I could. I'd be kicked out of training otherwise.

The first thing I noticed was that the Air Force jargon was utterly different. Formation, marching, and salutation were also completely different from how I had been trained in the Navy. It was initially shocking to me because I realized I didn't only have to re-learn basic customs and courtesies, I also had to find a way to rid myself of what I had been used to as a sailor.

Although the prior Air Force enlisted members seemed to catch on fast, I was sure those who came in from the civilian world were better off than I was. After all, this is their first introduction to the military. What they learned here was all they knew so far, so they only had to learn - not unlearn and relearn as I did.

Many of the prior Air Force enlisted deduced that I must have been in the military after they saw my Navy ID card on my armband. They were curious to know how I managed to commission into the Air Force from the Navy while still on active-duty status. My unique background and commissioning route were a first for them as well, and I worried that I couldn't live up to their high expectations.

I felt like I hadn't earned anyone's respect since I showed up to training, and I was deeply disappointed with myself. Now that I failed the very first test, I felt like I had lost all of it altogether. I wasn't sure what their perception of me was, and I cared about it for the wrong reasons: I thought I was letting the Navy pride down.

When training started, the entire class would have to march everywhere we had to go. Following lunch at the galley, someone needed to march the entire wing of students back to the hostel. However, no one wanted to lead an entire class of eighty-six students and look a mess, so the instructors and the high-ranking officers watched patiently, waiting to see who would volunteer to take on the task. No one did.

One of the instructors stepped out and requested in a very firm yell, "Who will lead the wing?" I knew: *This is my opportunity.* With my heart pounding in my throat, I stepped out without overthinking it. I felt worked-up, under pressure, and hyper-aware as I could almost hear the rest of the wing asking themselves, *How's he going to do it?* It kept me on my feet. I knew nobody was perfect... but I had to come damn close. It was my only option.

The training commander walked up to me as I stood at attention, ready to lead a wing of eighty-six students. He glimpsed at my Navy ID on my arm band, which I still carried around since I was prior enlisted as well, but from the Navy. Then he confirmed, "You were a Navy corpsman?"

"Yes sir!" I responded. For some reason, I sensed his respect and admiration after he knew I was a Navy corpsman.

"Carry on!" he yelled.

I led a wing of students on parade across the base while all the high-ranking officers looked on. You don't get a lot of chances to make a good impression in the military, and you almost never get a chance to recover from having made a bad one. A good impression could go a long way, especially with my rocky start. With this move, I'd not completely redeemed myself, but I'd managed to put myself in a much better place. Now I had to succeed.

A few things I thought worked in my favor. They knew how much boldness it took to lead a wing of trainees in the first week since most students didn't have much clue what was required of them. Everyone got yelled at. Now they knew my name, and they figured I was an African immigrant because of my accent. They didn't get that every day, I could tell. Some of them weren't exactly sure how to relate to me. Stepping out to lead that parade was a major turnaround for me personally, and I absolutely intended to capitalize on all that was working for me to become better in training.

While trying to make amends for failing my test, I did not only study harder; I memorized everything about the Air Force that came my way. I wasn't going to make the same mistake twice, not during this training. I made friends with one of the oldest and most matured prior Air Force enlisted. He explained and showed me a few things about the Air Force I needed to know to succeed, but most importantly, he warned me that I needed to seize an opportunity to display my leadership prowess, especially now that most students were still trying to figure their place in the mess we were all in.

After the first couple of weeks, I was relieved when we were all learning together and working as a team. Each of us tried to survive and help each other hang in there, and it became a symbol of our bond to poke fun at each other when one of us messed up. Once I hit my stride in the Officer Training School, it was obvious that there was nothing different between any of us.

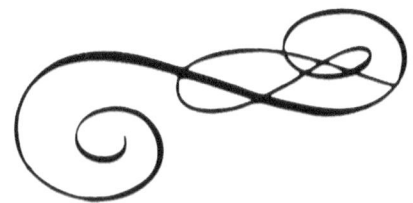

Chapter 19

MAXWELL AFB, AL: September 2014

The Sergeant Who Yelled.

D espite having prior military experience, I found myself in the same boat as my roommate.

My first roommate had been a college graduate for a few years before joining the military. He was brilliant, and he knew most of the academic portion of the training by heart. He told me he'd been studying for over a year while waiting for his training date.

I remember our first day together. He asked me questions which I had no idea how to answer. He reached into his bag and gave me a few copies of materials I should have studied before showing up to training, which saved me time and again as it turned out there was much more required of me academically than I had expected.

However, he had difficulty with day-to-day hands-on demands and military commands. Whenever the pressure mounted on, he got flustered, and that often didn't only land him in trouble, but me as

331

well. Since we were roommates, it was our duty to figure out how to help each other overcome our weaknesses. I had to learn much of that the hard way in the Navy, so knowing we could support each other through our respective weak points. I helped him train to get in shape and practice the commands until he caught on, and he helped me memorize the things I should have.

When I came to the U.S., I realized how individualistic Americans are. It is an essential part of the culture that is utterly different from Nigeria, where the society is more communal. The military is right in the middle. Somehow, they figure any group of the military is only as strong as its weakest link. This idea seemed to be the basis of all my military training, from the Navy to the Air Force.

Irrespective of the number of trainees in the same class, we were all responsible for each other, which trickles down from the wing level to the squadron, to the flight level, and all the way to the hostel where you share a room with someone else. One member's failure was the failure of every other trainee, although there were some outliers. Eventually, we all figured out that it was easier to progress if everyone else was doing well. The prior Air Force enlisted members were more experienced, and thanks to them, they worked hard with all the newbies to the Air Force, showing us the ropes and how the Air Force was a very different place with a very different culture.

As sailors, the Navy took pride in our ways of doing things. We marched and saluted differently from the Air Force. Our military jargons were different, and our customs and courtesies were much older and much more enforced across all chains of command. Thinking the Navy way in an Air Force setting was a bad idea, and I'd learned that the hard way.

It took me longer than it should to understand the fact that I was now in an Air Force training environment. Sometimes,

I thought I did and figured it out as the training commenced. However, I didn't quite accept the new rules quickly enough. It is one thing to think you are doing something right, but it is another actually to do it right.

This world seems familiar,
Like I lived this life before now.
I've been here before, my heart tells me—
Maybe that's why I know where I want to be and where I don't.
I try to run far from what I thought I once knew—
Things that I dread and things I don't.
Even so, I try to run closer to my dreams;
I think they are a better path to my redemption,
The condition for which I have been given another life.
There's someone somewhere that I owe my existence,
For many tried to destroy but can't.

The instructors could not help but notice as I re-learned everything, from adapting to new commands to folding my shirts, underwear, and socks. They yelled until they were red in the face while I struggled to replace my Navy ways with the Air Force.

One training day, when I was eating at the dining facility, often referred to as DFAC in the Air Force, one of the MTIs yelled in one of the loudest voices I'd ever heard.

"Hey, you!" came the loud voice from behind me.

It was distant, so I didn't think it would have been for anyone on my table.

Four trainees were eating at each table. The two students sitting across from me froze like they were about to watch someone die right in front of them. I stared at their frozen faces with a mouth full of food. We weren't allowed to look sideways or behind us while eating, so I froze too, praying the yelling wasn't for me.

The yelling continued, "Hey you! I'm talking to you!"

The two sitting across from me had stopped chewing their food to stare at me. I stared back at them, wishing that I could just swallow the food in my mouth and asked if that was for me. I could see it in their eyes, though: *You're about to die.* The more that yelling continued, the louder it got as he came closer to where I sat. The instructor sounded like he wanted to be acknowledged, but I knew it was a trap.

Finally, the voice was right behind my head. I could feel it. Then, very deliberately, he moved even closer and yelled into my left ear, "Look into my eyes!"

With a mouthful of food, I turned my head slowly sideways until our eyes met.

"Fix yourself!" he yelled again.

I adjusted my back forward and away from the back of the chair, where I had leaned back a bit without knowing. All the noise was for that simple reason. Two days later, during our funny stories session, my tablemates came to get me in my room to share what had happened, and we laughed until our stomachs hurt.

The truth was this was nothing compared to the countless yelling and punishments in my father's house. From my Navy boot camp days, I knew I was born ready for the military. Of course, the MTI would keep an eye on me in the subsequent weeks every time we sat to eat in the galley. But I wasn't going to make the same mistake twice.

Halfway through Officer Training School, I figured out a way to excel in every aspect of the mentally, physically, and emotionally demanding ten-week training program. I got a new roommate who was prior Air Force enlisted and had more experience than all the civilian newbies and me. I studied his ways and asked him for advice, and he was generous in what he shared.

I had many flaws as a sailor and an airman, but the military had been a journey not only for training but for learning whom and how to trust. By the seventh to eighth week of training, I was given the call sign "Doc," but they usually referred to me as "The Beast." Although I was the oldest in the entire class, I was also one of the fittest. I excelled in both academics and physical fitness, and finally felt ready, until my body brought everything to a screeching halt.

During one of the final tests, pain started to radiate to the rest of my body with each stride. I was only halfway through my run, but the tingling, numbing, and dizziness followed. The signs were familiar. I had felt them before while in the Navy, not once but twice. Both times, I ended up in the ER.

The second time I ended up in the Navy Medical Center San Diego ER while in the Navy, a commander walked into the room where I had been connected to several monitoring devices, and an intravenous infusion. He asked if I understood what had happened to me.

"Not really," I replied to the commander, who was also the ER doctor in charge.

"I just read your record. This is the second time you will end up here for rhabdomyolysis."

"Rhabdomyolysis?"

Although I knew what it was, I was still surprised to hear it, considering how close I was to dying from it the first time.

"Yes, you had it less than two years ago, and it was severe. Your kidney almost failed, but it came back around," he reminded me, but he sounded frustrated.

"Look," he continued. "I gotta tell you, if you ever come back here for the same issue, I will have to put you up for the med board. You don't seem to know how to stop. The third time might kill you! I know you feel like you're nineteen, but you're thirty-three. You have to start listening to your body."

This time I knew he was really angry with me. It was not uncommon for him to deal with people like me in the Navy and the Marines. Sometimes they have to be hard on us, even in the ER, just to get us to listen to them.

"Aye, aye, commander," I replied. He took another look at me.

"I'm glad you stopped this time, but don't let this happen to you again."

"I won't, sir."

The first time, I didn't stop. I felt weak and numb, muscles cramping, but I kept running. The dizziness set in, and the next thing I remember was the EMT paramedics struggling to find a vein to insert the IV.

I had passed out. I could hear my friends yelling my name to get me to say something, but I couldn't. When they wheeled me into the ambulance, I was able to speak, but my words were sloppy. Later, when I woke up in the ER, I noticed that a central line had been placed in my femoral vein because I had gone into shock. I looked at my legs, and they were both severely swollen. I couldn't walk on both legs.

Later, the doctors came in and confirmed that I had rhabdo, which was a short form for rhabdomyolysis. The term simply implied "breakdown of skeletal muscle due to injury to the muscle."

The risk with it was that the breakdown of muscle caused a lot of toxins to be released into my blood, too much for my kidney to get rid of. As a result, some people with rhabdo die from acute kidney failure. They had told me how lucky I was to have come back. Ever since my second rhabdo, I had tried to readjust how I trained. I hydrated as much as I could and rested well just before my physical fitness tests. But when the symptoms began halfway through my last run at the Air Force Officer Training School, I knew that was what it was.

I couldn't figure what could have caused it - I had taken every measure to avoid it. I didn't want to end up in the ER ever again, and I worried about how it was going to end for me if I didn't stop running. I heard my Navy doctor's words echoing in my head, telling me to stop and listen to my body. Still, I pushed, remembering that barefoot boy running through the Nigerian night's bush path with fireflies cupped inside his palms.

If I wanted to graduate with my class, I had to finish the race. Same as it was for that little boy, this was about strength and survival. So, I slowed down my pace instead of stopping. My body went numb. I couldn't breathe. Dizziness set in. I wasn't sure if I could make it to the finish line, but I could hear my classmates that were in the first batch of runners chanting, *Doc! Doc! Doc! Doc!* as the finish line came into my view.

I could barely walk afterward. My flight-mates came over to see how I was doing.

"Are you okay? You can't sit down after a run. You know you have to walk around," one of them said.

"I can't. My legs are cramping so bad," I responded, still struggling to catch my breath. I was still very dizzy but didn't say it. I didn't want anyone to know.

One of the instructors came around and asked if I wanted to go to the ER. I refused. While still sitting on the grass, the pain became worse, and one of my classmates with EMT experience asked my roommate to help him walk me back to the hostel. I could no longer stand on both of my feet which would last over an hour following the race.

As my classmates supported me on their shoulders, the EMT asked my roommate, "Did he finish the run, though?"

"What?" my roommate asked, grinning. "He's a beast. He is dying, but he still ran a ten- minute mile and a half.

My roommate then looked at me and said, "You're crazy, you know that, doc?"

I could barely laugh because I was in so much pain, but I smiled anyway.

Later, when I showed up to class, my instructors asked me how long I had been in pain during my last run. I told them it began halfway through the race. They looked at one another, and one of them said, "Good on you. That must have been really hard. You were the clear favorite before the race began."

On the last week of training, I reported to my primary instructors who were both Air Force officers, for my last briefing and feedback before graduation.

"How do you think you performed in this training?" They both asked. After looking at both of them in the eye, disappointment written over my face, I replied, "I think I could have done so much better if I had prepared for this training the way I should have." I continued, "I think I performed okay,"

They looked at each other and almost said in unison, "We disagree, what we are thinking is quite different!" They said. As I wondered what that was, they continued, if there's any student we have learnt from the most, that is you." Surprised, I wanted to know how.

"Amongst a lot of things that we learned from you in the past ten weeks, two things that all the instructors are unanimous about are: one, you never made the same mistake twice. From the beginning of your training, you picked yourself back up like a pro every time you fumbled, and never repeated the same mistake again." The first instructor explained. It never occurred to me I had been that way.

The second instructor continued, "Second, you think very differently from everyone else here. During the class and field exercises, we couldn't help but look forward to what you would say or do next, knowing the rest of the students and even the instructors, tend to approach the exercises with similar solutions."

I was surprised to hear him say that considering how I often thought my rationale didn't make sense to them sometimes while I attempted to articulate my responses to case studies in class. That was because, my points of view was often followed with silence and it was difficult for me to interpret how they had received it, including my classmates.

"Sometimes, we come back to the office, and between each other wondered how on earth you just came up with something like that in seconds. We know that you are older, more mature, and experienced, and this is especially why the Air Force stands to benefit tremendously from someone like you." The second instructor added. "The silence you often noticed in class after you contribute to case studies or respond to a question was because of how surprised we were. Even your classmates feel the same way."

This was when it made sense to me when my classmates once asked me during our nightly funny sessions, "how do you come up with your responses in class?" One of them once said, "I couldn't rationalize issues the way you do or come up with your recommendations even if I tried to, irrespective of how much time we are given to solve a task." It all began to make sense to me.

On the day of graduation, Tolu and the kids traveled down to Alabama for my graduation ceremony, my son was barely a year old and my daughter had just turned four a week before. During my oath ceremony, it was my wife who would pin on my new officer rank.

As I march through the windy marine
Way in the middle of the desert,
I see many faces made by the gentle washing of the rain.
It makes you wonder: where did they all go?
All I see are broken tracks and contours
Of what's left of the rock and clay:
Red, brown, and green.
Life couldn't be more complicated than the world below me,
But that's what makes it all beautiful.

Air Force Officer Training School.

Air Force Officer Training School – Pre-graduation dinner.

Air Force Officer Training School – Pre-graduation dinner.

Tolu pinning my officer rank during my officer training school graduation

PART 4:

Nuclear Missiles Operator

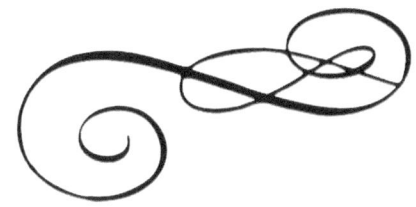

Chapter 20

VANDENBERG AFB, CA: October 2014
A "Doc" in Nuke "Tech" School.

The closer I got to the Lompoc military base, the less it looked like California. Lompoc was very unlike San Diego, mostly rural with farms. It wasn't nearly as bright or colorful as I was used to; there was practically nothing there.

It made sense. For a place where some of the country's most classified training and operations took place, it was smart to have such a small local population. As I drove into the base in my Air Force uniform for the first time, the gate security checked my ID and saluted me almost immediately. I acknowledged him but didn't salute back, so he saluted me for the second time. *Something's a little off,* I thought.

In the Navy, you can salute an uncovered officer provided you are covered, but they can only salute back if they are also covered. Otherwise, they would acknowledge you by responding or nodding. I hesitantly returned the salute before I drove into the base. Eventually,

I learned that in the Air Force, I had to respond irrespective of having a cover on or not.

I drove straight to the Air Force lodge, checked in, and rested for the rest of the day. The following day, I showed up at the training squadron office. They were expecting me and very much curious about what I looked like based on the unfamiliar name forwarded to them.

I couldn't help but get a kick out of the looks of surprise from almost every nuke officer I met. They heard my accent. They had never met an African immigrant in nuclear and missile operations. I'd imagine they wondered how someone like me got selected for a role such as this in the U.S. military.

Most of them were skeptical when they found out about my African background and my age. It wasn't the first time that had happened to me, as I looked much younger than my age. I'd have to show two ID cards to prove my age on several occasions.

I needed time to head out to town and search for accommodation for my family before they moved down to Lompoc to join me. The senior squadron officers suggested an apartment complex in town, and in less than two weeks, I set up our new two-bedroom apartment for Tolu and the kids.

I would soon begin training to become a nuclear missile operator—a highly classified training for select few officers in charge of the world's deadliest weapon. The training was going to last six months. I was excited, ready, and looked forward to it.

To whom is will safer?
Definitely not with us!
To whom much is given,
So little they have given back.

Music never dies,
As long as they are played.
Songs only have meanings
When they are written in words.

What gift could be greater?
To choose between good or bad,
Humanity or barbarism,
Morals or sin,
God or devil,
Love or hate,
To forgive or avenge,
To hope or to despair?

As I waited for my class to resume, I received a call from the training squadron office. When I arrived there, the two officers coordinating training for new officers took a long look at me. They seemed to have received surprising news about me, and I was more than a little worried about what that might be.

After an agonizing silence, one of them finally said, "You're a veterinarian?"

I took a deep sigh of relief and smiled.

"Yes, I am."

They had both pulled my record and were looking at it while I stood there just watching the shock on their faces. The initial skepticism about me was gone.

The female officer, a captain, looked at me and asked, "So what are you doing here? You are a doctor."

"Don't know. A special duty, I guess. This is what the Air Force wants me to do for now," I explained as casually as I could.

"We just received a call to send you down to Public Health on casual status," she said. "We will reschedule your training for the next class in three months. They said they could use your specialty over there right now."

Surprised, I replied, "Okay, Captain."

I'd only been there for two weeks. How could they have found out about me already? Vandenberg AFB was such a massive base with thousands of military members.

After showing up at Public Health, I met the flight commander. She was a captain as well. I took a look around, and I finally understood what was going on.

The U.S. military was fighting the Ebola outbreak in Africa. Given my medical background, Public Health wanted me to help with Ebola research and training to prepare our troops to assist in Africa before they were deployed. I felt right at home almost instantaneously. I was excited about the opportunity to use my medical skills, even if it were for a short time.

After a few weeks, the public health flight commander asked if I had a few minutes to talk. "I was going through your profile in addition to the work you have done here so far, and wanted to ask if you're interested in moving to public health permanently." She asked.

"I am open to the opportunity," I replied, "But I'm not sure if it's possible while I'm technically in training for another job."

If there was anything that I had come to understand about my life at that point, it was that if there were a path for me there, it would work out. If not, it wouldn't, but I would never shut the door to any opportunity. *What will be, will be.*

"I will talk to my commander and have him talk to your commander; maybe there's something they can do." The flight commander said. With that, I was dismissed.

Three days later, I received a call from my training squadron office. The squadron commander wanted to talk to me. When I arrived at his office, sitting behind a large, beautifully decorated brown desk, he invited me to sit across from him and went straight to the point.

"I received a call from public health," he said. "They are interested in you." He must have been in his early forties but looked much younger. He sounded friendly but professional.

"I agree with them. I think you will be a great win for public health if we could get you over there, so we don't put your years of experience to waste or have you start over a new career," the commander said. I nodded at him to continue. He then asked the same question the public health flight commander had asked me: "Are you interested?"

I replied with the same answer: I was open to that opportunity, but not sure which paperwork I needed to do. At that point, I was more interested in going where the Air Force needed me than trying to be in a set job or position. I was happy with the idea of alternatives and curious how it would all play out. *There will be no disappointments here,* I thought to myself.

"Good," he said. "Public Health is looking at the options to get you transferred permanently."

I nodded again, trying my best to hide my surprise at the quick progression.

"We will do whatever we need to do from our end. I want you to know that I will support you in any way I need to, even if that requires a letter or any form I need to sign," my training squadron commander said. I was amazed by the kindness of my commander.

Though I was relatively new to his squadron, he wanted the best for me. I thanked him and left, grateful to have people like him looking out for me.

About a week later, Public Health had all the information they needed to initiate the process. However, they were told that the nuclear career field manager, located in Air Force Personnel Center in San Antonio, TX, would have to release me to compete in public health. That meant he would have to sign a form that guaranteed my release from the nuclear career field should Public Health select me. I reached out to my career field manager to discuss our intentions, but he rejected the request.

"The only way I can release you from this field is if you're unable to successfully complete your training,' he said. "Either through failure to pass all required tests and exams, or through medical disqualification."

Public Health was disappointed, my training commander wished he could do something about it, but it wasn't his call. To be honest, I was somewhat indifferent to the issue.

We were in the military to serve, and we went where we were needed. Very few officers practiced within the field they studied in college. I thought it was a rare opportunity to become a missileer given my background. If I passed all exams in the coming months, I might be the first African immigrant to make it to such a highly classified position.

While on my casual status in Public Health, I reflected on the philosophical difference between researching viruses and my work as a nuclear missile operator. While I would eventually operate the deadliest weapon ever made by man to stop us from killing each other, for the time being, I was trying to prevent an infectious organism from killing us.

The ultimate goal between the two felt the same: to prevent people from dying. That was, and always would be, the most important thing to me.

Public Health eventually encouraged me to consider them if my nuclear training didn't work out, but I knew the only way that would happen was with a medical disqualification. I would never jeopardize my integrity to get what I wanted, even if it was an assignment I was so well suited for.

As nuclear training approached, I did a little studying on the topic. It was so simple, yet so complex: the existence of nuclear weapons could either wipe us out completely from the surface of the earth or, as it was meant to do, it could continue to prevent us from wars of mutually assured destruction.

We didn't have these weapons because we wanted to use them. We had them to prevent others that have them from using them. We had them in case we *had to* use them.

I believe in the originality of man,
The vision of a far desert covering the sky,
The mystery of where the source of the ocean might be.
I can spend the rest of my life trying to understand nature.

I believe in preference,
Not by choice,
But by a force that could never be explained;
To choose to open a door
Rather than the other in a silent room.

I believe in the spirit,
And things it could probably wish for after death.
I believe in the discontentment of man,
'Cause, that's why we are so damn good at our gifts.

I believe in moderation,
'Cause the greatest sorrow comes from
Things we desire the most.

I believe in things we cannot change,
Even when we're closest to the edge of the sky.
The need to understand——
There is a greater force we will never comprehend!
My life can't explain itself,
But I have my dreams to hold on to.

There will never be such a thing as
"The greatest writer of all time."
Like we are not the same,
Words don't come out the same.

I don't believe in body language readers,
It's like trying to understand the heart
And the mind of all men at the same time.
Still, a gift is a gift.

There's no such thing as perfect Love,
But you can live your life for Love.
Children will continue to be innocent,
And more than always,
Will grow up to make good or bad examples.

I believe in technology;
It's changing the world.
Merely the users,
Seem like mini-gods.

I believe in traveling the world,
What could be a better way to express
The freedom of our mind,
And see with your eyes
How much of nature is at our disposal?

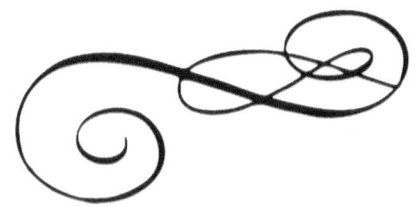

Chapter 21

VANDENBERG AFB, CA: January 2015
The Validator with an Accent.

After three months in Public Health, I finally reported to the Nuclear and Missile Operations tech school to commence training.

Before my first day in class, I had received a notification on where to report. I met my classmates—ten men and one woman from diverse races and backgrounds. After introducing ourselves, I discovered we were from various parts of the country. Our primary instructor walked in. He had a "weapon school graduate" patch on, so we knew he was a "whiskey"- an Air Force officer who had successfully completed the rigorous weapon school training.

"Welcome to class 1502", the young whiskey said. He asked us to introduce ourselves and where we came from.

Everyone noticed the shock on his face when I introduced myself and where I came from. He didn't ask me any additional questions, composed himself, and continued his introduction to the class.

"This class will be in two parts," he said. "The first half will be unclassified, which will be here in this class. The second half will be classified in a different part of the building." He pointed in the direction of the first floor of the building. "You will receive your flight suits in the next couple of weeks, but you will start your training rides before then," he said, sensing the confusion in the room and immediately taking questions before proceeding with a summary of what the training entailed.

As he spoke, I knew I'd have to devise a new strategy if I intended to succeed. *This is going to require a different approach from what I'm used to,* I thought. I had just learned about the Air Force. Now I need to understand the nuke community, which had never seen someone of my background. I knew I'd have to make some adjustments. For instance, I had to quickly learn to speak slower and clearer, briefly but concisely - just enough for them to clearly understand me, but not too much to completely mask my identity or accent.

"In weapon school, we had to earn our call signs," the whiskey said. "You will all get a call sign which is what I will be calling you throughout the length of the training."

After learning all the training rules, my classmates and I were granted access to classified training. The first half of the training was done in an unclassified environment. In this training phase, we learned the more mechanical side of the job: the weapon system, how the nuclear missile works, and maintenance as technicians.

At first, the training rigor was nothing compared to veterinary school. However, as we got further into classwork and practical simulations, as well as the unclassified instructions, this process became more intense than anything I'd experienced before in a unique way, largely due to the sensitive nature of the job. Most of my Navy training focused on medicine, physical fitness, and combat.

We learned how to pass information and give orders to the dispatcher. We learned to monitor *everything*. If a part of the missile broke, or if there was a fire, we learned how to detect that from where we were. If someone broke into the launch facilities—even if a rabbit ran across the missile field—we could see that, and we'd have to call it. Every missile alert facility was in charge of ten nuclear weapons spread across different state lines.

When the whiskey finally gave us our call signs, I got "Doc." I liked it - it was familiar, and had been a nickname of mine for many years, so it felt right.

The second half of the training was the more security-heavy classified part, where we learned how to engage with other countries, each other, and our government regarding our missiles. Everything was communicated through a series of letters and digits.

The repercussions for passing classifieds or taking our personal electronic devices into classified areas were grave. I had to be extremely careful. It was like nothing I'd ever done in my life, especially with the caliber of military folks and their very high level of clearance, dealing day-to-day with national security issues that I couldn't even discuss with my wife. Given my journey from Nigeria, I felt like one in a million to have such an opportunity.

One of the hardest parts of the training was learning the nuclear codes.

"If you can pass the nuclear codes block of this training, you have probably passed the hardest part of this training," the whiskey told us at the beginning of the training. True to what the whiskey told us, it was hard for most students to comprehend at first, but it came to me naturally for some reason. After class, I developed a simple breakdown of how the codes worked for my class. It was so good that the whiskey decided to adopt my work for subsequent classes.

After my instructor discovered my analytical talents and skills, he offered me a validator position for the training period, where I'd help critique the current curriculum and help develop a better one for subsequent classes. He was concerned, however, that I would struggle on the field because of my accent.

Once or twice he said, "Not because the doc is not communicating effectively out there, but I don't think there has ever been anyone like him on this job. Imagine someone receiving a call from him while in the capsule. He'll be surprising, and that will take some getting used to by the folks out there."

My classmates corrected him, saying they'd never had issues understanding me. Despite the instructor's feedback, I became the class's go-to for the weapon system. I passed all nine exams, more than thirty short tests, and the final simulation exam.

I'm not scared of the world,
But I'm fearful of time
And what its ticking hands might do to me
Before I can seize it.

Ever felt like you're ending your future,
Where it should have started?
Have you ever looked back into your past
And wondered how on earth,
You missed so much?

Only if a man knew what he was meant to be,
Only if he knew who he is,
Only if circumstances yield to his heart,
Then he would dine and dance with fate.

More often than not, though,
Many oscillate forty long years—
To reach a forty-mile path?
Whatever special forces you believe in,
Whatever your faith is in,
May it order your steps.

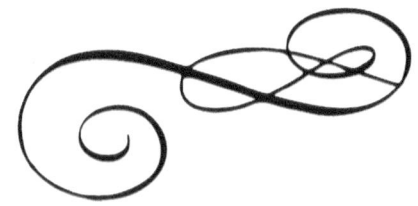

Chapter 22

VANDENBERG AFB, CA: June 2015

The Veterinary Surgeon Who Became a Nuke Officer.

After the six-month training, I graduated from a highly classified, perfection-driven, rigorous training program with nine other students. I celebrated with my family, both excited and daunted at all I would see, learn, and do when I started real operations.

The General of Air Force Global Strike Command led a ceremony where he read my story aloud and pinned on my nuclear missile badge. As he spoke, I thought about how I'd arrived on that stage, all from the promise I'd made as a child to become a doctor and come to America.

Throughout my adult life, my knowledge of medicine had given me my sense of worth and identity, and it had given everyone I knew that same perception that I could help in any situation. But that moment, I realized that my success in life wasn't defined by being a doctor. In fact, as the General pinned on my badge, I knew I might never work in medicine again.

And even though there would be many people who might see my new role as controversial or even unpopular, in my heart, I knew this was how I could do my part to save people, not just one at a time, but millions.

I stood on the podium, shaking hands with one of the highest-ranking military officials in the U.S. as he handed over my certificates. When I looked at my family before I walked back to my seat, my classmate's wife held my son, who was only a year and a half old. She and my son sat behind my wife and daughter. My daughter was now almost five years old. As Tolu clapped along with all the friends and family members of the graduates, I could see her teary eyes from where I was. I could feel how proud she was of me, even across the room. After a celebratory dinner that night, Tolu and I were cleaning up in the kitchen together. She told me it wasn't my graduation that had made her tear up, but pride.

"I had no inkling of doubt you would make it," she said. "At your graduation, I felt a lot of emotions. I couldn't help but think about what your past has done, but you have not let it stop you in any way, Deji. You left it behind but took your drive, love, and humility along with you and continue to focus on the future." Tolu stopped cleaning, held my hands, and looked into my eyes.

"If I have learned anything from you," she said, holding my hands, "it is that you know how to move forward. Though you had to start over, you find ways to move forward and take your family along." She looked at the kids and said, "Even though they are so little and probably won't remember any of what happened today, you have created a memory, a story they both need to know about when they are old enough and facing their own life challenges. The story you made today will help these kids tomorrow."

Tolu wrapped me up in a hug, smelling of dish soap. I felt her pride like it was my own, giving me the strength to keep going.

But the joy didn't last long. After graduation, I discovered I couldn't leave for my next base in Cheyenne. My newly assigned military primary care manager, an internal medicine specialist, had pulled my medical record from the Navy.

He discovered I was treated for rhabdomyolysis—the condition from exhaustion and dehydration—twice during some of my training. I wasn't ready to operate just yet: he decided to conduct further specialized testing before he gave final medical clearance for my permanent change of station.

The truth was that a job such as a nuclear missile operator was so highly specialized that you had to meet a specific minimum condition for physical and mental fitness. There was simply too much on the line not to.

My doctor put me up for the medical board, which in the military implied that they were considering that I might not be medically fit to serve at all.

I felt like I was being haunted spiritually. All my life, every time I was about to make headway and walk through another major door, there was always something there, just waiting to sabotage my efforts. By now, hadn't I made my own way in America and proven myself? Hadn't I done enough? Why was I still being followed by the family curse?

Tolu and I didn't know what to expect - we could so easily lose all that we'd worked for thus far. It was completely demoralizing. We'd have another six months before we'd know whether I'd gotten the job, but I'd never been one to sit back and wait. While I awaited the medical verdict, I helped create a history room for the training squadron, where historical mementos related to an Air Force unit would be preserved for people to visit and learn stories about that side of the Air Force.

Less than two months later, after the medical board looked through my medical records, they came to a decision.

My primary care physician gave me a call on a Monday morning.

"The medical board decided to return you to duty," he said. "We must begin your paperwork quickly to get you to your next duty station."

That moment, I understood with absolute clarity why my father said to me as a child: "Be patient in everything. If you can be a little more patient, you will achieve everything you set your heart to."

It was all I needed to assuage my worries. I promised myself to always remember to be patient whenever life started to veer off the path.

I informed Tolu about the news from the military physician.

"The med board results came back," I said, trying to contain my relief and excitement. "I am fit for nuclear duty, and we will soon be on our way to F.E. Warren Air Force base."

Tolu was excited about the news, but she didn't seem surprised. She had told me we needed not to worry about the new development because she believed it would all work out fine in the end. Whenever I asked her why she thought so, she always replied, "Because this is nothing compared to what you've been through. Besides, it always turns out great eventually." She added, "Your condition is not bad enough for the Air Force to kick you out. Disqualifying you from nuclear duties would have reopened the public health opportunity."

It finally started to sink in: this was no training or simulation. This was real. I had been entrusted by the President of the United States, the leaders of our military, and most importantly, the people of the United States to defend this country with my life.

The safety and future of the world rested in my hands.

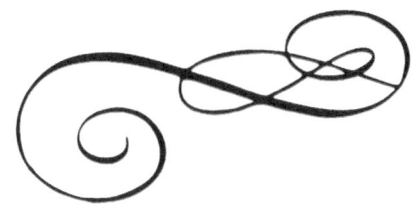

Chapter 23

F.E. WARREN AFB, WY: October 2015

The Deputy and His Commander.

As soon as I walked into my squadron's emerald green reception area, I saw Crotchet, my commander. He was standing behind one of the two computers, perched precariously on two old, worn-brown tables. He pointed into a tiny room filled with several large black cases.

"Take the case to Mike," he ordered.

Crotchet was the nuclear missile combat crew commander (MCCC), and I had just become his deputy (DMCCC). This was my first alert - how we referred to our job as nuclear missile combat crew members on a mission in an underground capsule.

As the new guy, I didn't think twice about Crochet's order. I walked past him into the small room and grabbed a solid case with *MIKE 01* embossed. It looked like a medium-sized briefcase, only with two holes at each end, meant for padlocks. On my arrival, I had been given a specific type of lock, and I'd noticed my commander had his hanging from the side of his flight suit. As I carried the case toward him, he turned and started down the hall. I followed on his heels.

He led me inside an auditorium with a massive projector screen and long glossy wooden tables on each side of the room. A few crewmembers in flight suits were already seated in pairs. Crotchet sat at the table, again with *MIKE 01* inscribed on a plaque, and the table marked *MCCC* at his place. I settled in the chair, and my side of the table was marked with a *DMCCC* sticker.

Soon the room was filled with crew members. Then the doors were shut for a classified briefing.

As eight other crew members from my squadron stopped by to congratulate me on my first alert, my commander didn't say a word. I knew this was serious business. I couldn't let him think for a second that I regarded it in any other way.

The projector came on, and the room went silent. The intel officer, sharp and concisely, announced the latest strategic updates and strategic planning for our respective missions.

Goosebumps prickled over my skin. I wasn't only going to defend the United States; I was protecting and ensuring that the entire world wouldn't collapse on itself. What amazed me most was that no one knew about us—who we were or what we were doing.

For the next thirty-two hours, the nuclear weapon system specialists directing various aspects of our mission took the floor and laid out specific mission requirements. After my commander and I verified all the relevant classified documents, we safely secured them in the big black case. He placed his padlock securely on one end of the box, and I fumbled to insert my lock into the padlock hole.

He stood over me, impatiently watching. Finally, I slipped the lock into place and tugged on it to ensure it was locked.

"Pull back on the lock and double-check it's locked securely," he ordered, although he'd just watched me test it. I tugged on the lock once again.

All five crews headed back to the squadron mission planning room for a follow-up strategy session while the leadership observed. It wasn't abnormal for us to make small talk with one another. People in this role—partner together on alert—composed a close team. Knowing a little about each other's lives was appropriate.

But Crotchet was reserved. He didn't speak to anyone else from the squadron unless one of us asked him a question. When I inquired politely about his family, he answered in short, clipped barks. I stopped asking. We settled into silence.

The squadron commander walked over to the front of the table and called me out to the front.

"Hey, Ayo," he said. "Come here."

I approached him, and he pulled my training patch off my right shoulder. Then he replaced it with a green operational alert patch featuring a skull and cross-missiles in place of the crossbones.

Now it was official. He shook my hand and congratulated me. I saluted back, and the room filled with applause. I didn't bother to hide my grin.

I grabbed the classified case, and Crotchet led the way out to the government truck that it had been my job to pick up earlier. I'd heard from other crews that the trip to Mike 01 would take up to two hours.

As with everything in the Air Force, there was strategic logic: first-alert missileers were often sent down there so they could get used to the distance. I climbed onto the driver's side and followed my commander's directions. I wasn't used to driving trucks, especially not a government truck, which is highly equipped with sensitive speed-tracking devices. I turned the ignition and poked along like a ninety-year-old man, the weight of my commander's eyes heavy on me.

"Better safe than sorry, right?" I said. "I have to get used to these trucks. I'm not a truck kinda guy."

If he smiled, it was faint. Then he said, "I'd prefer if you took your time."

As we exited the F.E. Warren Air Force Base gate, I grew aware of the nervous flutter inside me. In a few hours, I would be in charge of ten live nuclear weapons capable of annihilating millions of lives.

As we rode past the Wyoming highways to the unpaved back roads of Colorado, I thought of Ejigbo, where I'd grown up in Nigeria. The tall grasses, the field that spread across the horizon, and the deer that never stopped grazing on them. Tiny brown birds flew low along the road. Prairie dogs burrowed in and out of the small dry tracks on the farmlands. I had heard that there were so many of them that the farmers would pay the locals to hunt them.

Cheyenne is like a poem
Begging to be read.
She forces you under the blanket
With a paper and pen
As you try to comprehend the heart of the Midwest.

In the middle of May
Before the shoveling begins in the driveway,
You watch the snowflakes
As they fall on and around the new babes
Riding in the toboggan for the first time in the incline way.

Staring outside your window,
You wonder how beautiful the tree branches caught the snow,

And it's hard to put into words what the white earth holds.
It is a lovely thing to behold
When white Cheyenne in May glows.

After driving almost two hours, Crotchet showed me where to pull up—a few meters from the highly secured alert facility gate, which also had the inscription MIKE 01 on a signboard. There, there were two cream-colored buildings.

They were smaller than I'd expected, barely noticeable to anyone who might drive past. He radioed the security head, notifying him that we'd just pulled up on the access road.

I drove slowly inside, my nervousness replaced with calm as I paid close attention to everything happening around me. I'd trained rigorously for six months for this, but facing it now felt surreal.

The head of security double-checked our identities and gave us his reports. I understood a few things he talked about, but everything seemed to make more sense to Crotchet. As they spoke, the magnitude of the responsibility I was taking on sank in. I'd been trained to perfect my job as a U.S. nuclear weapon officer, utterly responsible for everything in my flight area, which included the missile alert facility we had just arrived at, the ten launch facilities where the nuclear weapons were deployed regardless of the locations, as well as the security forces protecting us and the weapons.

The elevator, which I'd only ever heard about in training, reminded me of lifts I'd seen in classic American movies as a boy in Nigeria. The front wall was graffitied with the names, signatures, and dates of services of airmen that had completed their tours there. As we traveled seventy feet below, my heart began to race.

But as I walked into the capsule, friendly faces welcomed me. Both commander and deputy stood up from the console chairs and shook my hand.

I thought as I looked around, it *can't be that bad. They've been on duty for over thirty hours, but they genuinely seem okay.*

I didn't notice much difference between my training and what I was now doing. The huge communication systems, the console from which we received messages, and the alarms should anything go wrong were all familiar.

I noted the out-going crew must have been familiar with my commander's personality, as they attempted to cheer up the atmosphere by sharing jokes. Crotchet remained laser-focused as he called me closer to show me how the changeover process worked. As the final portion of the changeover began, the out-going crew grew quieter, more serious, and laser-focused, just like my commander. They unlocked their padlocks from an immovable, impenetrable metal box where top-secret codes we used to verify launch orders were secured in the capsule.

I would never know my commander's padlock codes, and he would never know mine. For either of us to have access to the container, it will require both of us.

The out-going crew grabbed the briefcase, now empty, and said almost simultaneously, "Have a great alert, Ayo."

I certainly hope so, I thought. I was more than prepared to defend this country, but on my first official day on the job, I wasn't quite ready to experience an alert that was less than great.

I replied, trying to hide my nerves, "Thanks, guys."

After the massive blast doors were shut, the commander went off to bed in a tiny space we referred to as "the bed-mod" to rest before the night shift. And then, just like that, I was alone with the alarms, and capsule engine sounds… and also with my fear.

Anytime an alarm sounded, the reason could range from a minor, easily fixable electrical fault within the capsule to a security situation that would require a lethal security response. I glanced around, taking it all in. While the capsule was quiet, I thought about my family and friends.

Not all of them would understand my decision. I knew it would be disturbing to them to know that I had the keys to obliterating millions of lives. Only my wife fully understood how much I believed in the deterrent power of these missiles. I was certain that by sitting inside that capsule, ready to follow the orders of our president, I was helping to keep the world safe.

That morning when I'd kissed my children goodbye, I wondered what kind of example I was setting for them. *I am doing this for you,* I thought as I kissed each of them. *I am keeping the world safe for you.*

I spent most of my childhood wishing, praying, and fighting to be free from all the sadness and injustice around me. I fought to achieve that freedom to a great extent, not just for me but for my family. It was only natural for me to acknowledge the cost of this freedom. And for me, the cost was being down here - and understanding that the world might be a little safer because of it.

For three nights,
It's been a full moon.
For three days,
It's been so cold.
And in all these moments,
It's been so gloomy.

The thoughts of the silence in my life,
Every night without light,

And my past in my mind,
All begging to be unleashed
By the unburdened quill in my tote
That burns in my heart.
It is time.

An alarm sounded. I noticed the yellow banner on the visual display unit, which appeared similar to a computer monitor but much older. There were four of them: two on the commander side and two on the deputy side, attached to the right and left sides of the console. We can tell the severity of a situation just by the color of an alarm on the screen.

I prayed that nothing went wrong that I couldn't handle. As I fetched my technical data to figure out what troubleshooting actions were required, a call came over the phone. It was the mission lead.

"You know what that is, right?" he asked me.

"Yes, I do. I'm checking my technical data right now."

"Okay. This is a tricky one. That's why I called. It gets new deputies all the time. Make sure you read the warnings and notes after step five, and you'll be fine."

"Copy," I said. "Thanks so much, boss!"

Alone in my chair, I heard myself sigh in relief.

Missileers were damn great at watching each other's backs. If there was anything that anyone learned first in the military, it was the fact that we worked as one. That was the only way we could succeed.

As soon as I started going out on alert, I quickly learned that it wasn't uncommon for a more experienced crew member to come up on the phone when an unusual alarm popped up from a capsule monitored by a new crew member.

After Crotchet woke up to change over with me, he seemed surprised when I briefed him on what had happened.

"That's good," he said while he looked at the screen on the commander's side to verify my actions. "Most new deputies need help to get the actions right the first time."

"I did get help," I said. "Boss called right after it popped up."

"Good! I'll wake you up in the morning," he said, walking toward the restroom.

Following my first alert, I was sure that Crotchet might be quite rude and unfriendly, but he was, without a doubt, good at his job. Two weeks after we started pulling alerts together, he was required to give me official feedback.

When he asked me how I felt about my performance and knowledge on the job, I replied, "I think I'm okay."

He looked me in the eye and said, "I disagree."

I felt my insides drop.

"Your weapon system and emergency war order knowledge are far advanced for a new deputy," he continued. "And you are exceptionally calm, even when things start to go crazy. It takes a lot of experience to be able to do something like that."

I suddenly felt my heart swell. "Thank you," I said sincerely, confused but proud to hear praise like that from Crotchet.

In those first six months, I would learn a lot. I was the oldest amongst the line crew members, but many of them had more experience than I did on the field, and each of them made me a much better missileer. I observed my colleagues in the squadron and found at least one quality in each of them to which I could always connect.

Crotchet may not have been the easiest to talk to, but he was excellent to learn from. Others were so friendly, they made the most difficult tasks seem easier than they really were. Some impressed me with how their leadership showed how much they cared for others. No matter where we came from, there was a profound honor, respect, and commitment for each other and, most of all, for the nation we served.

Our position demanded a standard of perfection, which bound us closely. This was one of the many things I learned in that first year on the job. The capsule was a place that allowed my colleagues and me to bring life into sharp focus—to recapture where you came from, where you are, and where you were going. Most importantly, though, to listen to someone else from someplace else, and figure out how to build a lasting friendship.

Because when the time would come to go to war, both of you would probably never get the chance to hear the voices of your loved ones just one more time. We only had each other down there.

It wasn't long before I was no longer the new guy on the job.

After my first six months, I was sent out with a new commander, Lax. After the changeover, I took the day shift, and he went off to bed. When he woke up around 6:00 p.m. to relieve himself, I noticed a limp when he walked. Two hours later, he sat at the edge of the bed, gently rubbing his right knee. I noticed him wince.

"You okay?" I asked.

"Not really," he said. "My knee is swollen."

"It sure is," I told him. "I can see it from here."

"It's weird, though. I didn't feel any pain, and it wasn't like this before I went to bed."

I noticed the bluish discoloration. "You have a history of embolism?" I asked.

I had treated a couple of blood clots like this when I served in the Navy.

"How did you know?" he asked.

"I've treated these before. I know one when I see one."

"But that was a long time ago, though, and it wasn't in my legs."

I walked straight to the phone and called the flight commander's cell. "Sir, we're gonna have to burn through the commander backup. I think Lax needs to be taken to the ER as soon as possible."

Fortunately, we were at a site only an hour and a half from the base. Less than an hour later, the flight commander called to let me know he was on his way with the backup.

While we waited, I instructed Lax to prop up his swollen leg. I also urged him to take short walks around the capsule. "I'm glad it's you that I'm down here with," he said. "At least I know you'll save me if I stop breathing."

We shared a chuckle—but if our work had taught us anything, it was that in this job, we should be ready for anything.

A year and a half into my job, the world shifted.

The path America had taken following the 2016 presidential election and what it became divided the nation. We struggled to bring sanity back to the so-called nation of liberty.

This land afforded someone like me an opportunity to live safely in freedom, but the 2016 administration's rhetoric around nuclear weapons contradicted much of what my colleagues and I believed.

The daily humdrum of the capsule may have appeared superficial, but now more than ever, everything about our job was much deeper than it seemed.

Considering all the wars in every corner of the world and unprecedented nuclear tension, we, the missileers, had to continually remind ourselves about that call from the President of the United States that we hoped would never come. It felt just like when my father demanded to see me in his final moments - that same uncertainty and dread, knowing there was nothing I could do.

Just like I prayed for a miracle during my father's last days, I prayed for peace as tensions escalated. Russia. China. South Korea.

And a new president who wasn't afraid of confrontation. When North Korea launched an intercontinental ballistic missile with the potential to reach the mainland U.S., I wondered if the worst part of my job was about to become more than just a possibility.

As the threats continued to reach a crescendo, so did my awareness of the primary reason my job existed: deterrence. Now we had shifted to the possibility of going to war. Some said the possibility of nuclear war was unprecedented, others said it was imminent. I understood the deterrent power of my job better than any of them. And pressing the "button," annihilating cities, states, and nations, was a scenario every man should pray never happened.

For any missileer in combat at such time, death was inevitable. We literally signed on to die should the time ever come, to save America and her allies.

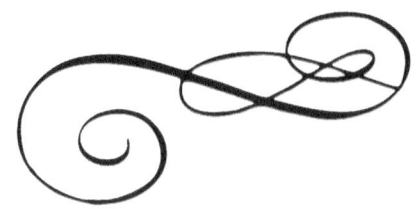

Chapter 24

F.E. WARREN AFB, WY: January 2017
The Nuke Officer and the Intercontinental Ballistic Missile (ICBM).

Besides the pride that came with the uniqueness of operating nuclear weapons, it was also a position that held the fate of all life on earth in the grip of just four hands. I learned how the capsule could be a place where two wrongs could be forced to become a right through honor, respect, and commitment.

Within about a year, I rose to the highest position on the field—mission lead commander, where I continued to help train new deputies.

The responsibilities of this role felt like another pioneering moment: I was setting a great precedent so that people like me could continue to have access to the same opportunities I was given.

From this point, I was in a position to help others use their lives and their loyalty to prove that just like any American-born citizen, we were capable of doing something worthwhile and benefitting the whole country - as long as we were given an opportunity to do so.

However, just before I became the mission lead, I experienced a few major setbacks - moments of prejudice that harkened back to my earliest days in this country.

Later, my flight got a new flight commander, the worst kind of flight commander. He hated my accent and, on several occasions, tried to manipulate my manner of speaking into an operational problem, citing "communication" as an issue for my performance.

When I was coming up for promotion, I asked him whether he could provide me with feedback on what I could improve on to continue to progress. Again, his feedback had to do with my manner of speaking. Even my instructors during my training had come around, no longer seeing my manner of speaking as a setback. So many of my colleagues had stood up for me. But now, on the job and in the case of this captain, I noticed that he was doing whatever he could to hold back my progress.

Somehow, it always boiled down to someone worried about my accent, or misinterpreting the context in which I spoke, or worse still, someone unable to interpret my expressions, or someone scared that I might out-perform and overtake them.

He silently stood for almost everything the military was against, and sooner or later, his real personality started to show: a racist who had no idea he was racist. The first time I encountered him was during one of my evaluations which he'd try to sabotage. Fortunately, there were other observers there to refute his claims. When he became my flight commander, it wasn't apparent until it was time for my upgrade to mission lead commander.

At first, during the leadership's meeting, it was him beating up on me about the way I communicated until finally, another new flight commander challenged him to tell the truth, "Just tell the truth, this is about his accent. You don't like it!"

He admitted it, and claimed others would have difficulty understanding me as well. They disagreed with him - I'd never had issues communicating with anyone in the squadron before he came to join us. The same flight commander who dared to speak warned him about the senior leadership discovering his real reasons for always trying to hold me back.

After being at the post for a long time and becoming highly experienced, I was upgraded to mission commander. Fortunately, the management disregarded everything he said and upgraded me. At that, I called a meeting with him.

After entering his office, I told him, "I'd like to close the door because I have a lot to talk to you about." I said in a gentle tone and friendly demeanor. He looked surprised but comfortable, and said it was okay.

After closing the door, I walked over, pulled a chair, and sat in front of him, his desk between us. He smiled and asked what he could do for me.

"Before you came down here, I'd never had issues," I told him. "I think you need to look inside yourself and figure out why. When you say people have problems on the job, and you're the only one bringing up the problem month after month, maybe you're the problem."

Now he had stopped smiling and seemed more surprised than when I had entered his office, but I was just getting started.

"Captain, let me ask you," I continued. "How many accents do we have in the squadron?"

"I don't know," he sniffed. "Maybe fifteen?"

"No," I answered. "We have twenty-two accents. Do you know how I know this? I know because I have to decipher how each of you speaks and what you're saying. I take time to listen, and if I don't understand someone, I ask questions. But you, you listen to my accent, not what I'm saying. Now that it's just the two of us here, would you say that you understand what I'm saying right now?" I asked.

"Yes, I can hear you clearly and understand what you're saying right now." He replied.

"Good. Why do you think you seem to understand me better right now?" I asked.

"I don't know. You are sitting right here, and I'm listening to you." He said as I tried to engage his eyes.

"That's exactly what I'm asking of you. That's what I do everytime in the squadron. On duty. Off duty."

"Remember the last time we were on crew together?"

"Yes, I do." He nodded.

"You said when immigrants decide to settle in the U.S., they must learn the new culture and find a way to integrate completely, even in the way they sound. You also said all non-Christians will go to hell."

He remained quiet but was beginning to have a hard time maintaining eye contact. He'd never expected me to confront him the way I did but also couldn't push back because he knew I was telling the truth.

"One day, if you find yourself in a more diverse, less classified base, you'll cause so much damage to so many careers and hold people back from progression because of how they sound or look, instead of allowing them what they've earned," I said, trying to speak in a clear, gentle tone despite being frustrated, angry, and disgusted at this young man.

"I can deal with you because I've been through much worse in my life," I continued. "But for new graduates, they'll explode if you treat them like this."

He looked like he wanted to say something, perhaps defend his actions - but out of visible shame, he remained silent.

"Captain, this is my highest principle: we are serving the United States of America. No matter what our accents sound like, each of us deserves dignity and respect. Our role is not only to evaluate people; we are supposed to care for them, to look out for them. And in nuclear missile operations, our job isn't to judge anyone. It is to protect everyone." I concluded.

I had taken on one of the greatest responsibilities to protect the people in this nation and the world. I had grown from a hungry, scared Nigerian child to a doctor, to serving the greatest country in the world, and still, I had to fight for respect.

I realized that no matter how far we travel in life, there will always be someone trying to slow our progression. Maybe my grandmother would say this was life's way of keeping us on our toes. I remembered her words: *Men may try to slow you down, but your destiny is in your hands.*

Not long after, I had another talk with him to let him know I understood what was going on. I played dumb and lectured him about racial diversity, cultural perspectives, and different communication styles. Why it was crucial that we were all different because that was the strength of the American military.

I advised him to try and see people the same and told him that those things he saw as faults in others were in fact their strengths.

I thought he'd listened, but then word about him having issues with gay officers started going around. We did have officers with various sexual orientations in the squadron, and this flight commander seemed to have a problem with them as well as with me.

What was most disturbing about this wasn't just the fact that we had people like these leading in the U.S. Air Force - and often at much higher levels. It was the fact that even when others around them knew for sure that the accusations against other officers trying to do their jobs were unfair, even when they witnessed these conniving, subpar, shallow-minded, and sometimes racist officers for themselves, even when it happened right in front of them, they kept quiet, unless it affected them personally.

Some of my colleagues later approached me to ask if I had any complaint I'd like to officially submit about my racist experiences with him. These were the same colleagues that knew how he had been treating me before I talked to him, but they hadn't considered it a major issue until they started to find themselves in the same situation.

As much as he deserved what was coming to him, I had to turn them down because I had already talked to the captain one-on-one. While I respected their decision to take more decisive disciplinary actions, I felt it would be wrong for me to officially accuse him of something he hadn't done to me since I addressed the issue with him. If he did it again, I would.

A year after my discussion with the captain, the entire squadron and our leadership saw this man's true colors. Just like I had given him a chance after talking to him, the squadron commander had done the same, but the captain would not keep his racial and religious opinions to himself. He continued to make homophobic remarks on duty after he'd been warned. When you're someone with the power to do enormous harm, it's important that you view all humans with respect. Official complaints went up to higher-ranking officials in the squadron, and the leadership decided it was time to dismiss him.

As I was overcoming this hurdle in my career, wars were being waged throughout the world. I felt an acute awareness that I wished others would understand: it didn't matter what country you came from, how you spoke, or what color your skin was. A nuclear missile wouldn't discriminate. We all shared the same risk.

As deadly as nuclear weapons are, imagine our world without them: a mixing bowl of cataclysm, never-ending carnage, intimately romanced by the blood-thirsty, power-drunk savages that men can so easily become, like we have done to one another in pre-nuclear times.

The advent of the nuclear age was a terrible thing, but in many ways, it successfully saved lives in numbers that we will never be able to count. The ICBM has a vital role to play in world peace. So, as much as we all strive to create a nuclear-free world, we must also bear this in mind that if by some miracle, our world became nuclear-free, we must ask ourselves if there's another weapon more deadly than a nuclear weapon in existence.

By the macadam beaching the bay,
She walks nimbly and weakly today.
Though I say today, nay! but allay.
Dreaming a dummy, wake to reality.
Crossing the bumpy?
Where's fidelity?
O, joy of Utopia.

If only we could have
No death and no rivalry,
No sadism and no racism,
No prejudice and no ethnocentrism,
No reneging and no prodigality—
All on deuce, none on nil.
O, joy of Utopia.

Would I see her? Would I hear her?
Rejoicing with much hilarity,

My absurd nation of penuriousness.
Who will make her one?
Where is the don?
Will we ever find one—
one to create our Utopia?

Epilogue

WASHINGTON, D.C.: October 2018

The Father I Became.

I heard of the river on the mountain:
Pellucid and still, shallow, and warm.
Take me there and lay me rest...

As I sat in a hole more than seventy feet below the earth's surface in a top-secret location, manning the world's deadliest weapon, it was exceptionally quiet.

I thought to myself, *How far have I come?* From the cusp of starvation in Nigeria to sitting in this capsule, it felt like I finally had a life I could be proud of, and a story that I hoped could inspire many people to act on their dreams.

Since October 2014, after I was commissioned into the U.S. Air Force, so much had been happening to my family and me. My life felt like water, trapped in a rock and making its way through the cracks

385

and hollows to see the sunlight. I was not only seeing the sunshine, but I was also bathing in it, and it was just the beginning.

In August 2015, after we arrived at F.E Warren, AFB in Cheyenne, WY, I received a call from my squadron.

"Hey, Ayoade."

It was one of my new flight commanders. The voice was recognizable, but he sounded a little excited.

"Congratulations!" he said. "You have been selected for Outstanding Airman Recognition. I need you to stop by my office tomorrow morning. We will draft a short biography about you. Sorry for the short notice, but the General of Air Force Global Strike Command arrives next Tuesday, so we have less than a week to put this together for him."

"General?"

"Yes, Ayoade. It's the General's recognition. He will be the one to narrate your achievements, tell your story, and give the reasons why you deserve a General's attention at the All-Call next Wednesday. I guess you understand why we must be prompt with the preparations."

I was astounded that I'd been selected for a U.S. Air Force General's recognition. It had been less than a year since I was commissioned into the U.S. Air Force, and I'd only been at the new base for a month.

Sometimes, it is wise to reflect on our path to the present and thank God for not granting those heart desires we so desperately wanted when we wanted them, I thought.

I reflected on how easy it would seem to any observer, especially a fellow immigrant, to assume that the rise to my achievements was quick and uncommon, given I'd only been in the U.S. for seven years. They couldn't see the decades of disappointments before - and during - those seven years, all part of my journey to this moment.

I was no longer that struggling Nigerian kid. I had a life worthy of appreciation and a story capable of galvanizing many into acting on their dreams. I had my own shortcomings - the insatiable cravings of my heart at the will of no one but myself, spending no time celebrating accomplishments - but I was no longer the same man.

I realized that I didn't know how to live life, and I hadn't been thankful enough for all the little things. I had only continued toward my goals, never stopping to enjoy the moment, and the accomplishments.

I thought about the countless times that did pass me by: times I should have just looked to the heavens with my eyes closed, my arms spread wide open, and enjoyed the soothing breeze on my face. I was constantly chasing the wind all my life, failing to see how it spread generously all around me. But I was changing.

When the General arrived at the All-Call, he asked, "How many of you know Ramon? Has any one of you met him?"

A few hands went up, but I tried not to focus on them.

"The first time I met him," the General continued, "I was at his graduation ceremony in California. In fact, I handed over his first Air Force badge to him." He scanned the sea of faces as he continued with his story. I suspected he was searching for my face. It would have been easier to find me if my daughter hadn't left my side to be with her mom, who was sitting in the back row to pacify our crying twenty-month-old son.

"Ramon came from Nigeria," the General said. "He is a doctor. He has a master's degree as well!" He laughed incredulously. "Can you believe that? Wouldn't that make you question why the military?"

I wanted to hide. I felt like the earth beneath me could open up and to consume me, and I would welcome it. I could hear my heartbeat faster and faster, and blood rushed to my head and my hands. "He came to the U.S. for graduate school, fell in love with the U.S. and decided to enlist in the Navy, and finally, was commissioned into the Air Force."

If only the General knew that my love for the U.S. had gone as far back as my childhood.

"You know, stories like these blow my mind—the reason why we recognize him today as a role model for all of us."

I must admit that I'd never felt so honored in my entire life. I never expected a General to tell my story to the public so captivatingly well, like he knew me personally. I felt proud of myself for the first time, and it wasn't only by my doing that I came this far. It was just time. My time, with the unflagging support of my wife.

It was an indescribable feeling to know that the decisions that I made, the actions that I took with Tolu's help, however absurd, were finally leading somewhere. My life could be used to minister, motivate, and officially used as a role model for a branch of the U.S. military. How I came from nothing to this would take a while to sink in, much longer than I'd guessed.

"Ramon! Where are you? He should be with us!" the General said.

"Here, General!" I answered, getting up from the sixth row of chairs.

"Come over here!" he ordered, gesturing with his left hand. "I need to show you to everyone."

As confidently as I could, I walked to the front of the podium where he'd been addressing us for almost fifty minutes. The General shook my hands and held me by the shoulder.

"We've met before, right?"

"Yes, General," I replied.

"I gave you your first badge at your graduation three months ago?"

"That's true, General," I answered with a smile.

"You know my wife and I can't stop wondering why you decided to join the military. If you don't mind, I'm curious—why?"

"It's a long story, General, but I can try to summarize the story behind my decision."

"Go on."

I summed it up for him as best as I could, and finally finished with, "The most important thing to me is that it makes me happy and I feel fulfilled to serve the people who need my help. I am living my purpose."

"Ramon, the Air Force is honored to have you," the General said. "You said exactly what I wanted to hear. I will take your story with me and share it with all the airmen at all the commands I will be visiting. You are a role model for many!" The General signaled to his aide, who handed him a coin.

It was a four-star General coin. He presented it to me as a token while I saluted him following my acceptance.

"How about your parents?"

"General, my dad died a few years ago, but my mom lives in Maryland."

"Great! How about my wife and I take a picture with you and your family? I will sign it, frame it, and then mail it to your mom with a letter so she can know of her son's achievements."

"General," I said, overwhelmed by this moment, "We'd be honored."

When you come from nothing to a new world, as I came from nothing to this one, you learn to earn your way through life. Words alone cannot capture feats. I have chosen to leave out just how much I've been through, because all the great things I experienced weren't by my own doing alone. I had a lot of help.

An empty barrel, they say, makes a lot of noise. At least in my own life, I have learned that coins can only be earned, no matter what's engraved on them.

True to his word, a few weeks later, my mom received a package in the mail—a framed picture of my wife and me, with the General and his wife. Also, a signed letterhead from General, USAF, Office of the Commander, Air Force Global Strike Command, addressed to my mom, stating:

"While visiting Francis E. Warren AFB, I had the pleasure of meeting your son. I was so impressed by his skills and enthusiasm that I wanted to personally write to let you know what a fine young man and airman you raised. His commitment and dedication to an often-thankless job are a testament to his character. Your son is exceptional!"

In spite of this, it didn't feel like enough. I had always craved achievement the way some men crave power, but I also aspired to constant perfection. I wanted my name to represent only the best. Many had tremendous respect for my journey, but I have never felt like I had done enough.

Time after time, though, a feeling of ungratefulness crept into my heart, showing me how much more I could have lost - my life making the top of the list. It showed me how demanding I'd been of life. How I frequently forgot to pause and appreciate all the small things that gave my life meaning, and how the things I beat myself up about were so trivial. How I needed to wake up. I needed to make peace with myself before my desires consumed me.

Nuclear Operations Tech School – Vandenberg AFB.

Nuclear Operations Tech School Graduation Ceremony– Vandenberg AFB.

General's recognition event.

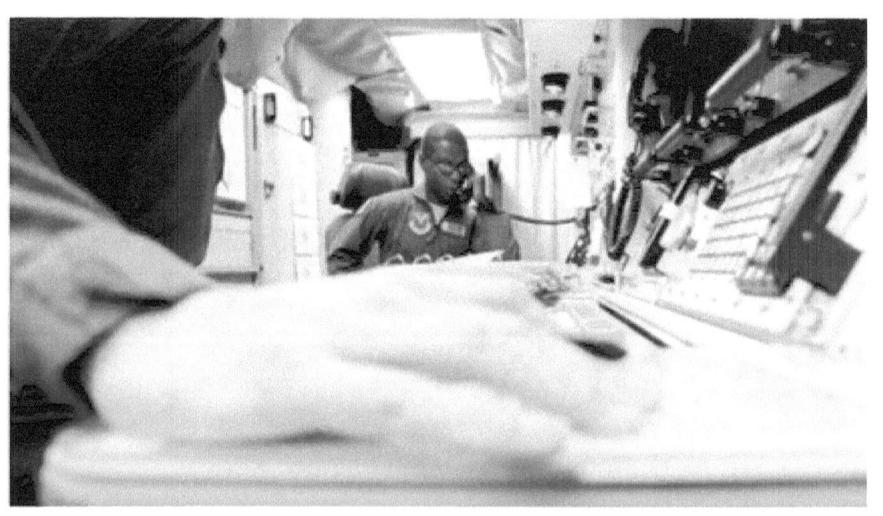

Mission Commander, Nuclear Alert – F.E. Warren AFB.

25th Secretary of the Air Force's recognition – The Pentagon.

USSF CSRO Civilian of the Year Award – The Pentagon.

Two months after I was selected for the General's award, Tolu asked me, "When was the last time you talked to Alhaja?"

"I can't remember. It's been a while," I replied.

"You need to call her," Tolu said. "It's about time you visit Nigeria to see her and my dad."

I agreed with her.

"You're right," I said. "I've been thinking about it, but it might still take a while. You know the drill with new jobs. I need some time to settle into this position before taking that much time off."

"Alhaja is ninety-nine years old. My dad is eighty-four. You have to find a way before it's too late."

My wife continued pulling my attention to a crucial part of me that I'd neglected for too long. Just when I realized how much I'd been taking for granted, she added, *They won't live forever, you know? It is time for you to make up for all the troubles Alhaja went through for you and your siblings.*

Tolu reminded me to look back at the memories of my past, those that taught me how far I had come, that I must keep close to my heart. I had so much going on in my life, both at work and home, but there was an uneasiness that never left my heart. The more I drifted into forlornness, the more Tolu persistently pulled me back to the things that mattered the most. I didn't think it was apparent, but she knew and was trying to help me understand what it was. She thought I'd kept away from the only love that I thrived on as a child for too long. The love instilled in me, the lessons and values I would find impossible to forget as a grown man. Alhaja's love.

Maybe I'd never let Alhaja out of my heart, but I'd been distracted badly enough not to keep in contact with her. How foolhardy I had been.

I tried to be more consistent with my calls to Alhaja and my father-in-law from then on, but they were still not as frequent as they should have been. Alhaja had gotten older since my childhood, but she still sounded as sharp as I'd known her as a child, just as my dad had predicted.

My wife's dad, a former international boxer, was still physically independent, as you could imagine. I'd been married to his daughter for six years but never met him in person. I didn't want to think about how they could be gone at any moment. I knew it to be true. I just hated hearing it.

Finally, I booked a flight to visit my father-in-law and Alhaja in Nigeria. I didn't tell Alhaja or any of my family members about my impending visit because I wanted to surprise them. However, I had kept in touch with my father-in-law about my plans to visit him, and he was preparing for my arrival, excited about meeting his son-in-law for the first time.

Time is a teacher
That gives you
The wisdom to know
You're a fool
When you're a fool.

It gives you an enviable future
If you learn to acknowledge it,
'Cause the portion squandered
Never comes back.

People will always be a reflection
Of what they spend their lifetimes doing,
So why live as though time had no end?
Why wait till tomorrow if today seems right?

Use your time wisely,
For if you waste time,
Time will disappoint you in the end.
Be wise, my friend,
And use your time well.
Be wise, my friend,
And use your time well.

Later in December, about a month before my trip, we received a call from my mother-in-law from Lagos.

It was almost bedtime when my wife's phone rang. Her dad was ill. His cold had progressed for a day or two, but it didn't seem grave. My wife later called him, and we spoke briefly. The following day, she called to follow up, but he had been admitted to the hospital.

He had been diagnosed with malaria and a few other metabolic issues they weren't aware of before his admission. I prayed and hoped that nothing happened to him and my grandmother before my arrival in Lagos.

My wife had never experienced such tragedies with loved ones and didn't know how to process the news about her father. The more I tried to encourage her to be unequivocal in her faith; the more she seemed to feel otherwise. She seemed to be sure her father's time had come. I tried to discredit such thoughts, telling my wife how prayers could change everything, but deep down, I was worried that I might not forgive myself for wasting so much time.

Beneath my confident demeanor, I was genuinely scared about losing my father-in-law before I could meet him, and Tolu sensed that. Countless times, she had tried to persuade me to visit Nigeria to meet him in person.

Undeniably, the love that binds a daughter to a father can intuitively tell us when we have lost a loved one before we do. Four days following the first call from my wife's mom, we received the terrible news: he was gone.

Although he was old, Tolu had a very hard time with his loss, which was unsurprising considering their bond.

I can hear them;
I can see them.
Like a sound from a broken pipe
Came the cries from dust.
Like rain
Came the tears from the sky.
The broken-hearted widow to be
And the unfulfilled promises!

Father!
That's what you are.
Love!
Yes! So intense you sacrificed all.
And Liberty!
The reason for it all.
A foundation for a new generation,
The best gift to any child.

The flesh might turn ashes,
And the bones might return to dust,
But the spirit will always endure.
The glory will live on,
So that the glorious can be engraved in gold.
I'd choose an immortal name
Over all the treasures of the world.

The airport seemed much smaller than I remembered when I had left many years ago.

It reminded me of my father's words to me as a child, how some things in life that once seemed mighty continue to shrink as we grow older. *Many things in life, especially the physical ones, will continue to appear smaller than you thought when you were much younger, just like each day will go by faster than the previous as you get older,* he'd said.

There I stood outside the airport, wondering why I ever thought Murtala Mohammed International Airport was such an enormous airport. What a difference time made. My wife's aunt and my mother-in-law's company manager waited for us by the pick-up zone while the driver pulled over just in time. My flight had been rescheduled for later in January, while Tolu was added to my flight schedule as well. We invited my mom from Maryland to Cheyenne, to help care for our kids.

As we drove to Lagos Island, I noticed that most parts of Lagos had changed over the years and looked a little better than they used to. However, the people hadn't.

Whatever it was that instituted and preserved the wrongs in the social system - especially the lapses in law enforcement - persisted. The heart-rending mentality of the average Nigerian had gone from fighting social injustice to accepting it as the norm in Nigeria.

After we'd arrived, my mother-in-law pulled me away to have a private talk with me. I wasn't sure why, but my wife had noticed that I still struggled with the guilt of not meeting her father when I had the chance to. My mother-in-law wanted to talk about it because she knew I didn't know what to do.

She said, "Daddy was a jolly man, full of life. He lived an accomplished life and never had regrets. The last thing he wants is you living with guilt about not meeting him before he left. He's not here with us physically, but he will always be with us. So, shake it off, and be happy because you have been nothing short of a great son-in-law."

Help me—
I'm traveling a one-way road.
Though lost on my trail,
I want to keep moving on.
My limbs get weaker,
So I keep crawling on my knees.
My shredded skin has bled,
Staining the sand red,
Yet it will take a miracle to see you.

Since your time has come,
Then mine's a forlorn hope.
The loss is mine,
And that's because we had
Only twenty days between us.

My wife told me a lot about her father, but not once did she mention how famous he was in Lagos. He was once a politician, the *Surulere Local Government Chairman* in Lagos State. This is the equivalent of a Mayor position in the U.S. Most citizens loved him for his integrity, honor, courage, compassion, and mostly his generosity. Alhaja needed some over-the-counter medications, which I promised to send over to her in Nigeria through a friend. However, I planned to show up instead. I decided to pay her a surprise visit on the third day following my arrival in Lagos.

I had a bag with Alhaja's medications and another bag of clothes that I had brought for my late aunt's children, as well as my cousins, nieces, and nephews, most of whom had no clue what I looked like. I made plans with one of my cousins who knew precisely where Alhaja now lived. She had sold all her investment shares to build a new house for herself on the outskirts of Lagos.

As planned, my cousin strolled into Alhaja's room while I hid behind the entrance door. She had been confined to bed and a wheelchair. She pulled herself to sit at the head of the bed while her back rested on the headboard.

Alhaja welcomed my cousin as he sat beside her, praying and chanting soulful rhymes. They were not empty words and were different for each of us, the grandchildren. I could see her from where I stood behind the door, but she couldn't see me. *How can she convey such profound love so easily with these words?* I thought to myself.

It was magic to listen to her put words together, especially in the presence of her grandchildren, that could probably comprehend only half of what she was saying. She was the only one who knew the *oriki* of every child born into the Ayoade family.

Oriki is a form of poetry, praise poetry, almost similar to panegyric poetry. It is a nonpareil cultural practice found amongst the Yoruba tribe of West Africa. It is fundamentally used to identify the different dynasties, ancestries, pedigrees, and for cajolery. It is a norm in Yoruba tradition for a person to have individual oriki after their familiar name, and as well, family oriki and sub-ethnic oriki. So, when being welcomed by one's grandparents, be it in the village or wherever they are domiciled, would usually start with them first mentioning one's oriki name.

However, Alhaja was different. As a child, every single morning, after prostrating to her, which was how male children greeted the elders, she kissed us on both cheeks, prayed, and rained oriki on each one of us, one at a time. We had individual oriki names.

As soon as my cousin stood up and backed away from her, I pressed on slowly towards her. She watched me as I approached her, mouth agape in incredulity, too shocked to utter a word. She couldn't believe what was in front of her.

"It's me, Alhaja. Ramon."

I sat in the same spot on her bed where my cousin had just stepped away from, both arms raised towards her as I leaned forward to hug her.

"Ramon? No, it can't be you. You didn't say you were coming home," she managed in a low tone beneath her breath.

I hugged and kissed her on both cheeks like she usually did to us.

"I know, Alhaja. It was meant to be a surprise. I wanted to surprise you. It's been such a long time, but you haven't changed a bit," I said as I sat next to her, feeling like the exhilarated little boy I once was.

As soon as Alhaja gathered her composure, she started praying and chanting my *oriki* at the same time. Usually, it took a few minutes when she did, and in those minutes, there was an overwhelming consummation of the spirit and emotions. A temporary discernment of a sense of purpose: where I came from, how much to be proud of about my esteemed origin, but most fundamentally, how important I was.

"I brought all your medications, Alhaja, just like you requested. I know you were expecting a friend to bring them over, but that was a distraction from what I was up to," I said with a mischievous smile.

She beamed at my attempt to make her laugh as she pulled her medications out of the bag, one after the other. My cousin passed me a pen so that I could inscribe on each of the bottles what doses to take. It was the easiest way for Alhaja to follow dosage instructions ever since I was a boy, so I knew exactly how to write the dosages and how to explain them to her as well.

"Ramon, you are such a blessing. You are still the same caring, selfless, generous little boy I raised," Alhaja said. "The things you said when you were a child, they came true. Your dreams, they come true."

"Well, Alhaja, I have you to thank for what I am today.

You are so important to me, and I can't thank you enough for all that love. You know I thought of how I could immortalize you and the great things you have done for all of us, so I decided to write about you just so the entire world might know your story even long after you are gone."

I hugged and kissed her again.

"So, when are you going back?" she asked.

"In about four days, Alhaja. My wife's father died. His funeral is in three days. I'm not sure if I'll be able to see you again before leaving for the U.S. because there are lots of people we still have to see."

I'd wished I could see her every day before my departure, but that wouldn't be realistic given our commitments in Nigeria.

"Whichever way, Alhaja, I will call you so we can talk. I won't be staying away for too long. I'll try to come over to see you every year."

She smiled and gave me another hug. How selfless and undemanding she'd been.

As we drove back to my mother-in-law's house, words could not capture how satisfied I felt. I'd been scared about Alhaja for so long before we'd left the U.S.

I can hear the cockcrow and see
Streams of gold running past the blinds.
It's time for my friends to fly out of their nests.
The Beautiful City of Lagos,
Friends, and roses,
But you seem to be my first thought.
Grandma, Grandma,
The Island Beauty.

It's more beautiful in the woods
When autumn leaves.
Red flowers?
It's anthocyanin!
Christmas illusions?
Grandma, Grandma,
Your beauty stretches farther than the eye can see.

Grandma,
Did I mention how old you are now?
I want you to know:
My heart reaches out to you always.
Though I'm so far away,
It will always be with you.
I'll never leave you to frailty,
My Island Beauty.

Amid the tight schedule, my cousin came back to me and my wife four days later, the same day we were supposed to depart from Nigeria to the UK. I wanted to visit his mom's grave, my late godmother, after visiting my dad's grave.

How could I ever forget her? My preclinical years in college would have been impossible without her. I bought flowers for their graves and couldn't wait to talk to them after many years.

As we galloped in and out of the potholes, which continued for several miles on the unpaved Ejigbo roads that led to my father's house, the memories of my childhood years in the town returned. They weren't flashes but vivid and real, like I was reliving them.

"Why would your dad choose this place to build his home?" Tolu asked me. "Did you really grow up around here?

"Yep. I sure did." I replied, casually, still relatively distracted by the state of the place that was once my neighborhood.

"Oh my God! How did you survive?" This time her question seemed to be more meant for her than for me.

"Believe it or not, most of my childhood was spent around here."

My wife continued to ask several questions without waiting for answers. She hadn't seen my father's house yet. She peered from both sides of the backseat windows like a child lost in a jungle.

I attempted to summarize the answer to her endless questions; however immensely disappointed at the level of deterioration of the inhabited town. Ejigbo now seemed like a desolated moorland found abandoned in the middle of nowhere, harboring people and degenerating buildings. It was hard to comprehend that people live in such a state day in and day out.

"I can't imagine how rough it must have been for you," Tolu mumbled, trying to place the reality of my boyhood.

"I see why you weren't ever interested in the idea of coming home sometimes," Tolu said.

"Yep." I nodded. "That's true, and that's because I can't fix all these. I mean, I wish I could. I want to, but I'm not in the right place and position to do so right now. Heaven knows it takes more than one man with a dream for a place like this to change this situation for the better."

As I continued to stare out the front passenger window, I wished there was a way that I could make the living condition of the people better than we witnessed and I thought of how many must have driven past Ejigbo and thought the same many years before, while I was a kid living in that town.

"Well, I can't move my father's grave from his house to anywhere else I consider a much better place. This is what he wanted, so I have no alternative but to keep coming here from time to time to see him. He's my father, after all. I can only deal with the torture of the ugly memories of this town and my dad's house each time I come around here."

As soon as my cousin pulled over in front of my father's house, my wife admitted how large my dad's house was - but could still not fathom why here, of all places.

After banging at the gate for a few minutes, one of the tenants finally came out to the balcony. The same balcony Alhaja sat with us many nights below the moonlight, telling us wonderful tales of our origin.

"Hello! Sorry to bother you so early. I'm here to put a flower on my father's grave," I announced to the tenant from the other side of the gate. I gestured to the grey-tiled grave in the corner of the compound.

The tenant had no idea who I was, and I had no idea who he was. It'd been almost twenty years since I departed the house for the first time on my way to college. There was no one that I knew, or that knew me in the house except for old street neighbors that I deliberately avoided. The reason we came early, so we could leave before they started to wake up.

Shockingly, the old water-seller across from my house was right in front of his house. I could recognize his figure in the dark shadow, but I managed to avoid eye contact with him.

Just like in my childhood days, he woke up at about 5:30 every morning. The locals purchased water and toted water-filled buckets away from his front yard. I disliked the sight of it - it reminded me of how far we trekked to fetch water when we were only kids.

Although tempted to observe what had changed, I deliberately refrained from inspecting the house, which no longer had flowerpots carved around the massive fences.

I knelt next to my father's grave, a much fancier version than how it was before I left Nigeria. My brother had used the lease payments from the house to remodel his grave. It looked charming, but I couldn't deny the sense of deja vu as I talked to him. It was the same familiarity when I knelt before my godmother's grave after placing her flower on her grave. I remember speaking to them by their graves in June 2008, announcing to them of my final departure from Nigeria.

I don't know when I will be back here, but I promise you that I will make a good name for myself," I said to my dad. *"I won't disappoint you because I know you always had faith in me.*

Dearly beloved father,
It's been eight years today
Since you've been gone.
I held your flowers by your grave,
Your words still engraved in my heart.

Like it happened only yesterday,
I stared at the smile traces
Left on your departed face.
You left my arms, My hands,
And I am standing six feet
From the edge of your new home.

I can't imagine how lonely
You have been for eight years.
Eight years I have missed you,
Eight years more I have lived,
'Cause you're gone!

As my wife and I departed Nigeria for London, my college best friend, Tola, had planned for a cab to pick us up from London Heathrow Airport and drop us at his house in Dartford. He had been married less than a year before, and the newly wedded couple had insisted on hosting us.

Our main reason for stopping over was for my wife to visit her half-sister, who had been sick for a while. My wife hadn't seen her in ten years, and by some coincidence, she lived in the same building as Tola and his wife.

Tolu wanted to reconnect with her. It would be impossible to visit the rest of my wife's family in the U.K., so a family dinner was scheduled for everyone to meet at a designated spot in Central London.

"Are you sure this is your sister's address?" Tola's wife double-checked with my wife when we arrived.

"Yes, it is," my wife replied. My niece, her daughter, sent it to me since this was meant to be a surprise visit. She has no clue we're here, but her daughter knows we'll be here today.

"Wow! It's this building! You know that?" Astonished, she asked in a rather thick British accent.

"What? This building?" my wife asked, shocked but pleased. It was one thing to live in the same neighborhood by coincidence, but in the same building in Dartford indeed proved how much smaller the world was than we knew.

"She lives upstairs," she said. My wife knocked on the upstairs apartment door while we all stood by the entrance door, staring at each other in anticipation of the face on the other side of the door.

It was just as we'd hoped for as Tolu and the lady on the other end of the apartment door hugged each other for as long as it took to make up for the ten years apart.

The sun reflects on the melting snow.
The leafless trees bend to the whistle of the wind.
And what becomes of the creases on the tarred roads
Is not much of a worry meant for them.
However, the wheels that run over them
While enduring four seasons in one day is.

If my wife and I didn't know better, the ultimate outcome of the short trip was the lesson we needed to learn as a married couple. Friends and families were like a glass cup, if we let it fall, it broke or even shattered, and we might never be able to put it back together.

Regardless of our recent experience in Nigeria, my wife would never understand entirely what life was like for kids like me growing up where I did. Despite this, she understood me, and the person I had become.

We returned to the U.S. after spending three days and three nights in the U.K. My mom returned to Maryland the day following our return. Nineteen days following our arrival back home, we received a call from my late aunt's husband.

"Hey! It's good to hear from you, sir," I exclaimed, thinking it was a follow-on call to our resolve to keep in touch more regularly with each other from now on, as I hadn't been doing so in the past years.

"How are the kids?" I continued.

"The kids are fine. It's about Alhaja."

"Oh, Alhaja? What happened to Alhaja?"

"She's gone. This morning."

It was a Tuesday morning, the twenty-third day of February in Nigeria, but still the night of my thirty-sixth birthday in the U.S.

"Alhaja? Gone?" I immediately sat up in bed.

I felt like the entire world had just come down around me.

"That can't be! I spoke with her a few days ago." Still in disbelief, I let out a long sigh of despair. All I wanted to do at that moment was to be with Alhaja, holding her and wishing the news I had just received wasn't true.

My wife, anxious to know what was going on, leaned towards me from her side of the bed, "What happened? Is Alhaja okay?"

"He said Alhaja is gone. She died this morning," I announced to my wife in a shaky voice. I felt unable to process the news, but my eyes got teary as I held the phone to my ear in the dark.

"Oh my God! She's dead?" Tolu asked in clear disbelief.

"What? How? What happened? She was fine last time we spoke," I asked shakily, like the explanations could change the news.

"I can't explain much, but Toro was with her. Maybe she could explain what happened to you," he concluded as he handed the phone over to my cousin, Toro.

"Hey Ramon, it started on Saturday night." Toro began. She sounded tired like she'd been crying for hours.

"She kept rolling uncomfortably in bed all night. She couldn't sleep. Earlier in the day, she was perfectly fine, making phone calls and talking to people on the phone."

I almost felt Alhaja's pain and discomfort as Toro continued explaining how it had happened. I desperately wanted to ask why they hadn't just taken her to the hospital, but I didn't want to make anyone feel any worse than they were already feeling. It wouldn't change anything, not anymore. Toro had been around and cared for her for many years. She certainly did not deserve any blame. No one did. "On Sunday, the home health care nurse came around to check what was wrong with her. She said her vital signs were fine except for her respiratory rate, which was higher than usual. She then asked if Alhaja takes heart medications or medications for other severe conditions."

Toro continued. "We told her that Alhaja had no other conditions that we know of besides her joint problems and bone weakness, so she takes only supplements and a few other over-the-counter medications. The nurse decided to withdraw all the supplements and over-the-counter medications Alhaja took altogether so she could monitor her."

"Did Alhaja say anything?" I asked Toro.

"We tried our best to figure out what the problem was, but she couldn't explain." Toro answered. "By Monday, she wasn't talking anymore, and she wasn't eating as well. We decided to take her to the hospital, but I realized she had stopped breathing when I tried to feed her on Tuesday morning," Toro concluded as she began to cry over the phone.

"God, Alhaja is dead," I said, frustrated. Tears were now running down my face. "I can't believe I just talked to her. I was really looking forward to seeing her again." All I could think of was that I could have spent more time with Alhaja.

"You shouldn't beat yourself up, Ramon. You have been an amazing grandchild to Alhaja. She talked a lot about you. How you provided for her and how you ensured she never lacked financially. I know that her soul is in a much better place right now," my cousin said.

I sank into a long silence, enough for my cousin to hang up, thinking I was no longer on the other side of the line. I tried to recapture all the moments we shared, but I could only remember a few, memorable enough to draw more tears from my eyes as I stared into the past with Alhaja.

"'Deji, be thankful that you got the chance to spend at least one more moment with her before her departure," Tolu said gently. "Imagine if you hadn't? Be happy and be thankful for Alhaja. She lived long, but think back on how she'd suffered for too long. Trust me. She's only gone to rest from the tribulations this world had consistently thrown at her. Don't cry but celebrate. How many of us will ever get to live up to ninety-nine years?"

My wife was right. Alhaja enjoyed the sweet and endured the bitter parts of human existence. She encountered numerous crushing circumstances, and I will never comprehend how strong her faith was to survive her ordeals.

Surviving one's children isn't an acceptable thing in my culture. In fact, it is considered a curse. Alhaja outlived her children. Each passing year she survived following the death of her children only kept more of her loved ones further away from her, all for the fear that Alhaja was probably cursed. It is hard to judge people for what they don't know, though, or to blame them for their superstitions. Alhaja understood that even during her most terrible times. Moments when she knew that those she once loved and raised as children, that also loved her as much, could turn against her in the hour when she needed their love, trust and support the most.

Alhaja knew that only God could judge those that judged her even when she was innocent, and how she had to keep loving those that shamed her.

"That's as far as they can see, Ramon," she often told me. "Don't blame them for what they think about me; it's one of the downsides to our cultural beliefs and how quickly we can become judgmental as humans. Many people believe that I'm cursed. Others said that I'm a witch, devouring my children to preserve my life. What they forgot to consider is that all the direful things that happened to me and my kids could happen to any one of them. No one will ever understand where your pain hurts the most until they suffer the same pain where you do. However, I will never pray that even my enemy suffered the same fate as mine."

My father's words of assurance many years ago when I was only seven came back to me: *Grandma is going nowhere, Ramon. She will*

always be around and will be for a very long time. I can assure you;
there is nothing to worry about.

After putting all the recent events into perspective, it became harder to bear the noise in my head telling me how I always needed to be better. I wanted to be more aware of the small moments, enjoy them, and be grateful for life, and my family. Count my blessings if I could and celebrate each if I could.

When the cataclysm of war becomes a story, it can be forgettable for the listener. But it is a never-ending battle for those who truly fought. The war that I fight within is a never-ending battle that follows me everywhere, pushing me to be the best example for myself. Now that I have a family of my own, a wife, a daughter, and a son, I am convinced that I need to do much better concerning every single aspect of my life. To be blessed with wisdom is a tremendous gift but ultimately useless without understanding.

Every time I close my eyes,
I want to live a perfect moment of my life.

You took a nail in the sky,
Where my losses died.
You gave me peace,
But my soul couldn't see.
You gave me shelter;
Your Love, where you wanted me forever.
You called me your child,
But like a bastard,
I never obliged.
You raised me a family
And proved you love me truly.

Still, you fill my soul with gladness
I'd never find anywhere else.

Selah! Selah!
I hear your voice calling.
Selah! Selah!
And in my heart, singing.
All you ask of me
Is a moment to pause and think.

In December 2017, two years after I had been stationed in Cheyenne, WY, my squadron awarded me the Nuclear Missile Officer Company Grade Officer of the Year. As a senior commander on the field, I wrote a motivational letter to my squadron, recounting a part of my journey. It read:

"For those who have lived, are living, or are about to live the capsule life, be proud of yourself and what you do. The honor is in the fact that most men, not only from the U.S., will never know what you do to keep them safe. It is the same honor and values that I committed myself to as a seven-year-old kid who promised a better life for his family in the U.S. and refused to relent until he got it for them. I came from nothing to this life. From Nigeria to the United States."

October 2018 marked the official end of my time on active duty as a missileer. Just before I left Cheyenne, WY, in August 2018, the wing awarded me a commendation medal for my time on alert at F. E. Warren AFB.

Once more, I had to navigate my next move. And for the first time, my wife and I had the opportunity to choose where we could relocate. We decided on the Washington, D.C. area, where my extended family was based and where we'd be just a short trip away from Tolu's family in New York.

I ended up with an exciting position as an Air Force nuclear weapon system subject matter expert in the Pentagon. The title alone sounded grand, and I knew that the Pentagon's criteria to fill a job like that were fierce.

After interviewing in late September 2018, as I added the final touches to this book, they called to offer me the job, and I readily accepted.

What gave me the greatest sense of security and accomplishment was that our whole family was living close together. We'd been through a lot, but finally, we were there together.

Today, each of my family members is gainfully employed. My mom and sister both continue to work in healthcare, while the rest of my family is either working in the information technology field or pursuing graduate studies in technology and engineering at an Ivy League school. Not once have any of them taken for granted the lives they now have and the opportunity to build for themselves and their own families.

Even my mother's dream from long ago to have a career has come true. In this country, she became a professional and financially independent, comfortable for the first time in her life. I would do anything to take care of her, but today, she doesn't need me to. Still, for all of them, I like to think of myself as their protector - though now it's through the work that I do.

Before I left Nigeria, I knelt before the graves of my father and godmother and promised to fulfill the dreams I had for the future of our family. I pledged to make a new life and care for our loved ones. Together, with my grandmother, they taught me to be strong and live a life of value to the world.

And that is what Tolu and I teach our children: when we are gone, the only thing that remains is our goodness. Through our travels as a family, we show them the world may *seem* big, but it's very small. The people they meet today, they might run into again tomorrow, so they have to treat others with dignity, respect, and compassion. We want them to live knowing that everyone from every part of the world shares the same desire for a meaningful life. And when all else fails, what remains is family.

How long has it been?
Up above the clouds,
His eyes have been.
I see the heavens from where I sit,
Wondering how I could watch still.

For every channel branching out from a river source,
I have no clue where the origin is.
Though my eagle glides faster than any car can go
And my crawl seems faster than my walk.

As I perceive the ugliness of the rocky expanse beneath me,
"She spreads to a world that we know nothing of,"
I assumed in the absence of any vision.
I thought about my daughter, my son, and my wife who gave them to me.
She will miss me still…
My children will remember me when they return home
Because that's what kids do when they're finally away from other little ones.

My once deserted life that felt so empty,
Devoid of the kind of Love I desperately sought,
Now filled with the kind of life I only dreamt of as a child.
No matter what becomes of me from here on,
I know there will always be the three that will never stop loving me,
So dearly, so unconditionally.

I hope that my children continue to travel and meet people from many other places to explore love, life, and the breadth of the earth. As they get older, I hope they realize that anyone can change our futures, not only those we're familiar with.

I want them to know that no matter how far you go in life, humility, appreciation, and respect for others will take you even further. It will be up to them to aspire for a much bigger and more daring life than mine, with hearts strong enough to overcome adversities, and dreams bold enough to build their lives wherever they choose.

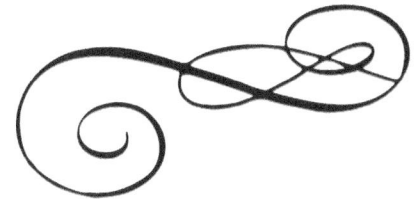

Acknowledgment

Starting with the most important acknowledgment of all; the Almighty God. Thank you for listening and hearing the prayers of the seven-year-old me. You never failed to veer me back on the path to your special plans for me, even when my frustration and desperation got the best of me as a lad. Sometimes, it is wise to look back and thank you for not granting those wishes we crave as humans and giving us the strength and patience to experience your plans. Somehow, it always makes sense in the end.

As a little boy, I'd say a few times, "I am going to move to the U.S. and marry a woman from Brooklyn, NY." That was not unusual for a Nigerian kid, growing up in the middle of nowhere and watching a little too much of "Coming to America." Like many dreamers, two decades later, the things I said and wished came true, but not without one thing that I'd never factored in, my wife, Tolu Ayoade.

My wife, the one that assured me that life could be equally simple and good, and not all are vile and wicked. That dreams are not to be given up on, and the paths to reach them, no matter how difficult, must be tread and trusted. You showed me love and faith, and how both give meaning to all mysteries only if I could exercise patience.

Darling, you gave me wings to fly when I could barely lift my arms. Your rare unconditional love defied every failure and every darkness. Indeed, after God, the only reason the pieces of me have fallen into place is YOU. My star has only continued to shine brighter because it found and aligned with yours. You are me, and I am you. I have come to hear myself smile, laugh, and feel the kind of joy that I'd never felt before you came into my life. Thanking you could never completely convey the gratitude in my heart for loving me the way you do. The years seemed to have rolled by so fast, but I have no worries because you're the one I'll grow old with.

To my children, Lani Ayoade and Mayowa Ayoade. The thought of you when I was younger, much before you were born, gave me the strength, courage, and fire to fulfill the promises I made to you and myself as a seven-year-old. I wanted a much better future for my unborn children if I were to have any, and here you both are. I can't imagine my life without you.

Lani, I named you after my dad because you remind me of the best things about him. You are intelligent, loving, caring, and thoughtful. You constantly strive to be better at everything you do. I can't wait to experience all the great and beautiful things you imagine. I pray that our world becomes a much better place as you grow older to understand it and that you will become one of the reasons it becomes a much better place for everyone.

Mayowa, you are so clever, handsome, funny, strong, and athletic. Even then, most parents would think the same of their kids, but when you are old enough to understand this, "you were a very clever child for a six-year-old." The words you say and the things you do make me smile, and I can't imagine ever coming home without receiving your special hugs.

My late dad, 'Lani Shakir Ayoade. You saw my dreams before I could understand them. You'd prove to us your words were better than your actions, that we needed to listen to them and not do the things you did. When I was 11, you told me, "It's good to be ambitious, but don't be over-ambitious. If you can be patient, you will achieve everything you ever desire. Be patient!" I can still hear your voice, advising me in the hallway. Thank you for your wise words, dad. I heard them, I've kept them to heart ever since, and they still guide me in the way I think and everything I do.

A special thanks to my mom, who gave up everything and suffered endless abuse just so she could be around to watch her children grow up to make something of themselves. You never gave up on any family member, no matter what. The beautiful things in our lives reflect your tireless prayers and sacrifices.

Grandma, Ayinke Ariyoh. Thank you for the best part of my childhood. You single-handedly shaped my perception and understanding of my heritage. You helped me understand the little boy that I was and the man I wanted to become. Your stories, your parables, I could never forget them. You taught me to always look for the best in everyone and the good in every bad situation. To have faith no matter my challenges, never be afraid to fail, learn from my mistakes, forgive quickly, and love ceaselessly. Your words are imprinted in my heart and will continue to linger for the rest of my life.

To my late aunt Sola Aibor, my godmother. You left before I could repay you for taking me in and treating me like your son during the most challenging times in my family. You fed me, clothed me, boasted about me to everyone about how much you believed in me. You loved me like any mother who loves her son and filled the vacuum in my life as a seventeen-year-old with hope. As I headed off to college for the first time many years ago, hundreds of miles away from home, you bought me my first groceries, a shirt, a nice pair of shoes, and a bowl of fried meat. You were the reason I would eventually make it through my preclinical years when I had no means of surviving in school.

To my five siblings: Abideen Ayoade, you are such a gentle soul, always seeking non-violent ways to resolve conflicts. Abiola Ayoade, my only sister. You are strong, loving, enterprising, selfless, and caring. Lateef Ayoade, the comedian of the family. More than half of the words out of your mouth made us laugh, even when the times were tough. Adetunji Ayoade, The Genius. It's still unbelievable how you always managed to fix every broken electronic at home, considering you were only a child. I'm always looking forward to learning something new from you, and thank you for always believing in me. Israel Ayoade, you will always be my brilliant, special little brother.

My cousins: Tope Adesina, thank you for bringing out my poetic side and being the only one I could write to during my lonely years. Toyin Oriolowo, you showed me what it means to be a black immigrant in America and the possibilities that lie within, early enough for me to leap into my future in the U.S.

To my best friends: Tola Oloko, sometimes, I wonder if I would have made it through the long years of vet school without you. You were the first friend I made on my first day in college. You stood by me through thick and thin. You always listened and never judged anyone. Once, when I couldn't afford my tuition and had a few hours left to my first preclinical exams, you showed up with all the money you had left in your account to make sure I made it through that academic year. Though we live on two different continents, ours is a brotherly bond that has stood the test of time. Sam "Chydo" Ezeribe, now and then, we make a best friend who connects with us more profoundly than any other friend. Chydo, I remember walking into your mom's cybercafe in 2001. In a few minutes, we both knew we not only shared dreams of moving to America someday, but we were also driven by the passion to create a better future for our parents and siblings. To love and protect our family and those around us and think less of ourselves was our perception of life and family. Both of us believed that our faith could move mountains, and this faith guided us on a path to living our dreams the way we envisioned and talked about it over twenty years ago. I remember writing the very first chapter of this book in your apartment when I had no place to stay, but you offered to share yours for free. I know that I am blessed to have you as a friend.

Mark Malatesta, you are more than a mentor. You are the first to believe in my story. You continued to encourage me to follow my dreams of publishing this book someday. You didn't stop at that; you helped a naïve immigrant like me navigate the literary world in America and pushed me to create top-notch products. You never got tired of my questions, and neither did you ever not respond whenever I needed your advice. I'm thankful to have met and known you, but most importantly, to call you my friend.

To Jeff Kleinman, Frank Weimann, and Sonali Chanchani of Folio Literary Agency, this book would have been impossible without the three of you. Jeff, when I received your call after returning from an exhausting extended mission, your interest in my work gave me the boost and the courage to continue with this book. As the first in my family to move to the U.S., I intended to leave an account for my children and the generations that would follow about their heritage. Why and how I journeyed here. How it all began. The challenges that I faced and what I made of myself. However, most importantly, my vision for the future. Jeff, your encouragement and actions showed me and assured me that the world needed to know about my story. You made me dig deeper and helped me form a narrative arc for the story. Without you, my account only seemed like an ocean of words and events without a destination.

Frank, you believed in my story. Your optimism and positive energy are infectious. You had a great vision and helped form a direction on the best way to get my story out there. I could never forget your words and actions supporting this book, but more importantly, your heart.

Sonali, I will never forget your tireless efforts in editing our proposal and coordinating the best approach to get my story out. You are simply amazing! You responded every time I reached out, never complained, and genuinely cared and wanted the best for this story. Thank you for believing in me and for all the time you invested in me.

This acknowledgment will be incomplete without thanking my military family, my brothers and sisters in arms. I am thankful to my friends, colleagues, and leaders in the U.S. Navy, U.S. Air Force, and U.S. Space Force, that helped shape me into who I am today. You are a huge part of my American story, establishing a solid root and foundation that I hope several generations of my family will build upon. You taught me excellence, how to lead, integrate, adapt, fight, and defend, and what it means to serve selflessly. Most importantly, you taught me greatness is impossible without teamwork. Like I often say, I did not only help save lives in the military; the military saved my life, for it is where I found my purpose.

Dr. 'Deji Ayoade (ah-yo-AH-day) is the first African immigrant to become a nuclear missile operator in the United States Air Force and serve in three U.S. military branches. He is an emerging memoir author and lifelong poet who strives to touch the lives of his readers through heartfelt storytelling. In addition to his memoir and companion poetry book, he is the author of *Selah! Selah! (Pause and Think): Poetry.*

Enduring a childhood chock-full of impoverishment and loss, storytelling was his safe haven, quickly becoming his way of envisioning a future he wanted to be a part of. Moreover, the power of the written word served as reassurance that he and his loved ones would one day leave all the hardship in Nigeria behind.

Besides being a Writer, 'Deji Ayoade has held the roles of Veterinary Surgeon, Combat Medic, Nuclear Weapon System SME, Senior Program Analyst, and U.S. Space Force Department of Defense Civilian at the Pentagon.

Underground is an emotive journey of restored hope and faith along the path of attaining the American Dream and communion with a higher power that was there all along. Page by page, a personal narrative is revealed to the reader—one brimming with trials and triumphs, grief and joy, loss and love in equal measure. Through poignant, candid, and vulnerable storytelling, 'Deji Ayoade shares his innermost stirrings of the heart and all the maelstroms they entail with utmost poise. Beyond the pages of outpourings by an American military man, this is a true story about a soul who, since birth, envisioned a thriving future for himself and the generations to come.